Universal Leaf
Tobacco Company

UNIVERSAL
CORPORATION

Maximum
Clearance
9'6"
No Trucks

Tobacco Merchant

TOBACCO PLANT

Tobacco Merchant

THE STORY OF
UNIVERSAL LEAF
TOBACCO COMPANY

Maurice Duke
Daniel P. Jordan

THE UNIVERSITY PRESS OF KENTUCKY

Frontispiece: A depiction of a tobacco plant
published in 1796 by Smith, Reed, and Wayland, New York.
Endpapers: (front) Universal's main office in Richmond, Virginia, in the
early 1990s (photo by Maurice Duke), and (back) a North Carolina family
gathered in front of a flue-curing tobacco barn around the turn of the
century (photo courtesy of Universal Corporation).

Library of Congress Cataloging-in-Publication Data

Duke, Maurice.
   Tobacco merchant: the story of Universal Leaf Tobacco Company /
Maurice Duke, Daniel P. Jordan.
      p. cm.
   Includes bibliographical references and index.
   ISBN 0-8131-1892-1 (acid-free paper)
   1. Universal Leaf Tobacco Co.—History. 2. Tobacco industry—
United States—History. 3. Conglomerate corporations—United
States—History. I. Jordan, Daniel P. II. Title.
HD9139.U63D85   1995
338.7'6797'0973—dc20   94-26776

To the men and women
of Universal Leaf Tobacco Company

Contents

Illustrations follow pages 52 and 148

Where to? What next?
        —*Carl Sandburg*

Preface

Universal Leaf Tobacco Company (ULT) was formed in 1918 when six American leaf tobacco dealers consolidated and extended a leaf tobacco buying business originally established in 1888. Leaf tobacco dealers make no consumer products. Their business is selecting, purchasing, processing, and storing leaf tobacco for sale to manufacturers, who then make it into the various tobacco products used by the public. As Southern businesses go, Universal can be considered to be an old company. It is also largely unknown because Universal markets no products directly to the public, advertises little, and prefers a quiet approach to its business. It is also an unusual company, and study of it reveals much about the United States economy as a whole, and about the economy of the South in particular.

Universal is the largest independent leaf tobacco dealer in the world. It deals in tobacco grown in all parts of the globe for the manufacture of tobacco products. The company's processing plants are located worldwide and employ over fifteen thousand people full time and seasonally. Headquarters are in Richmond, Virginia, with facilities in other states as well as in Europe, Africa, Central America, South America, the Far East, and Southeast Asia. Universal buys for resale in excess of 35 percent of all the tobacco grown in the United States.

To describe more precisely the company's function and purpose, some explanation of the leaf industry is required. Leaf tobacco is marketed in different ways throughout the world, but in all instances the grade selection and establishment of price has to be done by a corps of experienced tobacco experts. Because tobacco is a perishable commodity, it has to be quickly treated following its purchase to avoid deterioration.

In order to understand the need for leaf dealers, one need only be aware of the fact that during the height of the tobacco buying season in the United States some fifty-six auctions are operating simultaneously. Only a few of the largest manufacturers have found it feasible or economical to maintain a buying organization within the United States, much less worldwide, to cover such a vast market: but by using the services of a company such as Universal any manufacturer can be assured complete market coverage. With few exceptions, the world's manufacturers of tobacco products leave the selecting, buying, and processing to leaf dealers, who service huge accounts from country to country with tacit permission from the home office to rely largely on their own judgment.

Universal's business takes different forms with different customers. In some cases Universal selects, buys, and delivers the leaf to the customer for an agreed-upon commission. In other cases, business involves both the purchasing and processing of the tobacco based on a customer's pre-season order. On some occasions, immediate delivery and payment are made. In others the company finances the manufacturer until time of delivery. Finally, the company also buys for its own account for later sale. In such cases the tobacco is stored until needed.

The process of turning raw tobacco leaves from the fields into a finished product such as cigarettes, cigars, pipe tobacco, snuff, and chewing tobacco begins when the farmer harvests the crop and separates it into rough grades. According to government standards there are eight grades of tobacco, and six qualities within each grade. Also, there are eighteen different tobacco colors, plus several combinations of colors, making the various choices of colors, qualities, and types of tobacco number in the thousands. Because they lack the knowledge to fine-grade, farmers rough-grade only. They then take the tobacco to a warehouse and consign it for sale. Universal's buyers acquire tobacco on the warehouse auction floors through the process of competitive bidding. After purchase, the tobacco is transported to Universal factories where it is cleaned, sorted, regraded, and blended. There its moisture content is stabilized and it is packed, either to be stored for future sale or to be shipped directly to the customer, a manufacturer who makes and sells tobacco products to the public.

This book deals with all aspects of Universal Leaf Tobacco Company's history, including the purchase, treatment, storage, financing, packaging, and transportation of tobacco worldwide. The book also deals with the newly emerging Universal Corporation, a giant holding company whose interests are just now beginning to extend beyond tobacco into other commodities.

Acknowledgments

We owe a debt of gratitude to a number of people both in and out of the Universal Corporation, without whose assistance and cooperation this book would not have been possible. First and foremost, Thomas R. Towers, former president of Universal, gave generously, and with good humor, of his time and energy and was indispensable in helping to arrange interviews, sometimes having to put an extra twist of the arm on people who were busy in the day-to-day operation of the company. Although never dictating the content or format of the book, he made suggestions that made the finished product more accurate than it otherwise would have been. In the early stages of the project, M. Norton Howe Jr. rendered similar services. Jan Laverge, Gordon L. Crenshaw, Wallace L. Chandler, Henry H. Harrell, James M. White III, and Betty P. Grosclose have read all or parts of the manuscript and offered helpful suggestions.

A number of libraries offered assistance in the research stages of the book. Chief among them were those at Duke University, East Carolina University, the University of North Carolina at Chapel Hill, the University of Richmond, the University of Virginia, Virginia Commonwealth University, the Virginia Historical Society, the Virginia State Library, the Arents Collection of the New York Public Library, and the Library of Congress.

For providing personal papers or other useful information, we would like to thank the following: the late E.D. Allen, Robert E. Bateman, Beverly B. Brookings, the late Don F. Bell, the late L.F. Cary III, the late Mrs. H.W. Davis, O. Kemp Dozier, John C. Gorman, the late Robert M. Harrison, the late H.N. Howard Jr., Robert K. Krick, the late A.I. McOwan, Thomas D. Miller, Ann Morton, the late R.A. Noakes, Charles S. Norwood, Hunter R. Pettus Jr., William S. Powell, R. Robert Sengstacken, Mrs. Helen Marie Taylor, the University of Virginia Alumni Association, Dennis Williams, and Fielding Williams.

The following people offered special assistance during many on-site visits to Universal facilities from Florida to Canada: T.B. Bennett, James R. Carson, Mrs. Grace W. Coats, A.J. Criswell, Diane B. Jackson,

E. Agnew Galloway, W.A. Goodwin Jr., the late A.L. Hobgood Jr., James L. Kennard, Charles W. Kennedy, M.L. Dawson Lee Jr., W.J. Long Jr., the late O.K. McClenney, Claude G. Martin Jr., Glen McDowell, J.K. Moser, the late M.R. Nelson, W.E. Parham, Thomas Rose, Neleine Satterwhite, Edward M. Schaaf III, Duke Smith, the late Frank G. Tedder, C.W. Thomas III, Catherine Thomas, and James R. Williams.

Assistance of various kinds was offered by Sharon Adams, Linda Baber, Elizabeth A. Braswell, the late Robert L. Carlson, J.R. Chaffin, Beth Cheuk, Robert L. Covington, C. Cole Culver, John M. Gregory III, Betty Groseclose, Wirt L. Grubbs Jr., Ronald J. Karnes, Allen B. King, Terri Marks, Peter J. McAteer Jr., Peggy Phillips, Nancy Powell, Nancy Slaughter, and Dianne Sullivan.

Legal advice as the book was proceeding was given by Francis V. Lowden III and James M. White III. Technical information and assistance was supplied by Bernard S. Holt Jr. Editorial advice and suggestions for revisions were rendered by Dr. James T. Moore of Virginia Commonwealth University, specialist on the history of the New South; he read and edited the manuscript, but we hereby absolve him from responsibility for errors or oversights that might exist in the book.

The ground for this book was broken in the mid-1970s when Dr. Joseph C. Robert, a leading historian of tobacco, conducted the first interviews with several Universal personnel. We have made use of his interviews with the late James E. Covington Sr., the late Harry E. Hitchcock, the late A.I. McOwan, and the late Pierre C. Warwick. We would also like to thank Dr. Robert for his interest and encouragement while the present work was in progress. Stuart Christian also provided assistance by taping an interview with R.A. Noakes. Assistance with computer technology problems we encountered was given by Sharon Call and, particularly, by Lynn Graham.

In the process of writing this book, no one connected with Universal dictated the way we were to proceed nor what our conclusions should be. We were never denied access to materials we requested or persons we sought to interview. All conclusions drawn in the following text are entirely our own.

A special note of thanks is due our wives, Lewellyn L. Jordan and Elizabeth Anne Duke. The preparation of this book took a number of years, and on many occasions Lou and Anne helped as sounding boards for ideas. We cannot count the times they rearranged schedules to accommodate work routines and last-minute changes in plans.

1
The Heritage

From the bloodshed and destruction of the American Civil War, the United States rose in one generation to become the world's industrial leader. The American people were quick to recognize and celebrate what they perceived to be the rags-to-riches ascension of the nation's new economic elite, the Armours, the Carnegies, the Rockefellers, the Swifts, and others. Horatio Alger wrote over a hundred novels revolving around the theme of "pluck-makes-luck," and almost everybody accepted the proposition that society's leaders were those who deserved all they got by force of will and strength of character.

Often overshadowed by the attention given the new industrial giants were equally enterprising young men who came from farms rather than factories, from the rural South rather than the urban North, and whose rise from modest circumstances was no less dramatic than that of the captains of industry. In the tobacco business one could cite Washington Duke and his sons Brodie, Buck, and Ben of Durham Station, North Carolina, and a trio of Virginians—Richard Joshua Reynolds of Patrick County, Lewis Ginter of Richmond, and Jaquelin ("Jack") Plummer Taylor of Orange. The least known today of these early tobacco barons, Taylor improved upon his every opportunity until he eventually founded the Universal Leaf Tobacco Company, which has long been regarded as the world's largest independent dealer in leaf tobacco and is now the centerpiece of a billion-dollar conglomerate with diverse global operations.

Jaquelin P. Taylor started life in circumstances that were anything but modest. Born March 2, 1861, at Meadow Farm, Virginia, in the northern Piedmont county of Orange, Taylor had the immediate advantage of a distinguished ancestry. James Taylor, the first of the line, arrived in the Old Dominion from Carlisle, England, in the seventeenth century, and the family subsequently enjoyed both fame and fortune. James II became a militia colonel and a burgess and had been one of a handful of men invited by Governor Alexander Spotswood to journey from the long-established Tidewater region through the wilderness into the fertile Shenandoah Valley. The trek took place in 1716, and the governor honored the participants by making them "Knights of the Golden Horseshoe." James Taylor II liked what he saw on the lush western slope of the Blue Ridge and later received a crown grant of perhaps fifteen thousand acres there. One of the region's first settlers, he built for his family—and heirs—a home he named Bloomsbury.

Like the Jeffersons in Albemarle, the Marshalls in Fauquier, and the Madisons in Orange, the Piedmont Taylors cleared land and prospered in planting and in politics. Favorable marriages and large households extended their influence, and by the 1850s the family could claim not only scores of local and state leaders but also Presidents James Madison and Zachary Taylor, both sons of Orange.

Young Jack Taylor's parents were established members of the Piedmont aristocracy. His father, Erasmus, educated at the University of Virginia, dabbled in law but more seriously lived the life of a gentleman planter, while Jack's mother, Roberta Stuart Taylor, was the daughter of Captain John Ashby of Fauquier County and thus the first cousin of future Confederate hero Turner Ashby. In the mid-1800s, on part of the original crown grant, Erasmus Taylor built Meadow Farm. Erasmus and Roberta had eleven children, of whom Jaquelin, named for a Huguenot ancestor, was the sixth.

If Jack Taylor was fortunate in the place and family of his birth, he was much less so in its timing. A month after his birth in April 1861, a signal shot thundered across the harbor of Charleston, South Carolina, beginning not only the Confederate bombardment of Fort Sumter but the American Civil War as well.

Antebellum Orange boasted scenic beauty and a diversified economy, but war left its mark on the county and on the Taylor household. Tens of thousands of troops either passed through or encamped in the area, which figured prominently in the major campaigns of Second Manassas and the Wilderness and served as winter quarters for the Army of Northern Virginia in 1863-64. General Robert E. Lee pitched his tent near Bloomsbury and once entertained Confederate President Jefferson Davis there. General James Longstreet on one occasion established his headquarters on the grounds at Meadow Farm and on another was brought to the main house following his near-fatal wounding in the Battle of the Wilderness.

Although opposed to secession, Erasmus Taylor followed Virginia out of the Union "for good or ill." He became a Confederate staff officer in time for the battle of First Manassas in July 1861 and served intermittently until his surrender and parole at Appomattox in April

1865. His principal distinction was a lengthy stint as chief quartermaster for the corps commanded by General Longstreet, after whom the Taylors would later name a son.

Living directly in the path of war took its toll on the Taylor family, so much so that Roberta and the children relocated to Richmond. Although the fighting stopped in the spring of 1865, in some ways the worst was yet to come. In 1860 Erasmus held personal property valued at over twenty-six thousand dollars, a handsome sum for the times, but by 1870 that amount shriveled to only three thousand dollars. With a growing family and diminishing resources, Erasmus struggled to hold Meadow Farm; he was finally moved to reckless speculation in an attempt to recover his losses. Young Jack later recalled his family "living on very, very close rations," selling land and possessions, taking in boarders, and, as a last resort, mortgaging the estate itself. He also remembered his father's bold gamble to mine mineral resources there. Rail lines were laid, equipment was installed and shafts sunk—all in a futile attempt to extract iron ore.

The postbellum years thus compounded the hardships of the Confederate period, and the time came when Jack had to leave home both to make his own way and to help his family. In an earlier day he would have likely gone to a private academy and then to the University of Virginia, after which he would have embarked on a career as a gentleman-planter or lawyer-planter, in time inheriting some piece of the Taylor legacy. Instead, his education was limited to what he could absorb within the family and to a brief stint at The Meadows, a poverty-ridden school operated in nearby Albemarle by a kinsman of the Taylors and an ancestor of the future military giant U.S. Army General George S. Patton.

At the age of sixteen or seventeen, Jack left home for Richmond. He could not have known that the dusty road from Meadow Farm in time would stretch around the world to tobacco enterprises in dozens of countries or that his vision and drive would allow him to create what would become a multinational, billion-dollar conglomerate.

It should be said that Taylor did not travel alone. Although fate had deprived him of a princely legacy in a material sense, it had rewarded him in other ways. Necessity was his great teacher. His conservative temperament was founded in his youthful experiences of frugality and hard times and in the lessons he derived from the recklessness of his father. Jack would be energetic and enterprising but never financially speculative—and he would rarely buy anything he could not pay for. Taylor also took with him a love of family and place and a determination someday to restore Meadow Farm to its prewar splendor. Not the least of his assets was his name, one that would be known at each of his future stops. Because he was a Taylor he could get his foot in many doors along the way, but it was what he did that would open them fully.

How much young Taylor knew at this point about tobacco is uncertain. The leaf had been widely grown in Orange County, but the variety was the old Virginia type, likely cured by fire or air and thus unlike the bright, flue-cured variety on which his fortune would be made. It does seem clear, however, that he left Meadow Farm with the belief that, by diligent application, he could make money in tobacco. But first he would have to learn the business from the bottom up, which would be Richmond's initial contribution to the Taylor story.

Antebellum Richmond had been the tobacco capital of the world in an era when one city resident said the leaf was "in almost everyone's mouth, either for mastication, fumigation, inhalation, or discussion." By the 1870s, however, the adversity of war and the ascendancy of other tobacco towns had conspired to diminish Richmond's standing in the trade, though the leaf continued to enjoy preeminent status in the local community.

Jack Taylor arrived in the Virginia capital in 1878, just as the city was recovering from the worst effects of the national Panic of 1873. Through the family network he gained employment with one of Richmond tobacco's "Big Four" firms—namely Alexander Cameron and Company located at Cary and Twenty-fourth Streets in the city's tobacco district. Three Cameron brothers had migrated from Scotland before the Civil War and had established themselves as tobacconists in Petersburg, some twenty miles from Richmond; by the 1870s, their empire had expanded to include such disparate places as Australia and Richmond. The Richmond branch consisted of two operations: Alexander Cameron and Company, a plug factory run by Alexander; and Cameron and Cameron, which George oversaw as a cigarette- and cheroot-producing concern.

Cameron employed more workers than any other plant in Richmond, and Alexander's marriage into the Haxall family, long associated with the city's internationally famous flour mills, combined with his civic-mindedness to establish him as one of the town's foremost citizens. Cameron brands included "Venus," "Queen of the Seas," "Flower of All Nations," "Purity," and "Canuk." Managing one of the factories was William B. Taylor, perhaps a relative of Jack's and also a partner in the Taylor Brothers Tobacco Company, a well-known chewing tobacco firm in Winston-Salem.

Under the Cameron aegis, Jack Taylor entered the tobacco business as a common laborer. Later he would tell a grandson to expect "long years of fairly menial type work," his grandson later reported, "because there was no other way to learn anything about tobacco." For his first job he put labels on containers; he lived in the attic of the Cameron household. However humble the conditions, Jack Taylor was ideally positioned to learn about the tobacco business. Richmond's seventy-five tobacco factories ranked first among American cities and provided, in effect, a school as well as a testing ground for the fledgling entrepreneur.

The manufactured product of the 1870s was mainly plug or chewing tobacco with some attention given to smoking tobacco, snuff, and cigarettes. The latter product was positioned for a boom, however, and especially so under the leadership of the Richmond firm Allen and Ginter, which saw its daily output soar in the 1880s. In time, Allen and Ginter's "Richmond Straight Out No. 1" and "Pet" cigarettes would be known worldwide, thanks in part to Lewis Ginter's genius for advertising. His appealing if flamboyant boast was that the Allen and Ginter product contained only "the brightest, most delicate flavored and highest cost gold Leaf Tobacco grown in Virginia."

Although Richmond could rightly claim present and future primacy in cigarette manufacturing, it was losing its antebellum position as the nation's premier tobacco marketing center. On the eve of the Civil War, *DeBow's Review* had noted that "probably more tobacco was opened, inspected, and sold in Richmond than in any other city in the United States." The leaf arrived either loose in piles or tightly packed ("prized") in hogsheads, and it came by wagon, by boat, and by oxen.

From all points in the Tobacco Kingdom of Virginia and North Carolina, leaf found its way into Richmond, where state inspectors guaranteed quality and a local tobacco exchange oversaw sales both private and public. By the 1870s the erstwhile Confederate capital had serious rivals in small market towns throughout the burgeoning bright-leaf belt of North Carolina and Virginia and was experiencing strong competition from Danville, its neighbor to the west.

Following this shift in market focus, Jack Taylor left Richmond in 1881 to relocate in Danville. He had learned about the leaf and its manufacture in Richmond; now he would learn the business of buying and selling it in what locals claimed to be "the world's best tobacco market."

Founded in the late eighteenth century, Danville had long been a tobacco town. In its favor were good water and rail connections and a location in the heart of the area where bright leaf became king. Even before the Civil War, Danville had made its mark in the industry by implementing the loose-leaf auction system in warehouses built especially for the purpose. The "Danville system" spread rapidly, and by the 1880s ten large warehouses were active locally. A tobacco association conducted two auctions simultaneously, each selling at least 150 piles—which were larger than today's—per hour. In the year of Taylor's arrival, Danville sold over 30 million pounds of bright leaf, a figure far above Richmond, its closest rival. Add two dozen factories, and a local booster in 1885 could accurately assert that "the commercial and industrial life of the Town may be said to be almost wholly dependent upon the Tobacco trade."

Most of Danville's tobacco was sold to brokers, some 142 of whom were operating in the city by 1885. To buy low and to sell high was the dealer's art, and the 1880s was a golden age for speculative enterprise. Each sale tested one's judgment and nerve in what had become the nation's most competitive tobacco market.

The twenty-year-old Taylor entered this sink-or-swim trade under the tutelage of James G. Penn. Born in 1845, Penn had switched from manufacturing to dealing when he formed a partnership in Danville with John H. Pemberton in 1872. The enterprise prospered, and in time the company not only sold its leaf throughout the United States and abroad but also bought on order for the Japanese governmental monopoly.

Details are sketchy, but it is certain that Taylor became a successful dealer in Danville, earning enough money to take his first steps to save Meadow Farm from further deterioration and perhaps from the auctioneer's block. Taylor also recognized the boom-time potential of the bright leaf towns of North Carolina. Thus, with Penn's financial support, he moved again, once more following a trend. His destination was the hamlet of Henderson, where to the skills of a dealer he would add those of businessman and entrepreneur.

By relocating to Henderson, Jack Taylor became part of a larger movement of Virginians eager to profit from a growth in the tobacco business in the Tar Heel state. This trend predated the Civil War; production rose from 12 million pounds in 1850 to 33 million in 1860. This expansion had been spurred by the "discovery of a new type of leaf—the lemon-colored or bright leaf tobacco" and by the development in Caswell County of a new curing process utilizing charcoal-fired heat fed into storage barns by wooden flues. The result was a leaf that could be grown on sandy soil once regarded as unpromising for tobacco. North Carolina counties from Halifax to Stokes grew the new leaf in bulk and sold it in the traditional markets of the Old Dominion.

News of the quality of the bright leaf spread rapidly, in part because of an accident of history. In the spring of 1865, near Durham Station in the bright belt, Joseph E. Johnston's rag-tag Confederate army maneuvered to check a mammoth federal force under General William Tecumseh Sherman. Suddenly word arrived of Lee's surrender to Grant at Appomattox, and negotiations got underway for Sherman to receive a similar capitulation. Weeks passed and soldiers of the blue and gray, well over a hundred thousand strong, relaxed from the trials of combat and turned to the solace of tobacco. Many came to sample—and to like— the yellow and mild leaf of the Durham region. The armies soon left, but the soldiers took with them a fond memory of bright tobacco and spread the word of its quality.

Local farmers and entrepreneurs were quick to capitalize. John B. Green wisely changed the name of his smoking brand to "Bull Durham," thus launching a tobacco line soon familiar the world over. The Duke family—father Washington and his three sons—did well enough with their "Pro Bono Publico," but they also recognized the edge enjoyed by Green and his partners and thus switched in 1882 from pipe tobacco to the manufacture of cigarettes. This decision ultimately led to wealth the likes of which earlier tobacconists could scarcely have dreamed.

With a combination of innovative machinery, creative advertising, and competitive zeal, the family, now paced by son James Buchanan ("Buck") Duke, became industrywide pioneers and built an empire that in time included the American Tobacco Company as well as the world giant British American Tobacco. The number of cigarette factories in Carolina rose dramatically, and manufacturing centers developed in Durham, Winston-Salem, Reidsville, and elsewhere. The demand for Lord Bright likewise increased as the growing region spread into the Carolina coastal plain. Enterprising railroad executives also played their part as new market centers sprang up in the closing decades of the nineteenth century. Few of the new tobacco towns were so well located as the one to which Jack Taylor moved in the mid-1880s.

Although incorporated in 1841, Henderson had languished in its early years. The population had numbered a mere 186 in 1860. The war era had extracted its price, and a fire in 1870 had destroyed the town's business district. But suddenly the city's fortunes changed. The rapidly expanding bright belt offered new opportunities, cotton revived to the east, and several rail lines linked Henderson with cities in all directions.

Farmers had formerly taken their crops by wagon into Virginia, but on January 29, 1873, David Y. Cooper had conducted the first local auction sale in a nondescript wooden building. Just four years later Cooper had a handsome brick structure, complete with a marble slab embellished with gilded leaves courtesy of Richmond's Allen and Ginter, and Cooper claimed to be selling "more tobacco than any other warehouse in the world." Cooper enjoyed an extensive wagon trade as he serviced farmers from fifteen counties, garnering sales of 7 million pounds annually by the mid-1880s.

Cooper soon had competitors. By 1881, when Vance County was incorporated, Henderson claimed a population of two thousand as well as four "real streets, eighteen saloons, eight attorneys, several auction warehouses, and five tobacco manufacturers." By 1885 when Taylor arrived, Henderson was the location of four major houses, from fifty to sixty regular buyers, and several prize houses, one of which was five stories tall.

Jack Taylor wasted little time establishing himself in the expanding market. Danville had taught him the ins-and-outs of judging and buying tobacco, and he arrived with the advantage of financial support from Pemberton and Penn, whom he represented at the outset, and of Taylor kinsmen already well known in the community. His rapid rise can be attributed to his drive and acumen and to his ability to enlarge upon his opportunities.

After buying for Pemberton and Penn, Taylor formed his own company in 1886—a venture that by 1896 was referred to as "the great leaf shipping and exporting establishment of J.P. Taylor & Company, one of the largest in the South." Sometime within that first decade, Taylor also built or acquired a mammoth factory, hailed as "one of the most completely equipped" in the South. In the process he won the friendship of Buck Duke and of other aspiring tobacco dealers in the Tar Heel state.

J.P. Taylor also became president of the Henderson Storage and Inspection Company, incorporated in 1889, which was the state's first facility of its kind and evidence of Taylor's entrepreneurial spirit. The company stopped a large flow of tobacco to Richmond and Petersburg, and Taylor began to profit handsomely from handling tobacco as well as from buying and selling it.

Within a decade of settling in Henderson, Taylor displayed two other qualities that would propel him to later success: he was a good judge of young talent, and he was prepared to venture beyond his home base. Both points are illustrated in the case of Rommie Purefoy Watson. A farm boy from the region and a Wake Forest alumnus, Watson was still a teenager when he went to work for the J.P. Taylor Company in 1888. Seven years later he went to Wilson, North Carolina, one of the most promising of the new markets on the Coastal Plains, to establish R.P. Watson and Company, destined to be one of the largest dealers in the trade. Watson's silent partner and sponsor was Jack Taylor.

James I. Miller also caught Taylor's eye. Miller had arrived in Henderson in 1895 as an eighteen year old, with twenty dollars in his pocket and no guarantee of work. After warehouse employment distinguished largely by the fact that he married the owner's daughter, Miller took auditor positions with the telephone company and with J.P. Taylor. He was soon working full time with Taylor, who became a close friend and mentor. Miller's rise can only be described as meteoric. When the J.P. Taylor Company was incorporated in North Carolina in 1904, one of its partners was James I. Miller. His incentive-heavy deal with Taylor was "base salary, plus bonus and stock options." Ultimately Miller became president of the Taylor Company and a founder of Universal. In 1924 he broke away, relocated in Wilson, and formed a company bearing his own name, eventually doing business on a global basis.

While advancing the careers of younger men such as Miller and Watson, Taylor also began to venture into Kentucky, land of the burley and dark leaf, and showed some courage in buying, gun in holster, in the dark tobacco district during the violent days of the Black Patch War of the early 1900s. Taylor continued to be an active citizen in Henderson; he invested in several nontobacco enterprises and contributed much to the town's growth and development. Now in his early fifties, trim at six feet and 170 pounds, Taylor enjoyed an even temperament and excellent health. The latter he attributed to his forswearing of hot sauces and his adoption of the practice of "Fletcherizing," by which he chewed his food what according to an observer seemed an interminable number of times before he swallowed.

Taylor had a knack for quickly following trends in the industry, and in 1912, he aligned himself with the future once again—by returning to Richmond. Almost forty years had passed since he had left Meadow Farm and first settled in Richmond. The city, now with a population of over 132,000 had largely freed itself from the ravages of the 1860s, though war memories remained and were enshrined in monuments, sites, and commemorative observances. Richmond's tobacco mix was also changing. The town no longer claimed preeminence in market size or in production. Although large amounts of tobacco continued to be brought, sold, and manufactured locally, the city had lost its primacy in these basic categories to such competitors as Danville, Durham, Reidsville, and Winston-Salem. But to any tobacconist who could see the future, Richmond held several attractions. Popular taste in consumption was moving rapidly toward cigarettes and away from cigars, pipes, and chewing tobacco. The Virginia capital was destined to serve several major cigarette manufacturers, who were following in the footsteps of the industry pioneer in the South, Major Lewis Ginter. Richmond would also become a center for leaf dealers—entrepreneurs who neither grew nor manufactured tobacco but who, at risk, bought, handled, and sold it. Richmond's advantages in transportation and financial resources and its proximity to major markets added to its appeal.

In Richmond dealers had access to the three most desirable types of American leaf for cigarette manufacture: the low-nicotine bright or flue-cured tobacco to the south and southwest; the highly absorbent, air-cured burley to the west; and the long-burning, air-cured Maryland type to the north. Richmond was not beyond reach of other key markets—namely, cigar leaf from Pennsylvania, Wisconsin, and Connecticut, western Kentucky's dark-fired and dark air-cured leaf popular in snuff and chewing tobacco, and the flue-cured tobacco that spread down the Atlantic coast to South Carolina, Georgia, and Florida.

Jack Taylor's motives for relocating are unclear. Though he no doubt appreciated Richmond's strategic location, family considerations perhaps played a role. Married in 1895 to Katherine Wall of Maryland, he had lived comfortably in Henderson. But as children Mary and Jaquelin Erasmus began to grow up, Taylor decided to sell his house to partner James I. Miller and shift his headquarters to Richmond.

In 1912 Taylor took his family on a pleasure trip to Europe—his only visit there—and returned to take up residence in Richmond. The Taylors lived in rental property while an impressive house was constructed for them at 2325 Monument Avenue, a suburban street only recently farm land but rapidly becoming a fashionable residential address and one of the South's most renowned boulevards, which would be marked in time by impressive statues to honor Confederate heroes Lee, Stuart, Jackson, Davis, and Maury.

With the outbreak of World War I in 1914, demand for American tobacco soared, and Taylor took certain steps that served as necessary preliminaries to the founding of the Universal Leaf Tobacco Company in 1918. On June 30, 1916, the accounting firm of Ernst and Ernst presented reports on the financial status of the J.P. Taylor Company and its subsidiaries. A few days later, on July 11, came the incorporation of the J.P. Taylor Company of Virginia "for the purpose of taking over the business and property of the J.P. Taylor Company, a North Carolina Corporation, and continuing same as a going concern." For $814,815.85, Taylor of North Carolina was bought by Taylor of Virginia, which authorized initial capital stock of $1 million, divided into shares with a par value of $100 each.

Taylor became president of the new corporation and James I. Miller secretary-treasurer; lawyer Lewis C. Williams served briefly as vice president before being replaced by Thomas B. Yuille, late of the American Tobacco Company. Officers would serve as directors, and initial salaries were set. Legal counsel was asked to "domesticate" the company in North Carolina and Kentucky for purposes of doing business in those states. General offices were located in the Allison Building at 803½ East Main Street in Richmond's financial district.

By the time of incorporation, Jack Taylor had built a multistate enterprise. The company's business, simply put, was "to buy, sell and deal in, and deal with leaf tobacco whether for its own account or on commission." Assets exceeded liabilities by $720,000 and Taylor's financial management was adjudged by Ernst and Ernst as sound and "conservative." In addition to headquarters in Richmond, there were branches in Henderson and in the Kentucky towns of Lexington, Maysville, Carrollton, and Shelbyville.

Business was also conducted through agents elsewhere in the United States and abroad and through companies into which Taylor had bought or with which he worked on the basis of joint accounts. The Taylor-associated companies in 1916 included the W.A. Adams Company of Oxford, North Carolina; the C.B. Cheatham Company of Farmville, North Carolina; the Person-Garrett Company of Greenville, North Carolina; the R.P. Watson Company of Wilson, North Carolina; the W.A. Willingham Company of Danville; and the W.H. Winstead Company of Baltimore, Goldsboro, North Carolina, and Owensboro, Kentucky, among others. Cash deposits were divided among banks in Kentucky, New York, North Carolina, and Virginia.

It is clear that J.P. Taylor's business was not only profitable but extensive enough to deal in a variety of tobacco types. In addition to the flagship in Henderson, redrying and storage facilities were located in all major belts. In an era when a few hogsheads constituted a respectable sale, Taylor's customers were numerous in both this country and abroad, with two of the most significant being the Japanese monopoly and the legendary Nanyang Brothers of Shanghai, China.

The records of 1916 also reveal the names of several tobacconists who later became indispensable props in the Universal system. Andrew Jamieson (of W.A. Adams), C.B. Cheatham, James I. Miller, Thomas A. Person and his soon-to-be partner G.R. Garrett, W.H. Willingham, and W.H. Winstead were all leading dealers in their own right by World War I. Among the lesser figures of 1916 destined for larger roles later were Kenneth R. Edwards ("buyer, Lexington"), Robert L. Kimbrough ("Manager, Cynthiana"), J.B. Strickland ("Manager, Lexington branch"), William Donnell ("Manager, Springfield, Ky., plant"), and F.J. Weil ("Manager, Carrollton plant").

Working with these and other dealers, Taylor had become a master of the multiple deal, sometimes involving three or more participants. Joint accounts and ventures were common, as when a local company or partner might buy and pack the leaf on its own market with Taylor assuming responsibility for purchase, transportation and storage, and the ultimate sale. Then, as later, a man's word was his bond; written contracts were—and still are in the tobacco business—virtually unknown, with the system operating in a manner personal and informal, if a bit chaotic.

By 1916 almost forty years had passed since Jack Taylor had left Orange County taking with him little in the way of material wealth. He had started as a laborer in a Richmond factory and had moved with the trends of his day, relocating in response to opportunity. In the process he had mastered each phase of tobacco marketing and production and had learned the tobacco business from the ground up.

By 1916 Taylor ranked as one of the most prominent and prosperous dealers in America. With Meadow Farm reclaimed and his family settled in comfortable style, Jack Taylor, now in his late fifties, might reasonably have rested. But his enterprising spirit dictated yet another move. This move would be entrepreneurial, not physical, and it would propel Jack Taylor beyond his previous accomplishments in America's tobacco belts. Indeed, it would place him squarely in the center of a global stage.

2
Founding and Early Years

Universal Leaf was typical in many ways of corporations that came into being during World War I. At first, demand virtually guaranteed success and encouraged sudden and at times reckless growth, but a postwar depression brought disaster. The organizers of Universal aimed high and fell hard before they adjusted to a moderate course and finally achieved success. Along the way corporate leadership changed dramatically; virtually all Universal's founders retired, left the company, or assumed passive roles as younger men assumed control.

Although the exact date is unknown, at some point during the war years Jaquelin P. Taylor set upon a scheme to create the largest dealer organization in the world. He planned to accomplish this by combining his own holdings with those of several prominent tobacconists who formerly had been active in the American Tobacco Company, a trust "perhaps, the most amazing in all the chronicles of high finance." The company would buy leaf tobacco from the farmer, store it, and later resell it at a profit.

Under the leadership of Taylor's old friend, James B. Duke, the American Tobacco Company had been founded in 1890. The "trust"—as the company soon became known—combined the country's five leading cigarette manufacturers and controlled perhaps 90 percent of the market. Twenty years later, with Duke as president, American claimed 80 percent control of all aspects of the nation's tobacco industry, except cigars. This growth bred antagonism and eventually led to prosecution under the terms of the Sherman Antitrust Act of 1890. In 1911 the United States Supreme Court ordered the American Tobacco Company broken up, a task so complicated that, ironically, it had to be supervised by Buck Duke himself. From the wreckage emerged cigarette's "Big Four"—American, Liggett and Myers, P. Lorillard, and R.J. Reynolds—as well as an array of snuff, cigar, and other tobacco companies.

Jack Taylor knew many of the principal figures in the old American organization and shared their appreciation of the opportunities available in a competitive marketplace fueled by the wartime demand for tobacco. The mechanism for action was simple: Taylor had his holdings formally assessed; his prospective partners did likewise; and stock in the old companies was exchanged for stock in a new one.

After general principles had been decided, Taylor's lawyers —from the Richmond firm of Williams and Mullen—moved in to incorporate what became the Universal Leaf Tobacco Company. Early 1918 passed in legal preliminaries: on January 25, the Virginia State Corporation Commission issued a charter of incorporation. The following day a maximum of 16 million shares of capital stock was authorized, and on February 13, fixed capital stock was set at $10,750,000.

The new stock was exchanged on an agreed-upon formula for all capital stock of companies bearing the names of J.P. Taylor, Patrick H. Gorman, Oscar C. Gregory, C.B. Cheatham, and W.H. Winstead. Always conservative, Jack Taylor and his J.P. Taylor Company took all the 7,500 shares of Class A preferred stock as well as a controlling portion (52,000 shares) of two classes of common; Pat Gorman received 20,000 shares in common stock, and the other three individuals split the remaining 9,316 shares. (Stock allocations would be subsequently amended.) Bylaws were approved, and on February 28 a provisional board of directors was chosen.

On March 1, 1918, at the Taylor offices in Richmond, the lawyer-incorporators stepped aside, and the first real officers were chosen. Jaquelin P. Taylor became chairman of the board, with Thomas B. Yuille president. Vice president and secretary was William A. Willingham. Vice president and treasurer was James I. Miller, with Patrick H. Gorman serving as vice president. The assistant secretary-treasurer was S.J. Shivers.

Universal's initial leadership came evenly from the two founding sources: the Taylor group (Taylor, Willingham, and Miller) and the old American group, consisting of Yuille, Gorman, and Shivers. Shivers played only a secondary role before his death in mid-1919, but the others were men of consequence in the tobacco business.

Willingham (1872-1945) came from South Boston, Virginia, a town destined to provide Universal with key officers down to the modern era. He attended business school in New York, then returned home to begin over a half century's career as a tobacconist. After a stint with American, and also with Yuille, he formed his own trading company in Danville and then joined forces with Taylor, serving as an early officer of the J.P. Taylor Company of Virginia.

James I. Miller rose from clerk to become Taylor's right-hand man and resident manager of J.P. Taylor's Henderson operation. Born in 1877, he had by 1916 come to be one of three original directors of the

Virginia company, and in 1920 he replaced Taylor as its president. In the meantime Miller moved to Richmond and lived with his family in one of the city's best-known residences, the former mansion of Major Lewis Ginter at 901 West Franklin Street. Miller died in 1964.

Universal's first true president, Thomas B. Yuille, ranked among the leading tobacconists in the country. From an old-line Scots family in the Valley of Virginia, he started in the business as a buyer for Dibrell Brothers in Danville in 1886, when he was only seventeen years old. A few years later he joined the leaf department of the newly formed American combine. By 1901 he headed the leaf purchasing division of the trust and was a resident of New York City. After the breakup in 1911, Yuille remained with American as vice president in charge of tobacco leaf purchasing and manufacturing.

Five years later, Yuille left American to become vice president and director of J.P. Taylor in Virginia and no doubt helped to plan the formation of Universal. Serving on numerous boards in the financial and business communities in Richmond and in New York, he was re- garded as a shrewd individual and a tough trader. Until his death in 1934, Yuille brought to Universal not only standing in the leaf world but connections in New York City and within the old trust system.

From the American stable also came Patrick Henry Gorman (1873- 1946), who, like Taylor and Yuille, had risen to the top in the late nine- teenth century. Born in Raleigh, North Carolina, Gorman entered the business as a floor sweep at age thirteen. Five years later he made his first trip abroad "trying to get the English tobacco merchants to buy direct from him and not go through intermediary English tobacco bro- kers." At age nineteen he initiated the first sale held in Greenville, North Carolina. At twenty-one he headed the P.H. Gorman Company, a high- volume dealership in the emerging Eastern belt in North Carolina and was soon named president of the Greenville Tobacco Board of Trade.

Along the way, Gorman's interests expanded to include cigar leaf, and in 1900 he joined the trust to buy its cigar tobacco in Cuba, Puerto Rico, and the Netherlands. He became fluent in the Spanish language in the process. By 1912 he had become a director of American and vice president of the American Cigar Company. Four years later he resigned and "reorganized the Patrick H. Gorman Company as a worldwide com- mission buyer of tobacco" with branches in all major American belts and headquarters in Durham. His strengths included a knowledge of both cigar and cigarette leaf and a buying and selling organization that was strategically placed.

The original board of directors of Universal consisted of the five principal officers plus five other well-known tobacconists. The nonofficers included three men within the company—W.H. Winstead, Oscar C. Gregory, and William S. Luckett—and two—John B. Cobb and Joseph F. Cullman Jr.—from the outside. Gregory (1875-1930) and Winstead (1876-1962) were North Carolinians who had started in the tobacco industry at early ages and who headed Universal subsidiaries; Luckett, a Kentuckian, had been associated with Gorman at American Cigar and would be elected a Universal vice president in 1918.

The two outside directors—Cobb and Cullman—had in common friendships with several Universal officers and distinguished careers in the business. Moreover, both were positioned to help the fledgling corporation in markets beyond the Old Dominion. A Virginia native, John Blackwell Cobb (1857-1923) came from a prominent tobacco family and went on to become an expert buyer and eventually head of the leaf department of Duke's trust. Finally, he served as president of the American Cigar Company. Diversifying his interests, Cobb acquired holdings in drug and chemical companies and enjoyed a reputation for philanthropy in his adopted home of New York City.

Joseph F. Cullman Jr. was, simply put, a rising star in what was quickly becoming a dynasty in America's tobacco industry. His father, Joe Senior, was well established as a New York cigar leaf dealer and also had a brief stint on the Universal board in 1918 while Joe Junior, born in 1882, was serving in the military. In time, the Cullmans moved into the cigarette area of the business and acquired Benson and Hedges. Philip Morris later acquired them, and the Cullmans led both firms to success and expansion. Joe Junior, who died in 1955, is still remembered as one of the most important tobacconists of the twentieth century.

Universal's founding fathers were long-time tobacco men with excellent connections in all major leaf areas and also with the giant manufacturers who appeared after the trust was dissolved in 1911. Although most of Universal's leaders could claim only limited academic training, virtually all had grown up in the tobacco business and had prospered in an era of unrestrained competition followed by another era of consolidation that forced out many dealers and small manufacturers. A Virginia or North Carolina heritage also united most of the new officers and directors. Almost all, however, were in the final stages of their careers.

Although they were practical tobacconists, the founders were almost euphoric about the prospects of the corporation they pretentiously had named "Universal." J.P. Taylor predicted "the business to be had was limited only by the ability of the organization to handle and finance it." An early advertisement described Universal as "Dealers in Leaf Tobacco from Everywhere to Everywhere," and an early news story noted that "the company handles all grades and sells to snuff, cigarette, cigar, smoking, and chewing tobacco manufacturers." From the point of view of these men, there was no limit to the success that the company might enjoy.

In many ways such optimism was justified. By forming one company from many, buying power was consolidated, competition among partners removed or at least restricted, and uncoordinated sales made part of an orchestrated network. Moreover, financial resources were combined, processing plants shared, and orders could be filled "without delay for any class or grade of tobacco and upon any market" and at prices made attractive by volume buying. The new venture would be run by seasoned tobacconists, individuals united in the belief that profit was to be made by providing a service to foreign and domestic manufacturers.

The timing also seemed favorable. World War I had proved a bonanza for American tobacconists, especially cigarette manufacturers. Antismoking sentiment, never strong in that era, quickly faded; more and more women took up the cigarette habit. Oriental or Turkish blended cigarettes gave way to those made essentially from American leaf, and in 1917 and 1918 doughboys popularized American brands throughout Europe. Cigarette production in the United States rose from under 9 million in 1910 to well over 16 million in 1914 then to over 57 million in 1918. Cigarettes soon replaced cigars as the most popular form of smoking in America.

Tobacco, almost regardless of type or quality, was in demand, and the opportunity for profit was great. Each of the manufacturing "Big Four" had its own leaf-buying division, but each also bought from independents. Among the latter, consolidation was in the air, as the total number of dealers declined from four thousand in 1913 to three thousand in 1918. Preceding Universal as a major new combine was the International Planters Corporation, organized in 1916, with subsidiaries throughout the principal buying belts.

Functioning as a new concept in the tobacco business, the infant Universal would largely be a holding company. That is, it would "hold" varying amounts of stock in a variety of both subsidiary and partner companies, owning 100 percent of some and offering leadership to all.

To oversee this complex network, Universal initially had two administrative headquarters—one in New York City, which was responsible for sales and corporate administration, and another in Richmond, which supervised leaf purchasing and processing.

In 1918 New York City was a worldwide center in the tobacco trade. Most European buyers had their principal offices there, as did the giant American Tobacco Company and other leading domestic firms. The port itself was a leader in leaf shipping, and the city's financial resources were vital for large tobacco deals. The leaf barons of New York lived affluently and set the tone for aspiring companies throughout the industry.

Universal's New York office was located at 21 East Fortieth Street on the corner of Madison Avenue; the company occupied the entire tenth floor and part of the ninth. A dozen private offices decorated with Persian rugs opened from a spacious and well-appointed reception area. The tobacco sample room was as likely to be stocked with whiskey as with leaf—hospitality was the hallmark of the leading New York tobacconists.

Headed by the flinty Tom Yuille and the jovial Pat Gorman, the New York office was manned largely by former employees of the American Tobacco Company. In addition to running the company, the principal officers served as the sales force; other nonofficers worked in support of salesmen. The company's secretary and its treasurer each had assistants, and all enjoyed the support of a coterie of accountants, bookkeepers, clerks, and secretaries. At the outset the transportation manager was located in New York, as was a "book man" or accountant for each of the principal subsidiaries.

Universal's Richmond office remained that of the J.P. Taylor Company at 803½ East Main Street, occupying space that was relatively small and had its seedy aspects. Taylor remained the principal officer in residence. Also likely to be on hand were such leaf experts as K.R. Edwards and O.C. Gregory, who oversaw the buying and who had contacts with the "Big Four," several of whom also had leaf headquarters in Richmond. Through the Taylor Company, Universal also operated a processing plant in the city.

Universal boasted that it bought on all major markets, and this was made possible by a network of affiliated companies, all of which had been or were still independent dealers whose combined geographic range did in fact cover the spectrum of market possibilities. Universal had resident companies buying not only throughout the bright and the burley regions but also in cigar leaf and in such exotic types as western Kentucky's "Green River" and "One Sucker." Universal's control of affiliated companies ranged from one-third to 100 percent.

From the beginning, Universal affiliates had considerable latitude. "The operating people in each company," wrote one veteran tobacco man, were "almost autonomous." Universal might "supply help for financing and selling but in management...[it would] capitalize on the abilities of the partners." The companies Universal owned 100 percent, such as J.P. Taylor, were run by the front office. Universal's president traditionally was also the Taylor president, but affiliates in which the company controlled 50 percent or less functioned more like partners than subsidiaries. Some of the partners were old-time tobacco barons accustomed to success—and to success on their own terms. Typically, a subsidiary bought on designated markets, which were usually local, and used its plants, which were usually small, to receive, regrade, process, package, and store the tobacco for subsequent sale. Most had established their own clients, and, to complicate matters, some, like W.A. Adams, had foreign customers as well. A few subsidiaries also had their own subsidiaries!

As much as possible, Universal drew on the strengths of its subsidiaries and allowed them to continue profitable patterns that were well established, even if it meant one arm of the family might be competing with another in a given market—or even for a particular customer. Multiple accounts were common, with as many as four subsidiaries being involved in various phases of a particular deal. Tobacco might be bought by one subsidiary, processed by another, billed to a third, and sold by a fourth.

In the beginning not all the subsidiaries were leaf dealers. Within the Universal network were at least two steamship companies, a processor that "rehandled" tobacco for the African trade, a storage company, and a Kentucky distillery. Foreign subsidiaries included a tobacco company to cultivate leaf tobacco in Puerto Rico and Santo Domingo as well as a trading company as far away as Canada.

Business at the fledgling company was at the outset equal to Taylor's optimism, as Universal purchased about 10 percent of the market during the 1918 and 1919 crop years. In 1918 the company bought about 100 million pounds, of which 44 million were in turn sold to the Big Four and other manufacturers created by the breakup of American. The principal customer was P. Lorillard, long tied to the Taylor Company, with roughly 20 million pounds. Most of this business was sold on order, but some was disposed of on a speculative basis wherein Universal bought the leaf on its own and then sold it later—for example, to American, which purchased almost 6 million pounds in this way. It is significant that Universal did considerable business with the "Big Four," each of which had its own buying arm but none of which could cover all markets as effectively as could Universal and its affiliates.

In addition to doing business with the heirs of the old trust system, Universal sold heavily to smaller manufacturers, such as Continental (a predecessor of Philip Morris) and Stephano Brothers of Philadelphia, within this country and abroad. The demand for American leaf was so heavy that foreign sales were often made "on description"—as opposed to "on inspection"—of a sample, as manufacturers in Europe clamored for all the tobacco the United States could deliver.

Lesser amounts were sold to such substantial accounts as the giant British American Tobacco conglomerate, Nanyang Brothers in China, and the Japanese government monopoly. Again, sales came both from direct orders and from purchases made from the company's inventory. On-order deals promised sure, but often only modest, profits; a speculative purchase could bring either reward or disaster—selling prices sometimes fell as holdings increased. In either case, for its leaf procurement—and especially for leaf that went into inventory—Universal borrowed heavily, mainly from banks in New York. But, in both buying and selling, deals were made on a handshake: a man's word was his bond, and a man who broke his word faced ostracism.

Although Universal immediately established itself as a major dealer, competition came from such independents as Dibrell Brothers, an old-line firm in Danville, Virginia, from the newer International Planters Corporation, and from numerous family-owned companies. A government report in 1920 estimated that Universal and International together had bought "from forty to fifty percent of the tobacco that is not taken by the leading foreign and domestic manufacturers in the heaviest producing areas, with Universal's being the more active of the two."

Credit for Universal's successful launching must be divided among several of the founders at the upper echelons as well as among scores of individual tobacconists. But as the excitement of a new beginning gave way to the pattern of a daily routine, leadership settled into the capable hands of two men—Thomas B. Yuille, Universal's first true president, and, second in influence, James I. Miller.

The narrowing of authority to these two men resulted not only from the drive and talents of Yuille and Miller but from the retirements and deaths of other founders. J.P. Taylor, for example, resigned as chairman in early 1922, expressing his intention "to be relieved of all business responsibilities" in preference for the pursuit of personal happiness at Meadow Farm. Taylor remained an influential director until his death in 1950, serving along the way as a conservative voice on the finance committee and maintaining an interest in (and some influence on) company affairs. Essentially, however, he was an elder statesman in his late years.

Although shrewd businessmen and respected tobacconists, Yuille and Miller offered sharp contrasts. Yuille, the older of the two, had been educated by Buck Duke, and some believed that Duke himself had manipulated Yuille into the presidency of Universal in an effort to check the "unfriendly" consolidation of independent dealers. Though a Southerner, Yuille understood New York City and its world of banking, finance, and stock exchanges and preferred to live there in an affluent style at a prestigious address on Fifth Avenue. A short, genial individual, he moved comfortably in the elite circles of business and of society.

Miller was no less self-made than Yuille, but Miller's rise had been within the Taylor system and within a world that stretched basically from Henderson, North Carolina, to Richmond. He had relocated from the former to the latter easily enough and established himself as an earnest, upright individual, a director of several local institutions, and a popular Sunday School teacher at Richmond's First Baptist Church. Perhaps even before J.P. Taylor's retirement, Miller was the force behind the Taylor Company and served as the Richmond counterpart to Yuille. Both men contributed heavily to Universal's success, but within six years of the founding, both would be gone from the scene; each would take with him censure as well as acclaim.

Aided by Miller, Gorman, and to a lesser extent by others, Yuille presided over the company as it refined the disparate conglomerate of 1918 into a working and ongoing business system. Some subsidiaries were dissolved or liquidated; others were added as territorial responsibilities were rearranged; and buying in the bright and the burley markets was coordinated by a central committee. The Richmond plant—and others—closed, but space was acquired for relocation of the Richmond office in the new Richmond Trust Building at Seventh and Main Streets. In addition, foreign agents were hired for South America and the Far East, and ties were strengthened with long-standing representatives such as I.C. Solberg (in Norway), Frank Watson (who operated both in London and in Liverpool), Luis Almeida (in Portugal), and Charles H. Suhling (in Germany). In 1920 officer-director William S. Luckett established a European branch by converting an apartment on Paris's Champs Elysees into a luxury office complete with the obligatory Persian rugs. When Luckett fell ill, his fellow Kentuckian F.J. Weil replaced him.

Within top management, a finance committee was established in 1920; chaired by Yuille, it met monthly in New York. Later, subcommittees were named for both inventory and audit. In 1919, the president confessed his inability to prepare an annual report despite his "most diligent efforts" because of confusion within the subsidiary companies' stock holdings and because of the complex demands of new federal regulations. Townsend, Dix, and Pogson of New York City became Universal's auditors and issued the first of many annual statements; because of its simplicity and color, the report was called "the blue blotter." As for government regulations, the company survived a 1920 investigation by the Federal Trade Commission, which combed the tobacco industry for antitrust violations. The Richmond firm of Williams and Mullen became general counsel for Universal and its subsidiaries in 1922; Mullen himself would serve as a director for decades.

Universal's board met mainly in Richmond but occasionally in New York, and the annual meeting shifted from the third Tuesday in February to the same day in September, thus making it possible to have an annual report geared to the fiscal year. In these early years a sinking fund was established to begin retiring the company's large amount of outstanding preferred stock, and the officers approved numerous exchanges and realignments of stock among the affiliates. They also took steps to streamline the financing of affiliates.

Early on, the New York and Richmond accounting departments were consolidated in Richmond; a young bookkeeper named Harry Hitchcock physically guarded and traveled with the records, sleeping on them in the drawing room of a train from New York and supervising a team of Red Caps and taxis to move them.

A "contingent compensation" policy was also implemented. Initially only for ranking officers, it was later extended to include others in the company. Thus in the 1920s was born the forerunner of Universal's current bonus system. The plan also reflected the early development of one of the company's ongoing principles—financial incentives tied to performance.

Yuille also oversaw several plans to impose order on the expanding number of partners and subsidiary companies. In 1922, a single buying and processing arm was successfully established in the burley region under the name of Southwestern; a similar venture in the bright markets, called Southern States, had failed. More ambitiously, an attempt was made in the same year to consolidate most of Universal's non-cigarette leaf enterprises under one umbrella called Industrial Leaf. This new part of the business was to be funded by a complex arrangement in which Universal stockholders exchanged their common for Industrial's 8 percent preferred, with Industrial using the dividends of the company's common to pay for companies it took over.

In the category of corporate good citizenship, in 1922 Universal subscribed to government war bonds, contributed to the Japanese Relief Fund, and gave $250 to the Virginia Historical Pageant Association "in connection with the tobacco floats to be exhibited during Pageant week." As a pat on the back of a promising young employee, the board gave K.R. Edwards its congratulations and a check for $500 on the occasion of his wedding.

At a meeting of the board in Richmond, the directors professed surprise and regret at having received a brief notice of resignation, dated May 29, 1923, from President Thomas B. Yuille. Yuille stated simply that he was moving on to other challenges in the business. He had agreed to serve as chairman of Tobacco Products Corporation, then a vital cog in the Duke empire, and would also later serve as TPC's president. His departure from Universal must have been friendly, since he later returned as a company director. In one sense he deserved the thanks of the Universal family because, as its first president, he had played a central role in its construction, launching, and early voyage. And yet, he was also leaving it amid troubled times of financial distress.

When Yuille resigned the presidency of Universal in May 1923, the company's future was far from secure. After its founding in 1918, Universal had enjoyed immediate success, but as the decade of the 1920s got underway, financial difficulties plagued the infant corporation. Some problems came from adverse market conditions, others from flaws within the company, but all combined to produce Universal's first crisis. The solution came in part from the emergence of a new generation of officers headed by Frederick N. Harrison, whose twenty-two-year presidency began officially in September 1924.

Financial analysts would have little trouble spotting danger signs within the Universal system in the early 1920s. Bank borrowing rose sharply, inventory levels increased, the quarterly dividend on common stock was cut a third and then suspended entirely, and, most ominously, the company's capital stock depreciated sharply. Net profits fell from about $1.5 million in fiscal year 1923 to $950 thousand in fiscal year 1924. Also alarming was the borrowing by subsidiaries on their own authority and the virtual collapse of the giant affiliate, Industrial Leaf. Despite its youth, the company had already employed four treasurers and five assistant treasurers.

In some ways, Universal was a victim of the times. World War I had been a bonanza for American farmers and tobacconists alike, with its soaring prices, production, and profits. The war ended in 1918, but not, however, the farmer's optimism, and the 1919 and 1920 crops were unusually good. Then came a worldwide collapse in commodity prices triggered by overproduction combined with war-torn Europe's inability to buy and compounded by trade and credit problems.

The Great Depression for agriculture started not in 1929 but years earlier, and the entire nation buckled under a recession at the outset of the 1920s. Burley prices, for example, fell from 33 cents per pound to 13.4; in early 1921, bids opened between 10 and 15 cents only to plummet to between 3 and 5. Violence broke out in Lexington, Kentucky's great market, and buying stopped there and elsewhere. The farmers' bitterness led to a cooperative movement and to a Federal Trade Commission investigation of the industry.

The European market also collapsed. As James I. Miller reported in late 1920, overseas trade was "thoroughly demoralized," and England in particular was "badly congested with Bright tobaccos." Postwar instability and a glut proved too much for International Planters, which collapsed in 1922.

Management decisions also contributed to Universal's plight. As market prices fell, the company's speculative purchases rose. Universal built up a sizable inventory but began to find sales more difficult to conclude. The inventory included "old tobacco" that had been bought even earlier at higher prices. One major customer, Nanyang Brothers of Shanghai, had been badly oversold, and Universal was faced with the prospect of losing a valued client.

In retrospect, it is clear that Universal had grown too fast and with too little control over its subsidiaries. The multimillion-dollar Industrial Leaf conglomerate had been underfinanced from the start, and its push in cigar leaf came at the time when cigars were rapidly losing ground to cigarettes. Within the Universal family, new bank accounts and increased borrowing had proliferated, and borrowing had become increasingly expensive. Contributing to the problem to a lesser degree was the extravagance Universal lavished on its New York and Paris offices as well as on its principal officers.

James I. Miller also made unfortunate investments, though the situation is difficult to unravel. As president of both the Taylor Company and Southern States and as one of the principal organizers of Universal, Miller had amassed wealth and influence second only to Yuille's. When the presidency became available in mid-1923, it was offered to Miller, who declined, partly it appears because he opposed relocating to New York City. Perhaps he also let the opportunity pass because a story was already unfolding that would ultimately force him to leave.

Miller's fall from power was set against the backdrop of his own severe medical problems. During a slow recovery, Miller made a number of unfortunate investments. His worst decision was pledging $1.5 million for a huge tract of Georgia forest land that was no more than scrub timber. Miller had drawn heavily from his holdings in Universal stock for collateral and he needed cash from dividends to meet his interest payments. The cessation of the quarterly dividends on the company's common and the depreciation of Universal's stock crushed him, but apparently not before he was able to manipulate some of the company's assets.

Finally, on April 9, 1924, Miller's standing had become "intolerable," and he resigned as both officer and director to, he wrote, "go into business myself." Initially, he returned to Henderson where, with Universal financing, he founded the James I. Miller Company. In 1929 he relocated to Wilson, North Carolina, where his remaining decades were spent as a successful businessman, active churchman, and civic leader. Meanwhile, Universal spent years attempting to salvage something from the Georgia forest land Miller had purchased.

With Yuille's departure, the Universal presidency passed briefly to another of the senior founders, William A. Willingham, a Virginian who did not share Miller's distaste for living in New York City. Although only an interim chief executive (1923-24), the courtly "Mr. Will," as he was affectionately known, wasted little time before addressing the company's most pressing problem. Stockholders learned that a new policy of "strict retrenchment" was under way and that borrowing by subsidiaries was henceforth to be controlled by Universal's Richmond office.

Willingham further announced the curtailment of "endorsing notes of affiliated companies" and a goal of borrowing less and from fewer banks. On all counts, Willingham could justifiably claim some success, but the real recovery came later under the leadership of his successor.

Frederick Nash Harrison was only thirty-seven years old at the time of his elevation to the presidency on September 16, 1924. Although young and inexperienced in administrative matters, Fred Harrison brought to the office a number of assets, foremost of which were his family connections. Since their arrival in Virginia in the 1600s, the Harrisons had provided the colony, the state, and the nation with generation after generation of leaders. Fred Harrison's ancestors included a signer of the Declaration of Independence and two United States presidents.

Of Fred's four brothers, one was a businessman in Richmond; another a medical doctor in Danville; a third, James, headed the First National Bank of Maryland in Baltimore; and the fourth, Bob, had in 1919 become the president of Export Leaf, the buying arm of the world giant, British American Tobacco. Fred had maternal ties to a host of other Virginia statesmen. The time seemed right for a distinguished Virginia family to be represented at the head of a major, albeit troubled, Virginia-based corporation.

A second asset of the new president could be found in his own formative experiences, which not only shaped his character and values but made him an ideal transitional figure between the rough-and-tumble self-made tobacconists of the early twentieth century and the more sophisticated and better-educated leadership that was to follow.

Fred Harrison was the tenth of thirteen children born to the Reverend John H. and Anna Carrington Harrison, then of Virginia's Amelia County. Fred's father had been educated at the University of Virginia, had ridden with a Powhatan County troop under Confederate General James Ewell Brown ("Jeb") Stuart, and had been shot, captured, and imprisoned by the Federals. After the war, John H. Harrison had become an itinerant Baptist preacher serving five churches at a total salary of eighty-five dollars a year—plus an unspecified number of donated hams and chickens. He had at one time owned a small farm, but it had been lost to foreclosure. Although Fred would later joke about it, times were difficult in his youth, and, like other Virginians of modest circumstances, he recalled eating lard for butter.

When Fred was a child, his father died and the family was forced to move into sparse quarters in Danville where his mother, a strict and religious woman, became the principal influence in his life. While still a schoolboy in Danville, Fred entered the tobacco business; he would rise before dawn and walk to a local tobacco warehouse for his chores as a floor sweep. With the assistance of an older brother, he worked his way through the University of Virginia and graduated as a civil engineer in the class of 1911. After serving on the Panama Canal project and with engineering firms in California and Connecticut, he joined his brother Bob with the British American Tobacco Company. Bob's rapid rise caused Fred to fear talk of nepotism and to look for opportunities elsewhere.

In the meanwhile, Fred had caught the eye of the old American leaf czar, Thomas B. Yuille, who hired him to run Universal's W.H. Winstead branch in Owensboro, Kentucky, and also to work for Mr. Winstead during the Maryland season. Elected a Universal director in 1919, he was paradoxically both an insider and an outsider when he was chosen president in 1924.

Fred Harrison's third asset was his character and personality. On the occasion of his death in 1972, a close associate remarked: "I never heard anybody say an unkind or critical word about him, and I never heard him say an unkind or critical word about anybody."

Fred Harrison genuinely liked people, paupers and plutocrats alike, and people reciprocated his interest and affection—and trusted him explicitly. Though he would later be knighted by the King of Sweden, he never, as one acquaintance remembered, "put on airs"—a personal accolade in the South—and he always enjoyed the company of tobacco folk. He never had a personal secretary. Harrison's integrity and personal warmth were widely admired as were his donations to numerous charities—large and small—which he almost always kept confidential. Modest and soft-spoken, "a gentleman and a gentle man," he became the ideal diplomat to mediate disputes among his fellow officers and among the leaders who headed Universal's partner companies. Harrison, who had a way with people and was known for his stable character, inherited officers who would remain throughout his long tenure as president. Continuity of leadership in key posts helps to explain the company's success during his decades as the company's leader.

By 1924, to a remarkable degree, a new management team had been assembled at Universal. Of the founding officers, the chairman, the president, the secretary, the treasurer and most directors had resigned, retired, or reduced their responsibilities. Willingham continued to serve as chairman of the board from 1924 to 1945 and as a member of the finance committee. Remaining in New York City even following the closing of the office there and advancing in years, he seems to have played an ever-decreasing role in company management. Pat Gorman, though valuable in several areas, especially with cigar leaf purchases, resigned in 1929.

In this second, post-founding phase of Universal's management, the company officers were chairman of the board Willingham; president Harrison; vice presidents K.R. Edwards, Patrick H. Gorman, O.C. Gregory, J. Pinckney Harrison, and Mr. Will's brother E.W. Willingham; secretary Curtis M. Dozier Sr.; and treasurer Joseph F. Henderson.

The genial Dozier, whose Roman Catholic forebears had emigrated from France to the Virginia colony in 1683, was a mainstay in the state Republican party and also served as in-house legal counsel; however, he played a secondary role in management. But the other new faces— K.R. Edwards, Pinckney Harrison, and Joe Henderson—were real decision-makers and catalysts in the company. They would remain so for decades to come.

The oldest of the three, Kenneth Raynold Edwards, was born in Henderson, North Carolina, in 1891 and educated there and at nearby Trinity College (now Duke University). Starting in 1909 as a teenage foreman for the J.P. Taylor Company in his hometown, he was a vice president by 1914 and elected a vice president of Universal in 1921. As the older generation passed, Edwards became the preeminent leaf man in the company and remained so until his death in 1967. He influenced the purchasing and processing of millions of pounds of tobacco annually. To a large degree, the company's fortunes rode on his expertise.

A no-nonsense personality and an indefatigable worker, the stout Edwards had a keen eye for the leaf and for a bargain purchase. On the direct and rough-hewn side, usually sporting a large black cigar and being chauffeured about in a luxury car and always carrying with him a detailed knowledge of the current market situation, K.R. Edwards became the prime model of a "leaf man." Ultimately he earned the sobriquet "the Dean of Tobacco."

In sharp contrast to Edwards was the athletic and debonair James Pinckney Harrison, whose trademarks were sophistication, savoir-faire, and intellectualism. Although some associates took his increasingly discernible "broad A" accent and aristocratic manner to be signs of snobbery, none failed to acknowledge his brilliance.

Fred Harrison's first cousin and confidant, Pinckney was born in 1896, the son of a Danville, Virginia, lawyer who was an alumnus of the University of Virginia. Pinckney also attended Mr. Jefferson's University, as it was called by generations of Virginians, where he played both baseball and tennis and was active in campus life. Family financial reversals caused him to leave the university in 1916 and to serve briefly in the U.S. Marine Corps, in which he rose to the rank of sergeant. He entered the tobacco business during the war, and by 1919 at the age of twenty-three, he had become a vice president and director of International Planters, an early Universal rival. He went to Universal shortly thereafter, where he was elected a director in 1922.

Pinckney Harrison's lifelong strength was in sales, but his first major contribution to Universal was in the development of a significant profit center in China. There he replaced an agent with a company, then put in charge of it a tall raw-boned youngster who came from a family of nine off a hardscrabble farm near Reidsville, North Carolina. Pinckney's man was James E. Covington ("Covey"), who was destined to be one of the most colorful and important names in the Universal story.

In the 1920s Pinckney Harrison, who died in 1968, also made peace with Nanyang Brothers of Shanghai and in addition toured Europe to reassess Universal's standing there. Along the way, he won the Richmond city tennis championship for men's singles in 1926 and danced with his young wife, Nellie, almost literally around the world.

While "the Kingfish" Edwards dominated the leaf scene and Pinckney Harrison realigned sales, Joseph F. Henderson sought to reestablish the company's financial credibility. A Southerner who had migrated north, Henderson was part of a bank team that oversaw the liquidation of International Planters. Perhaps in that capacity he knew Pinckney Harrison or had come to know some of the Universal officers in New York. At any rate, he joined the company about that time and in September 1923 became its treasurer, thus ending the nearly annual turnover in that position. His accounting skill, conservative temperament, and strong ties with the banking community were welcome additions to the Universal system. Through the decades, Joe Henderson also served as one of the company's chief troubleshooters. He died in 1964.

Although youthful, Universal's new management team applied an old remedy to the company's financial ills: expenses were cut and new revenues aggressively sought. The formula was easier to state than to implement; however, results were positive, and by the fateful year of 1929 Universal was in a strong position. It had overcome the problems of the early 1920s and would continue to prosper during the Great Depression.

Retrenchment, which had begun during the Willingham interim, was accelerated. The far-flung and costly empire of Industrial Leaf was liquidated under the hand of Pat Gorman, as were other suspect or unprofitable enterprises, most notably Tropical Leaf. Small savings were achieved when the Paris office was made less luxurious and the New York headquarters was reduced to a branch. Less borrowing from fewer banks also helped, as did a tightening of control over the financial dealings of Universal's affiliates. Building on a 1923 resolution to "make straight loans to the subsidiaries instead of endorsing" their borrowing, the company established its authority over joint accounts with affiliates in 1925.

Using Richmond as its corporate headquarters placed Universal in contact with the leaf departments of most major American manufacturers and with the American branches of many European buyers. New offices in the Richmond Trust Building even inherited the Persian rugs!

The company continued to buy up its own preferred stock and held the line for several years against paying dividends due on its common. The annual meeting of stockholders was changed from the third Tuesday in September to the third Monday in October. While Universal cut back and streamlined, it also sought to generate additional revenues. Acquired from the residue of International Planters was the stable J.M. Edmunds Company of Danville, Virginia—the predecessor of today's Virginia Tobacco Company. Meanwhile, Eastern Leaf came into being to take advantage of market opportunities in Durham, North Carolina, and the W.H. Winstead Company entered the Pennsylvania market for cigar leaf. Across the board, Universal showed a more aggressive buying policy.

More significantly, new profit centers abroad were established in the form of Universal Leaf Tobacco Company of China and Canadian Leaf Tobacco Company. The company salvaged what it could from Miller's Georgia land purchase and, under the leadership of treasurer Henderson, sought to generate revenue from its cash surpluses by investing in "the New York call money market." To stimulate the business of its partners and subsidiaries, Universal accelerated its effort to help local managers buy into their own companies, and it invested heavily in plant improvements.

A Universal chronology from 1924 to 1929 reveals the nature of the company's recovery. In 1925, net profits rose to over a million dollars from fiscal year 1924's $179,365, and in November a *Wall Street Journal* headline trumpeted "UNIVERSAL LEAF MAKES A COMEBACK." A 1926 government report listed Universal as "probably the largest leaf dealer" in America, and the board voted a two-for-one split in Universal's common stock, although it changed from one hundred dollars per share to no par value. Further, for that year its gross sales rose 37 percent, and stockholders were told that "substantially all accounts payable have been liquidated, leaving your company about free of debt and with bank balance of more than $1 million."

In 1927 Universal posted an eleven-to-one ratio of current assets to liabilities, and the company was listed on the New York Stock Exchange "with no mortgages or funded indebtedness." In 1928 return from stocks in subsidiaries rose 44 percent. In 1929, gross sales totaled over $20 million and the company had a cash balance of $1.2 million, unlimited lines of credit and no bank loans outstanding. With fixed assets of over $3 million and a surplus of over $5 million, at year's end, Universal's board declared a special 5 percent dividend "payable in common stock of the Company" and also took steps to allow employees to buy stock in an expeditious manner.

Universal's recovery is all the more striking when viewed within the context provided by the fate of its rivals. International Planters was the largest of the dealers to fall in the early 1920s. From a World War I peak of 4,139, the number of independent dealers fell to 2,501; some consolidated and some went under while Universal sailed forward with a new generation at the helm.

3

The China Company
Strikes Gold

While Fred Harrison and the new management team set about to revitalize Universal in the mid-1920s, his cousin Pinckney was organizing a new and important subsidiary nearly half a globe away. Although its legal name would change more than once and although it would have more than one subsidiary itself, "the China Company," as it was called, proved immediately successful and contributed markedly to Universal's profits up to World War II and for a brief period afterward. It also provided some of the company's most colorful characters and dramatic moments.

The story might be apocryphal but is nevertheless revealing, and it is certainly too good not to tell: according to one account, when Buck Duke first heard of the invention of the cigarette machine, he called for an atlas. He paged quickly through the book, not for the maps but rather for their demographic information. His eyes spotted "Population: 430 million." Duke exclaimed: "That is where we are going to sell cigarettes." *That*, of course, was China.

Tobacco had been grown and consumed in China for centuries before Buck Duke's day, but Duke's efforts made the Chinese people enthusiastic about cigarettes. First through the American Tobacco Company and then through the British American Tobacco Company (BAT), Duke introduced mass cigarette importation and marketing, then local mass production and cultivation in a combination that ultimately led to mass consumption and profits that few tobacconists thought possible anywhere. Starting in 1890 and relying on carefully selected talent and advertising, Duke raised his sales in China to 1.25 billion cigarettes by 1902, to almost 10 billion in 1912, to 12 billion in 1916, and finally to 31 billion in the early 1920s.

Chinese cigarettes depended heavily on flue-cured blends, a need that was met by major imports from America. The peak was in 1931 when 124,207,000 catties (a catty equals about one and a half pounds) were supplied. The BAT also pioneered the growth of indigenous flue-cured leaf, with the volume increasing from 2,640,000 catties in 1916, to a peak of 231 million in 1937. Although hundreds of Chinese manufacturers arose to challenge the BAT dominance, none did so successfully. Some, like the Nanyang Brothers, Hwa Ching, and Dah Tung Nan, all of Shanghai, developed substantial enterprises, and they too added to the demand for tobacco purchases.

The focal point for much of China's tobacco trade was Shanghai, "The Pearl of the Orient." Strategically located on the coast of the East China Sea near the mouth of the Yangtze River and bays to the south, Shanghai was China's largest urban area and its most important commercial center. On terms dictated by western powers in the nineteenth century, Shanghai became a "Treaty Port" and, as such, was "administered mainly by foreigners." Within the city, large and specified areas known as "concessions" or "settlements," essentially "self-governing . . . enclosures" were "set aside for foreign residents in which local administration (police, sanitation, roads, building regulations, and so forth) was in foreign hands and financed by local taxes levied by the foreign settlements." Foreign citizens—and goods alike—were subject to limited taxation by the Chinese. Even beyond the settlements, foreign influence prevailed over local authority.

For many westerners prior to World War II, Shanghai was Shangri-La, a place in which a small amount of foreign currency went a long way, and life's amenities and excesses were inexpensive. Villas, polo horses, tennis and golf, night clubs, gambling, fine food and drink, "the world's longest bar," cultural events, daily comforts administered by a half dozen or more servants—all were within easy reach of Americans whose income by standards back home would be modest.

Of the companies that combined to form Universal in 1918, some had already been involved in the China trade and would continue. Universal worked initially through an American, George Happer, in Shanghai, subsequently making him the company's agent for China, Korea, and Japan. By 1924 the operation had expanded to branch status, but with disappointing results: with several million dollars at stake, a large contract with Nanyang had fallen apart. At this point, Pinckney Harrison came forward.

Regarded by some of his contemporaries as a visionary, Pinckney had unorthodox ideas as well as sound ones. With keen intelligence and assurance, he often saw long-range possibilities; the judgment of time proved him correct on some occasions and wrong on others. With China, however, Pinckney's analysis was rewardingly on the mark.

Harrison's contributions in China went beyond only seeing Universal's potential there. He also sold the idea, organized a new company, replaced the former agent with Jim Covington, and, for years, served as Universal's liaison with China. In May 1924, Harrison won board support for organizing the Universal Leaf Tobacco Company of China "to carry on a general leaf tobacco business in the Orient with the principal office in Shanghai." Two months later he gained approval for the operations there to include a sales-and-profits protocol, a loan guarantee of up to six hundred thousand dollars, and the transfer of Universal's previous holdings and personnel to the new company. Already he had set about making peace with Nanyang Brothers. As if that were not enough, Harrison also benefited from an accident of timing. An intense Chinese nationalism welled up in 1925 with the BAT as its most logical target, thus inadvertently causing the BAT to be sympathetic toward other western ventures. Native businessmen also opened the door to what had previously been a BAT-dominated local clientele.

Finally, Pinckney had double good fortune in acquiring available office space. The company secured quarters on the second floor of the Asiatic Petroleum Company Building owned by Shell Oil. It was ideally located for business purposes in an attractive commercial area of town fronting the Whangpo River, which flowed into the Yangtze near its mouth on the China Sea. And, its address was Number One, The Bund— with "Number One" carrying the coincidental benefit of meaning "most important" in the Chinese value system.

Pinckney now realized he needed a director in Shanghai, and he found him, unemployed and walking down the street in Danville, Virginia. Whether Pinckney Harrison had known James E. Covington before that chance encounter is unknown, but a short conversation led to a longer one and ultimately to Covington's being sent to China. "Covey" went first in a general capacity, soon became vice president and manager, and subsequently was named president of the China Company.

Born into a large family on a small farm across the Virginia state line not far south of Danville, Covington had known hard times as a youngster. With only a limited education, he had done factory work in Durham, had retailed "Little Recruit" cigars in Pennsylvania, and had served a tour with the British American Tobacco Company in China before returning to a short-lived job, once again in tobacco, in Danville. Somewhere along the way he had developed ambition, drive, a forceful personality, and a salesman's ability to sell himself and his product.

There would always be a raw-boned and rustic country boy inside

Covington—an unsophisticated presence that many people found attractive and which he would use and at the same time try to overcome. Tall and angular, the red-haired Covington could exude unsophisticated charm or, on occasion, he could behave true to stereotype and explode in anger. Some of his rough spots were smoothed by his gracious and polished wife, Annie Stuart James, daughter of a prominent politician and publisher in Danville. China and Mrs. Covington combined to advance considerably Covington's social skills. The process carried him, said one contemporary, from following the backside of a mule to being mounted in the saddle of a polo pony.

Over the years, Covington made fifty-two trips to China and lived there more-or-less full time for over a decade. In the twenty-one years in which he had a responsibility for the China operation, profits were made in all but one—and attractive profits at that. Except indirectly, the China Company escaped America's economic despair and turmoil in the 1930s. "We didn't know about the Great Depression," noted one former China hand. "We didn't feel it."

The nature of the business from the mid-1920s to Pearl Harbor was fourfold. First, ULT China imported American tobacco for sale in China. Second, it bought native leaf—from Chinese dealers and from local farmers—and sold it mainly to small Chinese manufacturers. Occasionally native tobacco was also sold to combines like the Nanyang Brothers or even to the BAT when they ran short of certain grades or to manufacturers in Europe and Scandinavia. Third, Covington's men processed tobacco for Chinese companies. And, finally, and of least importance, the China Company traded in an opportunistic way in a variety of miscellaneous items ranging from sewing machines (sold to Nazi Germany) to products made by American Machine and Foundry (AMF), for which one of ULT China's salesmen served as an agent. The entrepreneurial spirit was so prevalent that Covington once cabled Richmond to send him a "boat full" of American automobiles, which could be sold at a nice profit in Shanghai, but the directive came back "to stick with tobacco."

In its heyday in the 1930s, the China Company consisted of the corporate headquarters at Number One, The Bund, two redrying plants, two or three storage facilities, and three or more buying stations in the country's interior. In general, a handful of Americans, headed by Covington, supervised a multinational staff and a large body of Chinese laborers.

The laborers worked in groups and were supervised by a "Number

One" man in charge of the workforce. Tough and unsympathetic to physical weakness, the Number One, also Chinese, considered it routine for a one-hundred-pound man to shoulder and carry a two-hundred-pound load of tobacco or for several of them to pull a loaded hogshead of some one thousand pounds half a mile by hand.

Covington's management system was relatively simple. He made his expectations clear, delegated heavily, and kept a sharp eye in all directions. "He'd be the first to pat you on the back," remembered one coworker, "but also the first to raise hell if anything didn't work out." In his spacious office, Covington's desk was located so that he could see, if he chose, anyone entering the company's main door and also anyone getting off the elevator on the second floor itself. To an authoritarian temperament he added the trappings of an executive—tailor-made clothes, servants, and a seven-passenger Nash automobile. In short, there was never any mistaking who ran the business.

Covington oversaw the company's entire operations, but his special strength was in making a deal. Indefatigable in sales, he was as shrewd as he was diligent. He particularly understood the importance of "face" (self-esteem) to his Chinese customers. "In China," recalled one Universal veteran, "everything was 'face.'"

Unlike some rival dealers, Covington took the Chinese into his home—an ultimate compliment in the East—and entertained them royally there and elsewhere, always on guard to protect their sensibilities and to reassure them if a socially embarrassing situation arose. Covington knew how to put on a show for customers, even at the expense of his American staff. Once, for example, a guest accidentally put a foot through a lower pane in a French door leading to a terrace. Covington allowed no time for embarrassment to set in. "Oh, don't worry about that," he responded. "Watch this!" He kicked out another pane himself.

In sales, at various times, were also J. Fuller Malone, a happy-go-lucky North Carolinian who earlier had sold Buick automobiles in Shanghai and who could buy leaf as well as sell it; George Arbogast, a genial New Yorker and the AMF agent Pinckney Harrison had hired on a ship; Cliff Sutherland, a Virginian who had been sent from the main office in Richmond and who eventually would take charge of all sales of American leaf in China; and, to a lesser degree, George W. Macon and J.C. Waddell, two youngsters whose roles were more in leaf procurement and processing than in sales and whose subsequent careers in the States made them two of America's best-known tobacconists.

Backing the sales force was an office staff headed by A.I. McOwan, a tough Scotsman with a background in accounting. McOwan had been born in 1898; as a teenager in the British navy during World War I, he had survived having two ships shot out from under him. He later joined the BAT in China (where an uncle had lately been a missionary). Though his native countrymen rightly called him "MacAw'n," he was destined to be "McOw'n" to his American coworkers after having been recruited by Covington in the mid-1920s. Although these two strong-willed individuals clashed on more than one occasion, they also worked together to assure the successful day-to-day operations of the China Company.

Mac had full responsibility—broadly defined—for company records. Inventory, prices, sales, factory reports, and other items often changed daily, and current, accurate numbers had to be at hand. Mac also handled such financial matters as paying taxes in China and to the United States, preparing monthly balance sheets and annual reports, overseeing the payroll, and supervising foreign exchanges as well as petty expenditures. Chaotic conditions made China an unorthodox but genuine "tax haven," and payments were made largely "to keep the appearance of proper conduct."

As office manager, McOwan supervised an administrative staff that at one time reflected in national origin nine different countries. Almost all of these people were on straight salary. Two key assistants were Randolph Suri, a multilingual Swiss-born bookkeeper, and Mary Kammerling Frisch, a German secretary whose loyalty to the company would stand severe tests during World War II. The bookkeeper preferred using an abacus to an adding machine, but Mac was tolerant because he perceived no loss of efficiency or accuracy. While Americans came and went, McOwan was the closest thing to a permanent fixture in the China Company, serving it from the mid-1920s until after World War II, which included his incarceration by the Japanese from 1942 to 1945. He died in 1988.

Universal's American staff was augmented by Chinese businessmen who worked on a commission basis and whose roles as intermediaries were absolutely critical. Foremost was L.T. Yuan, Universal's "comprador" (the native man who arranges things). The comprador system was widespread in China and made possible another business reality, namely "the squeeze." At all levels extra payment was required for the delivery of goods and services. Call it a tip, a kickback, a bribe, an unofficial tax, an informal service charge, or paying for favors—the squeeze was not only persuasive but obligatory and was accepted as such by Chinese and foreigners alike.

"As prominent in Shanghai as a Chinese could be," the elderly Yuan was a politician and businessman, and he knew well the needs of Universal's customers. He might see them separately or accompanied by, for example, Jim Covington, to effect a deal. Under Yuan was L.T. Tsao, his assistant; Mohan Zee, "the greatest salesman in the world" and a man whose association with Universal would span decades and pass into the generation of his two sons; George Su, who eventually sold both Chinese and American leaf; and O.K. Lee, a businessman and Yuan's successor as comprador. In leaf procurement and processing, Universal's man was H.C. Chao, missionary-school educated, fluent in English, able, and respected.

American leaf was sold to the Chinese on a sample basis, with delivery taken from Universal's storage, usually after inspection. As in the United States, business was done on a handshake. Close contact with customers enabled Covington to cable anticipated and exact needs to the Richmond office, though on occasion he also went home for consultation and to visit the markets where he made himself conspicuous by buying all the tobacco he could for resale in China.

In the mid-1930s, fifteen or more American dealers had offices in Shanghai. Most operations, however, consisted of only a sales representative and his comprador. Universal had by far the largest operation in terms of personnel, volume, and scope of business; and few rivals could match Universal's range of sales, with customers from the BAT to Chinese manufacturers of all sizes.

Universal enjoyed several clear advantages over other American dealers in Shanghai. Covington's operation was larger and more versatile, and he drew upon the resources of a parent company that could extend financial aid, guarantee loans, and provide American leaf in any amount and from any market. In addition, Universal Leaf Tobacco of China had a competitive edge because it also bought and processed native leaf, thus establishing multiple ties with Chinese manufacturers.

Universal might process tobacco owned by a Chinese manufacturer, or it might sell him Chinese leaf owned and processed by ULT. Or a salesman might suggest the desirability of buying a combination of native and American leaf for a particular Chinese cigarette. Through its AMF connection, Universal also provided machinery and replacement parts.

So substantial was the processing business that in 1935, in response to a report by Pinckney Harrison, Universal in Richmond established a new company, Lien Hwa Leaf, "for the primary purpose of rehandling native grown tobaccos in China for the Company—and others." Lien

Hwa ("feeding or nourishing" in Chinese) was also set up to allow important Chinese to buy into the Universal network.

Universal's first processing plant in China dated from the 1920s and was located on Yulin Road within the International Settlement. Its season lasted six months, during which it ran two shifts of perhaps 130 to 140 workers each. Chinese were hired by the Number One. Women were paid forty cents a day, and men earned eighty cents; family teams were common. The combined wage, by Shanghai standards, was not unattractive. Coopers, who also worked under the Number One, were better paid. Americans were amazed at the strength, agility, and energy of Chinese laborers, who could handle 250-pound bales all day long.

The plant was small by American standards, and the process was simple. The ultimate purpose was to prepare newly purchased leaves for storage. The tobacco arrived tied in bundles, was checked for foreign matter, then cleaned by mass-steaming. Next it was hung on sticks, which were then placed on racks that were carried by moving chains through a shed for redrying. The leaf was heated, then cooled, then steamed again to bring the moisture content to the level required for storage—about 12 percent. Finally the tobacco was packed into hogsheads and taken elsewhere for storage.

Although the labor was menial, the redrying process had to be done carefully or the tobacco would be ruined. Machinery was unsophisticated—often consisting of J.P. Taylor Company discards—but knowledge of it was necessary for preventive maintenance, repairs, and smooth runs. This expertise came from the United States in the form of young tobacconists hailing mainly from Virginia and North Carolina and bringing with them experience they had gained working within the Universal system.

Redrying skills and a knowledge of leaf were essentials, but so were the qualities of a tough foreman. The men who came to Shanghai were usually single and looked at their service there as a chance to advance within the company while seeing the world. Pay was higher, and an American dollar bought several times in Shanghai what it would in the States. An assignment was given in exchange for a four-year contract, with the promise of a paid three-month vacation at tour's end.

Throughout most of the 1930s, the Yulin Road plant was managed by J.C. ("Ches") Waddell, a native Virginian who earlier had switched from pre-law studies to a floor sweeper's post with the Taylor Company in Richmond. Waddell had risen to a foreman's position when Pinckney Harrison sold him and especially his mother on the idea of young Ches's going to China. He arrived in Shanghai in 1930 at age twenty-five just in time to arrange shipment home for his predecessor's body.

Initially the Yulin Road plant consisted of Waddell and 130 Chinese workers. With study, he soon picked up an elementary knowledge of the local dialect, or at least enough to get the job done and to recognize that the melodic phrase he always heard on his arrival meant "old big nose is coming." Facing down a coopers' strike, he also learned that he "was the National Labor Board" and that a two-by-four plank could expedite negotiations.

Waddell worked hard, played hard, and soon moved into other areas of the Chinese operation. In time he bought heavily for the company from the leaf transported to Shanghai by Chinese dealers. In a lot across from the factory, the Chinese leaf would be placed in rows of 250-pound stacks, and Waddell would buy half a million pounds or more each day during a buying season of two or three months.

Waddell had begun to move into sales when, in 1938, he decided that two tours were enough. Now the head of a young family, he also took seriously warnings from a Japanese friend who told him bad times were ahead. Waddell's decision to leave China did not sit well with Covington, who apparently had been grooming Waddell to take over the China operation. Back in the States, however, Waddell later made his mark as a mainstay of Universal's buying staff. He finally did return to China, but only for a sentimental journey after his retirement. To his surprise, many of the old landmarks had survived World War II as well as the Chinese revolution.

The Shanghai plant where Waddell worked was the first but not the largest of Universal's China properties; the second eventually had two redrying machines as well as a larger capacity and labor force than did the Yulin Road facility. Located up the China coast from Shanghai in the resort town and port city of Tsingtao in western Shantung Province, it had been purchased by Covington and Harrison at a cocktail party in 1934. Chinese manufacturers had originally built the plant to circumvent Universal's processing dominance, but they had had difficulty operating it and had damaged a whole year's tobacco crop. Universal's technical assistance was requested; then the Chinese sold out. Covington later said the price had been steep but the ultimate reward substantial.

First manager at Tsingtao was George Macon. A native of Henderson, North Carolina, and a J.P. Taylor employee since 1931 when he was only twenty-two, Macon first arrived in China in 1936 and ran the night shift for Waddell in Shanghai. As the business at Tsingtao increased, a second redrying machine was installed, and eventually other men were brought over to assist in the plant and with the buying. Joining Macon were Charles Jackson, Henry Towler, and Rolf Gerber, the latter destined to die as a result of wartime incarceration by the Japanese. Before his return to the States, Macon also figured in one of the most perilous moments in the history of the China Company.

The Chinese had long grown tobacco, but their proficiency in Virginia types came only after the arrival of BAT experts who provided seed, technological assistance, and economic incentives. Chinese flue-cured tobacco came largely from Shantung Province but also from Honan, where the leaf was similar to the American Old and Eastern Belts.

Although inferior in many ways to American leaf, Chinese tobacco was in great demand within the country. Universal bought it regularly in Shanghai and eventually established three buying stations in Shantung Province, which included Tsingtao. The buying season lasted roughly from October 1 until just before Christmas. Purchases were on speculation, and prices were set at a percentage of those on the current American market.

Universal's three stations were on the main railroad line out of Tsingtao several hours into the interior; each consisted of a simple bamboo shed or two within or near a walled village close to the railroad line. Although China's "warlord era" had almost completely passed, militaristic activity and terrorism had not, and much of China still lacked any nationally recognized authority. One scholar estimates that in 1930 in Shantung alone, "31 thousand unorganized troops and bandits, in addition to 192 thousand regular troops, were living off the countryside." "Banditry flourished in all parts of the country," he continues, "and robbery and violence were commonplace." Kidnapping for ransom was widely practiced. That grim reality helps explain some otherwise strange aspects of Universal's buying network.

Arrangements in the buying provinces had been made in advance by Universal's highly respected leaf comprador, H.C. Chao. Universal's designated buyer lived in the walled village under the protection of the local Number One. A Chinese banker came in to handle the money, and likely a BAT contingent also would be there. Conditions were primitive by western standards, although Americans usually brought their own supplies and servants.

Accompanied by up to fifty soldiers with fixed bayonets, the Universal buyer left the village and took up his position at a shed made of bamboo poles with a deep thatched roof, sawtooth style, its opening facing north to catch the true light for judging tobacco. Farmers brought their leaf in carts and wheelbarrows—sometimes using their wives as draw horses. The leaf was displayed in rows through which the buyer walked, preceded and followed by armed soldiers. Offers were made that farmers could decline by exclaiming *pu mai* ("no sale"). For deals struck, tickets were drawn that were redeemable locally in Chinese dollars by the farmer.

Aided by the Chinese labor force, the buyer combined the purchased leaf into bales, put them into a packing machine, and stacked it all. When enough tobacco was accumulated, it was packed into a gondola car at the nearby railroad; then, accompanied by guards, it was shipped to Tsingtao for processing or for shipment and processing in Shanghai. Waddell, Fuller Malone, M.R. Doggett, and other Americans bought in Shantung, but by the late 1930s the buyers also included a Greek (Karas) and two Russians (Surin and Socolof).

Success in Shantung led to the establishment in l935 of a buyer station in Honan Province, where conditions were even more primitive and perilous. The BAT, which had been active there, welcomed Universal as a way of diffusing antimonopolistic antagonisms. The local Chinese dealers, however, were hostile to the idea of additional competition. Such was the scene faced by Universal's new man in Honan, George Macon, at the age of twenty-six.

Not long after establishing himself at the buying station, Macon was invited to a conference in the local BAT compound. Accompanied by bodyguards, Macon arrived in good order, but outlaws struck. A shootout took place just five feet away from Macon, leaving the head BAT man and six Chinese dead. Had it not been for quick action by one of his bodyguards, Macon might have been one of the victims. Renewed buying led to other difficulties, and the Honan experiment was abandoned.

Twice in the 1930s Universal's China operation was jeopardized by the outbreak of fighting between the expansionist Japanese and the tenacious but politically factionalized Chinese. In 1931 the Japanese invaded northern China, and the resulting war, though spasmodic and short-lived, reached Shanghai with tragic results. Macon, Waddell, and others in time became part of a volunteer militia force, a kind of instant home guard, called out to help the 4th U.S. Marines and other regulars protect the International Settlement from intrusion. Home guard soldiers were issued arms, barriers were constructed, curfews enforced, and defensive positions established. In October Pinckney Harrison reported "unsettled conditions" in China but predicted that business would not be hurt in the long run—and indeed the crisis passed.

Much more serious was the outbreak of violence in 1937. This time carnage and destruction entered even the foreign enclaves, and Universal's men saw war's horrors close at hand. Furthermore, in the aftermath, Universal had to deal with the mercurial Japanese—who came to control much of the Shanghai area—rather than with the essentially cooperative Chinese.

With little warning, violent confrontations occurred again in Shanghai on August 13, 1937. Air raids, fire bombings, infantry attacks, and hand-to-hand combat followed one another in rapid succession. Over a thousand civilians died when a bomb landed in the center of a busy intersection not far from Universal's corporate headquarters in the Shell Building.

Momentarily cut off in the confusion and destruction was Universal's storage facility on Dalny Road. The one American on duty there was Henry K. Towler, age twenty-seven, a native of Charlotte County, Virginia, and only recently arrived from the States. Towler got one telephone call through—and was told to stay put. He had little choice, as street fighting soon engulfed and isolated the plant. Although terrified, Towler did have the presence of mind to keep an American flag flying conspicuously above the building. When a truce was called and a rescue party appeared, Towler was holding on to the pole itself, the flag protectively—from a symbolic view at least—wrapped around him.

Although Universal's people would be exposed to life-threatening situations in the future, no occasion would prove as bloody as that terrible day in August. Towler, who tried unsuccessfully for years to blot the memories from his mind, still could not help remembering them in detail fifty years later. Trapped at the storage facility, he had watched in terrified horror as the fighting progressed door to door.

"We made sure that we hung an American flag out," Towler recalled. He telephoned Waddell and reported that he was trapped. "You could see them killing each other right and left in hand-to-hand combat," he said. "[The Japanese] would bayonet the Chinese—and they weren't soldiers either—anything that came along that was Chinese. They would throw them up on a pile and get behind them . . .using them for barricades. I got so scared . . . I was afraid they were going to come and get me next."

Later, Charles Jackson and Towler attempted to move their personal effects during a temporary truce. While changing a flat tire caused by broken glass, a bomb hit nearby. Body parts rained down on the car. This would have been frightening by itself, but the men also knew that just a few miles away uncounted Chinese women had been raped and slaughtered. "I have tried to forget about that thing for so long, but . . ." Towler said half a century later.

After more fighting and another truce, Waddell and two other company employees went through the combat zone—with Japanese and Chinese soldiers poised on opposite sides of the street—to inspect the Liaoyang Road storage facility. The brick structure seemed at first to be in sound condition despite a few shell holes and occupation by the Japanese. "Thank goodness this hasn't been hit," Waddell said. He unlocked the front door and was shocked when he stepped into a roofless interior; an incendiary bomb had destroyed all but the four walls. Also destroyed was two hundred thousand dollars' worth of American tobacco.

By November, the fighting had subsided, leaving the Japanese in control of much of Shanghai, including a large portion of the International Settlement and Universal's plant and main storage. As Universal sought to extricate its holdings in tobacco and the holdings of its Chinese friends and customers, the squeeze system expanded to include the Japanese. For a time the company used tennis courts in the French Concession to conduct its business.

Tsingtao also fell to the Japanese, and special arrangements had to be made to permit Universal's Chinese labor to work in the redrying plant there. Another difficulty came with a Japanese edict designating its own military paper, without value anywhere else, as the only official currency. One of Covington's last China maneuvers was designed to circumvent that policy. He learned that a large American naval vessel was lying at anchor in Tsingtao's bay and that American sailors were having to exchange their U.S. currency for Japanese paper for shore liberty; he struck a deal with the admiral in charge: under the eyes of the unsuspecting Japanese, Towler and others took suitcases full of the Japanese issue to the ship, where it was exchanged for checks from the National City Bank of New York. Covington had his American dollars, the sailors their Japanese script.

Despite these and similar interruptions, business continued, and by 1939 and 1940 it had returned to a profitable level. The company even introduced a new line dealing in Indian leaf, which was shipped for sale in Shanghai. By this time Covington had followed Waddell home, and the China Company's nucleus had contracted considerably. Macon was still coming and going, but the China regulars were now Arbogast, Sutherland, Fuller Malone, Crawford Peace (a redrying man from North Carolina) and McOwan. For them the real drama came in 1941—and Malone, Peace, and McOwan did not get out in time.

4

A New Profit Center
to the North

As Pinckney Harrison and James Covington were developing Universal's China business, other company officials were pioneering in Canada and in various cigar-leaf districts of the United States. These three profit centers had much in common. In each case, a younger generation of entrepreneurs took over an enterprise of modest proportions and turned it into an impressive operation. Each company operated on a relatively autonomous basis, and each featured an essentially self-made man whose individual drive and acumen led him to a dominant position not only with a key subsidiary but within the geographic region. In the 1920s and 1930s, China and Canada represented Universal's foreign operations and, coupled with the cigar trade, discussed in the next chapter, they offered both a colorful and lucrative addition to the customary business in American cigarette leaf.

In what today is the part of North America known as Canada, Indians grew tobacco long before the arrival of Europeans. East of the present-day Lake Huron and north of Lake Erie in the sand plains of southern Ontario, tribes cultivated the leaf and used it for trade, ritual ceremonies, and medicine, as well as for pleasure. Jesuit explorers commented on its abundance and diverse uses, which included being smoked in pipes four or five feet long. Native tobacco was "strong flavored and sun cured," and its seed was collected and planted by early French settlers.

The nineteenth century witnessed significant commercial production in Canada, largely in burley-type leaf, which was air cured. The first Canadian crop of flue-cured "Virginia" tobacco was grown in 1900 in Leamington, Essex County, Ontario, by two brothers from North Carolina working for an affiliate of the American Tobacco Company. "Bright" tobacco caught hold, and newspapers in Virginia and North Carolina published notices of jobs for enterprising tobacco farmers who were willing to come north and ply their skills.

Many who responded to these calls were youngsters right off the farm, such as Red Parham, later an internationally known tobacconist, who arrived from North Carolina in 1921 and stayed several years. Parham and his coworkers "spent winter months in a tobacco processing factory, teaching the workers how to grade and tie the tobacco, and during spring and summer, were buying or growing and curing the tobacco."

Some of these American farm boys arrived with visions of polar bears and mountains of ice, only to be pleasantly surprised by the often temperate climate and picturesque farmscape in Ontario's "old belt" of Essex and Kent counties and later, to the west, in Norfolk, Oxford, and Elgin counties. The adjoining province of Quebec had long grown tobacco, mainly non-cigarette types, but flue-cured was not introduced there until 1930 and its production would never rival Ontario's.

From its founding, Universal had dealt on a modest scale in Canada. Affiliates there included Gensior and Import Leaf of Montreal, and some business was also conducted with local manufacturers. But Universal's serious commitment came in 1925 with the founding of a new company with broad aspirations.

From Universal's headquarters in New York City, William A. Willingham had monitored Canadian developments, and in June 1925 he presented Pat Gorman and other directors with a tentative plan to organize a new company in Chatham, Ontario. In the short run, the step was taken to accommodate a Canadian customer, Tucketts Company of Hamilton, Ontario, but the long-range purpose was to make an early entrance into what promised to be a new source of marketable flue-cured leaf; although projected customers were Canadian, Willingham also saw export possibilities.

Later that year the Canadian Leaf Tobacco Company (CLT) received its charter and commenced operations to "buy, sell, handle, and deal" in Canadian tobacco. Of the two hundred thousand dollars' worth of stock authorized, Universal held about two-thirds, with a first option to buy the rest. But, as much as possible, the new enterprise was to have a predominantly British Commonwealth flavor—thus the name—with American influence being kept in the background.

The first company officers consisted of prominent Universal officials—with Willingham as president, Dozier as secretary, and Henderson as treasurer—but the man responsible for on-site operations was a newcomer to management. At CLT, Herbert Worth Jackson Jr., then in his late twenties, found his first opportunity to demonstrate the qualities that in time would make him president of Universal itself.

Jackson came from a distinguished Tarheel family that dated from the seventeenth century and included governors, judges, president Andrew Jackson, and the notable editor-writer-cabinet officer Josephus Daniels. Born in Raleigh, Herbert moved as a child to Richmond where his father served as president of the Virginia Trust Company, as Herbert's brother would later.

From Richmond's exclusive McGuire's University School, Jackson went on to the University of Virginia, where his college days overlapped those of Pinckney Harrison. Jackson, a mathematics major, completed his studies in three years, served as student body president, and maintained superlative grades. Bad eyesight threatened to keep him out of World War I, so he memorized the eye chart and joined the field artillery as a private. Soon a second lieutenant, he years later recalled that he "saw no action," but he did admit to having been "kicked by two mules."

Young Herbert forsook an opportunity in banking, not wanting "to sit on a stool all my life adding figures," and in January 1919 went to work for the J.P. Taylor Company in Richmond as a clerk. Obligatory service in the factories and on the markets came next, followed by his first test as a manager. He rose from vice president to president of Canadian Leaf by 1928.

Much of CLT's initial personnel (including Jackson) came from the Universal organization in the States. The first plant in Chatham was in a building vacated by a lumber company; the task of transforming it into a tobacco enterprise would be assigned to Ira C. Huff, a Taylor man from Henderson and for many years CLT's factory manager. "All business" and "a man of few words," the efficient and hardworking Huff believed "nothing was impossible." Eventually a senior vice president, he served Canadian Leaf until his retirement.

Overseeing the coopershop was Wyatt Cheatham, a black Richmonder and a veteran of the Taylor Company. An expert hogshead maker, Cheatham taught the trade to others, including Russell French, a native Canadian Indian who worked at the plant until his retirement, as did Cheatham. The first redrying man was a Kentuckian from the Taylor Company. From Southwestern and the C.T.W. Argue Company came Robert C. Hodgin as accountant, office manager, and assistant secretary. Quiet and good natured, Hodgin served the Canadian branch of Universal for thirty-five years.

A key man in leaf was Clarence L. O'Brian, a North Carolinian formerly with the British American Tobacco Company. O'Brian had come to Canada in 1924 to grow flue-cured tobacco in Ontario, but the next year he joined the new Canadian Leaf Tobacco Company as buyer and leaf inspector. He rose quickly to vice president and in 1931 became general manager as the on-site executive representing Jackson, who by then had returned to the States.

During his six years in Canada, Herbert Jackson not only established a profitable company but also established himself within the Universal system. He impressed people with his sincerity and with a manner that was down-to-earth yet gentlemanly. He worked hard and expected others to do the same. He inspired people by placing trust in them, and he was both accessible and a good listener.

Nothing if not systematic, Jackson was rarely caught unaware, and his ability with numbers and his mastery of detail were such that one employee suggested that "his head was a Burroughs adding machine." Frugality was a working principle with him; he even saved envelopes from incoming mail to recycle as note paper. A spittoon, to accommodate his chewing habit, always stood nearby. Surrounded by a young family and with the natural splendor providing endless opportunities for his outdoor interests, Jackson enjoyed perhaps the most contented days of his career.

Herbert Jackson must also be credited with hiring his eventual successor as CLT president and the man who would be in charge on-site from 1942 until his retirement in 1970—namely, E.D. ("Ed") Allen, one of Canada's most colorful and successful tobacconists.

It might be said that a coin toss brought Allen to Canada while a fifty-dollar bill helped keep him there. The coin toss in a North Carolina drug store determined which of three friends would respond to a Raleigh classified advertisement for two tobacco workers in Ontario; the fifty-dollar bill came from Ed's father with the injunction that he should be his own man and never fear having to walk home.

Allen was born into an old-time tobacco family near Creedmoor, North Carolina. As far back as anyone could recall, his people had been "somehow or another in the tobacco business"—as large growers, warehouse pioneers, and employees of various companies. His grandfather had been in the first wave of southerners coming to Leamington to work flue-cured tobacco, and Ed, a recent graduate of King's Business College in Raleigh, was favorably disposed to head north himself. He followed not only his grandfather's footsteps but also his advice to take plenty of long underwear. From 1927 to 1930 Ed Allen worked in southern Ontario, helping to plant the first tobacco ever in some places and later growing his own.

Allen heard of a possible job with Canadian Leaf, arranged an early morning interview with Herbert Jackson, and by 10:30 A.M. found himself "in the grading room and working." His first impression of Jackson, destined to be his life-long friend and business colleague, was that he was "very dignified, high class, well educated . . . the type of a man I would like to be associated with." In the 1930s Allen rose through the ranks as leaf tobacco inspector, buyer, sales representative, head buyer, assistant factory manager, and leaf superintendent. In 1942 he replaced the seriously ill O'Brian as general manager of CLT. All the while, Jackson, in Richmond, served as Universal's liaison with the Canadian arm and kept watch on operations there.

Even as Canadian Leaf was being founded in 1925, the principal flue-cured belt was moving westward—away from the pioneer area around Leamington and Chatham, along the north shore of Lake Erie toward such small towns as Tillsonburg, Delhi, and Simcoe. As the migration accelerated, so too did the pressure for Canadian Leaf Tobacco Company to accommodate it. In 1933, with C.L. O'Brian as the prime catalyst, it acquired, as a wholly owned subsidiary, the well-established firm of Norfolk Leaf in Tillsonburg. CLT got not only Norfolk's business but, more important, its plant, which, although old, was expanded under leadership of factory manager Charles W. Thomas Jr. Another North Carolinian and an alumnus of its state University, Thomas had joined CLT in the late 1920s as a buyer and salesman. An extroverted person and a "good hand shaker," Thomas also "could figure more angles on most anything you can think about of any fellow you ever saw." Beginning in 1933 he served successively as vice president, director, and manager of Norfolk Leaf. (His son C.W. Thomas III is currently president of Universal's major Canadian subsidiary, Simcoe Leaf.)

Meanwhile, the Chatham plant continued to operate. The facility survived a fire in 1931 and, in 1937, a flood so bad a row boat was required to inspect the damage on the first floor.

Canadian Leaf Tobacco's bread and butter account came to be Macdonald. Started by Jackson, increased by O'Brian, and firmly established by Allen, this relationship was carefully nurtured so that as "their business grew, our business grew." An old-time manufacturer named for its eccentric but successful Scottish founder, Sir William Macdonald, the Montreal corporation scored heavily during World War I by giving free to soldiers its popular cigarette brands, Exports and British Consols.

Macdonald, a private, family-run company, was headed by an equally private individual, Walter M. Stewart. A "man of few words"

but whose "words were his bond," Stewart distrusted high-powered salesmen and complex situations alike. He easily formed a close bond with
the direct and down-to-earth Ed Allen. Perhaps 80 percent of their business was transacted by telephone, with payment by certified check.
Stewart kept few records; he believed only two books counted: the check
book—"you spend so much"—and the bank book—"you save so much."
His wife, May, was an active partner in what was run—and run successfully—as a true "Mom and Pop" operation.

Later the government insisted that Stewart keep more complete
records and that he appoint a full slate of corporate officers.
Unintimidated and wily, he named family members to every post, including a son-in-law then incarcerated in Germany in a prisoner of war
camp. When asked about the conspicuous omission of his own name
from the list, he replied: "I'm just the owner."

Canadian Leaf's final expansion of the 1930s took the company
abroad when it established a branch in Southern Rhodesia in 1938.
The move was made "mainly as a service to English customers who
were interested in Rhodesian tobacco" but also with an eye toward export possibilities elsewhere. Again, Universal sought to maintain a Commonwealth flavor and to get in on the ground floor of a potentially
active business.

Sent to Rhodesia to begin operations was William H. Burroughs, a
North Carolinian with a Duke University education who had been a
buyer and leaf inspector for CLT since 1932. He established a base in
Salisbury and worked closely with a local dealer, Kileff, which processed, packed, and sometimes bought for CLT. Burroughs left, but
returned in 1939 and again in 1940, accompanied on the later stint by
Mr. and Mrs. Ed Allen. Business broadened to the point that CLT was
buying on Rhodesia's three major markets—Salisbury to the south, Fort
Jameson to the north, and Limbe in Nyasaland. Operations, however,
were disrupted by Germany's submarine warfare and ceased for the
duration of the war.

No account of Universal's presence in Canada before World War
II would be complete without at least a brief discussion of an unusual
venture there. Although not directly related to Canadian Leaf Tobacco
Company, it did involve Universal officials.

In 1927 William A. Willingham, Patrick H. Gorman, and other
tobacconists founded Club LaSalle on a section of scenic wilderness
leased from the Canadian government. Essentially a fishing and hunting camp, Club LaSalle was located in Quebec Province about one hun-

dred miles northeast of Montreal. Measuring perhaps sixty square miles and encompassing a dozen or more lakes and rivers, the tract was originally accessible only by air. A rustic lodge encouraged male companionship, and ample provisions (a major portion of which were of the alcoholic variety) and skilled Canadian guides kept life from being too spartan. Regulations were few and the organization informal, with Willingham and other Universal officials serving at various times as president. Membership evolved into one largely of ULT and Philip Morris officials; among the latter, Joseph F. Cullman III was especially active.

At that time Wirt H. Hatcher Sr. of Philip Morris and J. Pinckney Harrison and Herbert Jackson of Universal were also quite active in the club. Later a number of top people at Philip Morris, namely George Weissman, who succeeded Joe Cullman as chief executive officer of the company, Ross Milhiser, Clifford Goldsmith, Hugh Cullman, George Macon, and Hugh West became members. From Universal the membership included Gordon Crenshaw, Thomas Towers, Howard Cone, Stuart Christian, and Reece Holloway.

For years a number of Philip Morris and Universal top officials made frequent visits to this "remote and wonderful place," as Crenshaw remembered it. Although the group could not be characterized as expert outdoorsmen, the retreat was a source of enjoyment for all members. Moreover, LaSalle played a major part in developing the friendships between Philip Morris and Universal people.

Thus by 1941, Canadian Leaf had firmly established itself as a reliable profit center for Universal. Its operations had expanded smoothly, and its on-site management and personnel were stable. The continuity of its workforce was strong as most employees remained with the company until death or retirement. One veteran recalled CLT as being "a homespun, family-type of a company."

Two images of the American South. *Above,* tobacco grows at the base of the
Robert E. Lee statue in Richmond, Virginia, around the turn of the century.
Below, in typical fashion, this ox and mule driver has rolled his hogshead over
the muddy roads of nineteenth-century Virginia to market in Richmond. The
trumpeter at the right is signaling the start of the sale. Both photographs,
courtesy of the Valentine Museum, Richmond, Virginia.

Jaquelin P. Taylor, the major figure behind the founding of Universal Leaf Tobacco Company, at about age sixty-five.

Top left. Frederick N. Harrison, Universal's president from 1924 to 1946 and chairman from 1946 to 1950. "Mr. Fred" was sometimes called "the peacemaker" by company employees. *Top right,* Herbert W. Jackson Jr. joined Universal at the bottom ranks. Known for his conservative stance on all business matters, he served as company president from 1946 to 1965 and chairman from 1965 to 1966. Photo by Dementi Studio. Under president and later chief executive officer Gordon Crenshaw (*bottom left*), Universal became a worldwide company. Crenshaw served in the company's top post from 1966 to 1988. Henry Harrell (*bottom right*), current Universal Corporation chief executive officer, joined the company in 1966 and today oversees a worldwide diversified company. Used by permission of Cliff Bruce Studio.

Universal's China facilities at Tsingtao in the 1920s. The redrying plant at Tsingtao could turn out about 7,200 pounds of tobacco in ten hours.

The J.P. Taylor plant in Goldsboro, North Carolina, as it looked in the mid-1950s. This was the site of Universal's first "super plant." Photo by Overbee Studio.

Universal's headquarters at 201 South Third Street in Richmond, the nerve center of Universal from 1954 until 1968. The Victorian structure at the far right housed the company laboratory, one of the first in the tobacco business. Photo by Photographic Services.

A modern-day farmer stands beside his pile of flue-cured tobacco in a North Carolina warehouse.

Shown here in the early 1970s, K.R. Edwards was a Universal vice president before he left to form his own company, which later became a leader in the tobacco business as a Universal partner. Photo by Reuben L. Johnson.

R.A. "Bindy" Noakes (*left*), a native of Liverpool, England, a major figure in Universal's business in Africa, and Jan Laverge, the main force behind Universal's foreign operations, pictured in the early 1980s.

Billy "the Senator" Pritchard, seen here about 1980, was a legendary Universal tobacco buyer from the 1950s until his death in 1987.

The late John Leavell, a Universal buyer and company officer who covered all markets during his long career, points out the quality of a bundle of tobacco to a member of the Japanese Tobacco Corporation about 1975.

Gabriel "Gabby" Kremer poses with his daughter Nicola and son Dion in the mid-1970s in front of the airplane he used to evacuate Universal personnel from war-torn Angola during the revolution.

Harry Hitchcock, the force behind Universal's cigar-leaf business in Pennsylvania, as a young man traveled the entire Eastern Seaboard in search of new customers.

A.L. Hobgood, a nephew of K.R. Edwards, became the president and chief executive officer of Universal partner the K.R. Edwards company. Shown here in the late 1970s, he ultimately became a director of Universal Corporation.

The administrative section of the plant in Sintanjin, Korea in the 1970s. Korean tobacco is exported worldwide.

James E. "Covey" Covington at left and George Macon pose with their families in front of the Great Buddha in Kamakura, Japan, in the late 1930s during a brief layover on their way back to China from the United States. *Below,* shown here in the early 1980s, Edwin W. Humphreys, nicknamed "the Rattler" by some subordinates, is still known as the toughest taskmaster ever at Universal. His vision, however, paid off in the construction of the "super plants."

5
Cigar Leaf Tobacco

At the turn of the twentieth century, America's favorite tobacco product was unquestionably the cigar, and consumers spent more money for cigars than for cigarettes, snuff, chewing and smoking leaf combined. Cigars were made coast to coast, usually by small manufacturers who numbered in the tens of thousands, with strong concentrations in New York and Pennsylvania. Production hit four billion in 1890 and rose to seven billion in 1906. Significantly, when the giant American Cigar came into being in 1901, it controlled only one-sixth of the market.

There were cigar brands for every pocketbook, and retail outlets often made their purchases directly from an army of tobacco's finest showmen, the cigar drummers. As described by Joseph C. Robert: "Some wore high silk hats and frock-tail coats. Most sported double-breasted vests, across which flashed lodge emblems on massive gold watch chains. The cigar drummer entered the dark little tobacco shop, grasped the hand of the dealer, slapped him on the back, and passed along the latest stories. The heavy accordion-type sample case was unstrapped, specimens redolent of vanilla and rum rolled under the nose, a couple cut open to prove the genuine long filler." "Then salesman and retailer," Robert continues, "proceeded to the important part of the business, the premiums that went along with the cigars: so many pictures of actresses and prize fighters as display cards, a wall lighter, cigar cutters, and matches, not to mention a mantel clock if the order were sizable."

Leaf for American cigars came from both foreign and domestic sources. Cuba, Puerto Rico, and Dutch-controlled Sumatra provided the imports, while native leaf came largely from the Connecticut River Valley, which extended northward from Hartford into Massachusetts. Other regions that supplied cigar leaf included the Miami River Valley in Ohio; the region in and around Lancaster, Pennsylvania; and several areas in Wisconsin. In general, the Connecticut Valley was the oldest growing region, Wisconsin the newest, Pennsylvania the largest.

Cigar leaf itself came in three types, initially categorized by use as filler, binder, and wrapper. Traditionally, filler provided the cigar bulk or core and binder secured the filler in a cigar shape, wrapper being the outside cover. Cigar leaf was also used in such products as chewing tobacco.

Although Universal was organized to deal in all types of tobacco, most of the founders had scant knowledge of cigar leaf. The exception was Pat Gorman, who was equally at home in cigarette or cigar leaf and whose experience included years in Puerto Rico and a stint with American Cigar. Gorman moved quickly to establish Universal in Wisconsin, where in 1919 he organized the Jefferson Leaf Tobacco Company, headed by former American official W.T. Jefferson. Gorman also helped set up the La Plata and La Regional Tobacco companies in Puerto Rico, and Dominion and Tropical in Santo Domingo.

Closer to home, Universal also had a packing plant in Ohio and bought through dealers in Connecticut, Ohio, and Pennsylvania, and on the Dutch markets in Amsterdam. The company also had close ties with the Cullmans of New York City and did some Pennsylvania business through the W.H. Winstead Company, a founding Universal subsidiary.

Despite these initiatives in the 1920s, the company's cigar interests turned sour. Jefferson, La Plata, and Tropical were all merged into the ill-fated Industrial Leaf and failed when it did, although Industrial's liquidation took years to complete. Other losses were heavy, and by the late 1920s Universal's cigar-leaf business had shriveled to a negligible level, as Pat Gorman left the company to head American Cigar. Although no one could have known it at the time, what appeared to be Universal's cigar nadir was in fact its real beginning. A story was about to unfold in the person of Harry Hitchcock, a bookkeeper turned cigar baron. Against strong odds, Hitchcock would in time build Lancaster Leaf into America's largest dealer in cigar tobacco.

Harry Hitchcock was born in Baltimore in 1897. He was the son of a professional singer who had lost his eyesight. The Hitchcock family had a vaudeville show and also operated one of the city's first motion-picture theaters—an unlikely heritage for a youngster who aspired to be a Methodist minister. His father's sudden affliction interrupted Harry's education and his career plans, but in time he made his way through night school and the YMCA School of Accounting.

For a while Harry kept books, but he came to believe that he was "such a little cog in such a big wheel . . . that nobody would know I was there unless lightning hit me." He decided to leave even if it meant a cut in pay, and looked for work where "you were noticed if you did something worthwhile."

In June 1919, coming off the Baltimore streets on the arm of his blind father, Harry Hitchcock entered the office of the W.H. Winstead Company on Redwood Street (formerly German Street until World War I, when anti-German sentiment forced the change). Henry Winstead hired Harry as a clerk. Working "forty hours a day," he established himself as "a good numbers man" and "as the man with the figures." His tax expertise attracted the attention of Gorman, whom Hitchcock described as "like a father to me," and other Universal officers in New York.

Hitchcock later moved to the Richmond office, where he swallowed his Methodist pride in order to advance his career and became part of a Baptist Sunday School class taught by Universal's James I. Miller. He next was reassigned to New York City as one of the accountants for Industrial Leaf. Along the way his friendship with Gorman grew stronger; Hitchcock prepared Gorman's income tax forms, a practice he continued until Gorman's death decades later. With the collapse of Industrial, Hitchcock returned to the Winstead Company in Baltimore, where he received a startling proposition.

By 1927 experts agreed there was no future for a young man in the cigar business. Cigarettes had passed cigars in popular taste, and, consequently, in sales. Hundreds of dealers and manufacturers failed. Universal's poor showing was only part of a nationwide trend. The company's top management apparently had lost interest—or perhaps patience—with cigar leaf, but Henry Winstead thought one more low-risk effort might be worthwhile. Winstead himself confessed neither knowledge nor personal interest, and his own experience in cigars had been limited and unsuccessful. Still, he had a vision and shared it with his peripatetic accountant. Simply put, Winstead proposed that Harry accept a reduction in pay, leave bookkeeping, and relocate to York County, Pennsylvania, for the purpose of developing a cigar-leaf business there.

At this point in his career Hitchcock knew nothing about cigar leaf and in fact had never "bought or sold a pound of tobacco" in his life. He might have added that he was a nonsmoker and a missionary Methodist and that he would be attempting to enter an industry alien to him. "How do you start? What do you do?" he asked. But opportunity was knocking, and Hitchcock did not hesitate. Winstead's advice was straightforward: "The safest way to do it is to get options on tobacco without buying it, take samples and show them to prospective customers at a profit, and don't buy until you already have it sold." Winstead also supplied the name of a small dealer and acquaintance in York County, which was the location of a number of cigar manufacturers and was within reach of others in Ohio to the west and in Lancaster, Pennsylvania, to the east.

With Universal's blessing, the new enterprise operated as the cigar-leaf department of the Winstead Company. Harry became a Winstead vice president; his compensation was set at twenty-five dollars a week and 10 percent of the profits, which was a considerable cut from his yearly salary of six thousand dollars with Industrial Leaf. Pat Gorman was pessimistic but promised to help if he could.

In York County, Winstead's reputation proved to be of assistance, but from the beginning, it was Harry's show. "I personally kept the books," he later recalled, "and I also had to buy and sell the tobacco. It was 'a one-man band.'" Initial results were promising, and he soon made the correct decision to relocate "across the Susquehanna" in adjoining Lancaster County, the center of Pennsylvania's cigar-leaf industry. There Harry rented a small processing plant at Mt. Joy. He hired Jake Bowman, "a little country packer," as manager of purchases. For his administrative headquarters Harry chose the office of a former soap factory at the corner of Prince and Seymour Streets in Lancaster. Joining him as bookkeeper was Stanley Altland, who would eventually become a vice president. A skeletal staff kept overhead at a modest level.

Cigar leaf might be bought from a dealer or even a manufacturer, but more commonly it was purchased as a whole crop "in the barn" and from the farmer who sold it either as the quality "wrapper" long filler (80 percent) or the poorer farm filler (20 percent). In time, Harry's buying was done by one or two full-time, salaried supervisors who oversaw the work of from sixty to seventy seasonal buyers, "most of whom were tobacco growing farmers who worked on a per pound basis," he recalled.

Hitchcock's men bought not on order but "against indicated needs" of regular customers. The profit margin was often only a penny a pound, giving birth to the sobriquet, "Penny-a-Pound" Hitchcock. His goal was to get to the farmer "before anybody else with an offering price."

Lancaster tobacco was "Pennsylvania Seedleaf" or cigar filler. The area's limestone-rich soil produced a "heavy-bodied, thick, dark-colored gummy leaf" with good aromatic potential—that is, an ideal tobacco for the body or core of a cigar. In the region's diverse farming population were many Amish—hardy descendants of Swiss and German immigrants and steadfast adherents to the pure and simple values. Because it was labor-intensive and non-technological, cigar leaf seemed an ideal crop for the Amish, whom Hitchcock came to regard highly.

The Amish did not consume tobacco and even preached against it, but they grew it well and, Hitchcock believed, kept it alive in the country.

As it developed, Hitchcock's business was in "scrap," the least expensive type of cigar filler. Scrap might be breakage or residue after the stem or mid-rib had been removed to make the more expensive "long filler," or it might be simply a less costly grade or "farm filler." In either case, after curing by fermentation and storage the leaf would be shredded for blending with higher grades into the filler proper in an era when cheap cigars sold two for a nickel. In short, Hitchcock had opted for the Model T of the trade, not the Cadillac.

Hitchcock's success or failure ultimately depended on his salesmanship, and he soon discovered talents of a high order. His approach was straightforward: "I took samples," he recalled, "and went out to see a Pittsburgh manufacturer who had small factories around the country." When the manufacturer asked why he should start buying from Universal, Hitchcock replied, "You and everybody else I call on are presently buying their tobacco from somebody else. If you have an open mind and will look at our samples, while I don't pretend to have had previous experience in this, I can assure you that you will get tobacco fully up to the sample and at that price. Now if our price is competitive and better tobacco at the same price, or is good tobacco at a lower price, I would think in your position you would want to buy what you can to the best advantage."

To directness, Hitchcock added diligence. Tracking down "a couple of thousand small cigar factories" all over the east coast, he "drove a car fifty thousand miles a year, [and] averaged a thousand miles a week." He called on Hava-Tampa for twenty years "before I sold them the first pound of tobacco"—and then developed a substantial business there. Harry told a similar story about the giant Swisher, ultimately his largest customer.

Along the way Hitchcock collapsed twice from exhaustion, but he also made friends—like Joe Cullman—who simply enjoyed his company and who occasionally passed some business to him even when they did not deal with him directly. And, of course, friendship, always a mainstay in the tobacco world, could lead to business, as in the case of Gorman, who was as good as his word and placed a significant order from American Cigar.

Harry was alert to all possibilities. If he could not sell a manufacturer any tobacco, he turned the tables and asked if the manufacturer had any tobacco to sell him, some undesirable tobacco "to get rid of." This type of deal often provided an entrée and established a relationship in which Harry the buyer would later became Harry the seller.

Of course the fundamentals never changed. "Not having name brands," recalled Hitchcock, "what we had to sell was service, and the basis of it was integrity, and trying to do for other companies something we could do better than they could do for themselves." And, we "always did what we said we were going to do."

That last commitment was critical. Having been taken advantage of as a young salesman by customers who reneged on deals, Hitchcock was especially concerned about being "as good as his word." To encourage his customer to behave the same way, Hitchcock often prepared written contracts. Nor did he hesitate to go to court over a broken agreement.

He became outraged by what he called "parasitic dealers" who claimed an annual commission on any subsequent business that developed from a deal they had made. Under this system a dealer who sold some of Harry's tobacco to a manufacturer in, say 1931, would claim a percentage payment on any direct and later business Harry himself did with that client. Hitchcock and others fought this common practice, and today it is unknown.

The former accountant also put a stop to what had been a long-standing problem with Universal's cigar business. In the early 1920s "credit losses" were sustained on tobacco sold on long terms but not delivered for up to six months or even a year. Hitchcock's policy was to bill the purchaser monthly carrying charges "until the tobacco is delivered . . . and then we want to be paid." Once customers agreed, and thus reduced Harry's costs, he then cut his prices and gained a further competitive edge.

Hitchcock's operation prospered into the depression decade of the 1930s. Branches were established in such cigar-leaf regions as Wisconsin (Viroqua Leaf Tobacco Company, headed by the son of W.T. Jefferson; and others); in Versailles, Ohio; and in Windsor Locks, Connecticut. In the latter, Universal worked through a dealer, Howard Russell, who also bought on his own account.

Each month, Hitchcock sent a strong balance sheet to Richmond, and, except for an occasional visit by the company treasurer, Joseph F. Henderson, Richmond allowed him to operate almost autonomously. This freedom lasted until 1941 when Henderson and others recommended that Hitchcock's operation be reorganized into a company entirely separate from W.H. Winstead, which was essentially a cigarette-leaf venture. Part of the reason was obvious: the child had outgrown the parent, and the cigar department had been making "more money than the Winstead Company in total."

September 1941 saw the formation of the W.H. Winstead Company of Lancaster, Pennsylvania. Legally it was a Virginia corporation authorized to do business in Pennsylvania and specifically "to handle cigar leaf tobacco, used principally in the grinding of scrap, but also to trade in cigarette tobacco of lower grades." The new company had a book value of two hundred thousand dollars. Hitchcock was named president and general manager.

In keeping with the long-standing Universal policy of encouraging stock ownership—and thus a genuinely vested interest—by heads of affiliate companies, Harry Hitchcock had an option to buy up to 40 percent (eighty thousand dollars' worth) of the stock issue. He amassed thirty-five thousand dollars by mortgaging his home and selling "the gold out of my teeth"; Universal loaned him the balance of forty-five thousand dollars to be repaid out of future dividends. Years later, in 1967, when Universal bought him out, the company's book value had risen to $12 million, and Harry's percentage was then worth $3 million. It had been, Hitchcock said, "a fairy-tale development."

6

The Depression
and the Great War Years

Despite the excellent comeback from near disaster that Universal made
during the 1920s, it was anyone's guess what fate lay ahead after the
stock market crash on Black Friday, October 29, 1929.

As mentioned earlier, the tobacco world was experiencing a depression of its own as early as 1921. In that year the burley market
almost collapsed, and Europe—Great Britain in particular—was also suffering from a glut of bright tobacco. But what was unfolding in the
winter of 1929-30 was different. Problems suffered earlier in the decade were ones the tobacco industry could correct. But now the nation
itself was in deep, nearly cataclysmic, trouble. By 1932, stock market
prices had dropped to one-sixth of their 1929 worth, and American
exports were roughly half of what they had been three years earlier.
Worst of all, at the nadir of this collapse nearly 15 million people who
wanted jobs were unable to find them. To many, it seemed as if America
itself was about to crumble.

Tobacco, however, has long been considered a depression-proof
business (except at the grower's level), and so it proved to be during the
early 1930s. To be sure, Universal was not unaffected by the Depression, as witnessed by President Harrison's report to stockholders in September 1930: "The general business depression throughout the world
has to some extent affected the sales and profits of your company," he
stated. "Mr. Fred" then noted that "a substantial reduction in operating
expenses has been made during the last six months," indicating that
Universal, like other businesses, had been forced to retrench. "However," Harrison optimistically continued, "we anticipate a satisfactory
volume of business during the coming year." And despite the fact that
dollar volume for the year ending June 30, 1930, was down from the
previous year's, Harrison nevertheless proclaimed, "Your company is
in sound condition."

Indeed, such was the case. For example, during 1930 the board of
directors put into operation a company stock-option plan for officers

and key employees. More than $329,000 worth of common stock was purchased and sold at "attractive prices."

In addition to being financially sound in 1930, the company extended from Richmond to a sprawling complex of plants scattered about the East Coast and numerous foreign countries. It owned facilities in Richmond, Danville, and South Boston, Virginia; Goldsboro, Henderson, Wilson, Tabor, Kinston, Fairmont, and Lumberton, North Carolina; Mullins, South Carolina; Hughesville, Huntington, Carstow, and Chaptico, Maryland; Louisville, Lexington, Shelbyville, Cynthiana, and Owensboro, Kentucky; and Shanghai, China. The China facilities were functioning well. Other plants owned by Universal's subsidiary companies in the early Depression era were located in Greenville, Winston-Salem, Farmville, and Oxford, North Carolina; Clarksville, Tennessee; Hopkinsville and Henderson, Kentucky; Lynchburg and Petersburg, Virginia; Chatham, Ontario; and the Dominican Republic. The company also had agencies in cities in Europe, Asia, Africa, South America, Australia, and Canada. All these operations were overseen by a staff of thirty-five in the Richmond office.

The company's consolidated balance sheet for 1931 reflects the extent of Universal's business, and it does not read as if the country were in a depression. Although total dollar volume was still down— roughly equivalent to that of the previous year—the regular 8 percent dividend on the preferred stock and the regular dividends on common stock were paid. Universal also continued to acquire its own preferred stock, and $252,000 worth of it was purchased, leaving the total amount outstanding at $6,555,200.

In 1932, the bright tobacco crop was unusually small, and for the first time in its history the company paid no bonuses. But the following year, when economic woes were lessening, Harrison reported: "Your company is in a splendid condition." In 1935, with the dollar volume up to $18,000,000, he used the same phrase, substituting the word "excellent" for "splendid." In 1936, Universal boasted six wholly owned subsidiaries, and for the second time in its history, gross revenues exceeded $20,000,000 reaching $20,972,515. It was never again to drop below the $20,000,000 mark.

Business as usual was not the key for Universal in the 1930s, however. During and just after the Depression, new social programs were inaugurated with President Roosevelt's "New Deal," and the government began grading and regulating tobacco. In addition, Universal hired several people who would ultimately bring a much broader and more long-range vision to company leadership. Most important, although still firmly entrenched in the American South, Universal in the 1930s increased its interest in foreign markets, an action that was to pay enormous dividends following World War II.

Because Universal has never offered products directly to the public, it has always been a low-profile company, one unlikely to attract those seeking to regulate the tobacco industry. Nevertheless, the Roosevelt administration's interest in the tobacco business had an oblique long-term effect on the company, ultimately paving the way for direct governmental involvement at the highest level by way of the 1964 Surgeon General's report and the anti-tobacco laws of the seventies, eighties, and nineties.

In the 1930s the New Deal moved the federal government deeper into the daily lives of working Americans, continuing a trend that had begun with the Food and Drug Act of 1906, the Draft Act of 1917, and World War I controls. During his campaign, Roosevelt had often spoken of the "forgotten man," and by all accounts the tobacco farmer fit this stereotype. Auctioning off their leaf for an annual pittance, the nation's leaf growers were receptive to the ideas set forth in the Agricultural Adjustment Act of 1933. The tobacco section of the AAA focused solely on the plight of the tobacco farmer.

One important Depression-era law was the Tobacco Inspection Act, the purpose of which was to aid the farmer in pricing his product. Because farmers often had little or no contact with the world beyond their local towns, they were not in a position to know the prices tobacco would bring on various markets. According to the government's reasoning, they were therefore at the mercy of predatory middlemen who might defraud them by misrepresenting prices. Moreover, farmers were among those hit hardest by the Depression and therefore received a good deal of attention from the federal government. It was not until 1941, for example, that farmers' incomes reached the level they had enjoyed on the eve of the stock market crash twelve years earlier.

Becoming law on August 23, 1935, the Tobacco Inspection Act authorized the secretary of agriculture to impose an inspection system on any leaf market he designated, if he was able to gain approval from two-thirds of the growers using the market. Under the act, the secretary was also required to assist the tobacco farmer by publishing and distributing information regarding supply, demand, and market prices of the leaf. Actual grading was based on a subdivision of leaf into seven classes and types. Although Universal's buyers were influenced more by their own judgment than by the opinions of government inspectors, the precedent of government involvement in the tobacco business at the grassroots level had clearly been set.

Labor unions, another outside force that impinged on the tobacco world in the 1930s, had little influence on Universal, and what influence they had was limited to the partner companies. The unions' most conspicuous successes during the decade centered on manufacturers rather than leaf dealers, who would, however, feel the effects of organized labor following World War II.

Universal also had to deal with government directives such as the Social Security Act, which became law within two weeks of the Tobacco Inspection Act. Designed in part to establish a national and state sponsored system of unemployment insurance, the act immediately caused headaches in Universal's factories because government requested information did not exist and furthermore was impossible to obtain. But the government viewed it another way.

One case in point centers on the experiences of Hugh West, who was with Universal for twenty-five years before he left to join the Philip Morris Company. Given the job of collecting biographical data on some fifteen hundred hand-stemmers in the Henderson plant, West soon discovered that few workers knew their own middle names, that their last names were often the same as their mothers', and that many did not know their father's name or even their own date of birth. West collected the information as best he could and forwarded it to the government, but within two weeks 75 percent of his forms were returned as incomplete. West was assured by the government that all blanks on the forms must be filled in, whereupon he approached the problem the only way he saw possible: he fabricated the data. He made up names and arbitrarily assigned birth dates. Known only to West, many people in the Henderson area officially shared West's birth date.

Not only outside forces changed the tobacco world during the 1930s; inside ones played a role as well. Traditionally, American tobacconists were rough-and-tumble entrepreneurs with little formal education and a fierce adherence to the work ethic. In the 1930s, however, under Harrison's direction, those entering the Universal system brought with them different backgrounds. For the first time in its history, college-educated young men were recruited into the company.

Why Harrison chose the kinds of men he did is anyone's guess. Most likely, however, he saw in them something of his own image of what an up-and-coming young man of the 1930s should be both morally and culturally. Mr. Fred was a committed Christian, a member of one of the oldest families in the Commonwealth, and a philanthropist who financially aided many friends in the difficult years of the Depression, during which his salary remained in the upper half of five figures. In addition, he paid the way for more than one needy youngster through college or seminary.

Harrison apparently recruited new people with an eye to what they could become if properly nurtured. Among them was Pierre Warwick, a member of a socially prominent family who had to leave the University of Virginia without his degree because of a reversal in family circumstances. He later became one of Universal's master traders. Another was Edwin W. Humphreys, an unemployed metallurgical engineer who had been raised under trying circumstances following the death of his father. He was later to become the father of the super plants, facilities that would change forever the way tobacco was processed and would bring handsome rewards to the company. There was also Jan Laverge, a native Hollander of Huguenot descent, who brought with him a mechanical engineering degree and the willingness to work his way up from the bottom in a foreign country. This he did, and he became the father of Universal's foreign operations and remained one of the major forces in the company for some six decades.

These young men and others entered the Universal system under the tutelage of such crusty war horses as Lewis Gorin, at Southwestern; Frank Mills, of J.P. Taylor, at Henderson; Morgan Boyd, in the dark-fired area; and K.R. Edwards, who was in charge of leaf purchasing during those years. Men such as these, who formed the backbone of the Universal world, expected absolute obedience from those who worked under them. They were no-nonsense types who did not care what their subordinates thought or wanted to do. Pete Walker, a Universal supervisor from 1938 to 1966, explained his relationship with his subordinates. "If you were hard to handle, I had to get tough," he said. About his colleagues, he noted that "they knew damned well that I knew my business and they knew damned well that I wouldn't take any crap. So we didn't have any trouble."

Nor were these young men's entries into the tobacco business easy, or for that matter even civil by modern standards. John Leavell's initial encounter with the Universal family serves as a typical case in point. Over forty years later, Leavell, a college graduate, remembered the reception he received from R.L. ("Blackie") Kimbrough his first day on his first job at the Goldsboro plant during the Depression. "I reported to him at 7 o'clock in the morning on the 10th of September 1932, and he took one look at me, got up from his desk and walked all the way around me just like I was a horse. And he said, 'I'll say one thing: you're the sorriest looking bastard I ever saw. Tell me one thing: why do those sons of bitches in Richmond send me everybody that don't know nothing? Well, Goddamn it! I reckon we can use you.'"

In an atmosphere such as this, after the senior man had grudgingly accepted the junior he usually called him "son," while the younger always responded with "sir." The professional gap between the two was clearly defined and was never crossed for social occasions, those in charge considering themselves duty-bound to hold their charges in line and extract the utmost from them. Newcomers who played the game found their load lighter after the first few years. If good enough, they eventually became the company executives and in turn demanded the same from their subordinates.

It would be unfair, however, to characterize these hard-liners as tyrants. Often without a subordinate knowing it, his boss would go to bat for him behind the scenes. A beginner—"young little boys," as the widow of one factory manager recalled them—might start as a floor sweeper, move to the prizery, then be placed in charge of drying or stemming. A few seasons later he might be found driving for one of the regular buyers and occasionally filling in during the sale. When many men reached the level of buyer they had fulfilled their ambitions; others, however, with an eye toward further horizons and perhaps with qualities that led them to be more carefully groomed by their superiors, came back to Richmond and went on into managerial positions and ultimately the executive ranks.

In this rigid caste system superiors' decisions were unilateral and praise and announcement of promotion given privately. Walker, for example, recalled K.R. Edwards approaching him on one occasion without warning and saying, "Come here, son." The older man took the younger one out of earshot of other employees, "where nobody on God's green earth could hear him talk, which was his point to begin with," Walker recalled. "He turned around and looked up in my face and said, 'Son, you ain't making enough money. I'm going to raise your salary a hundred dollars a month, retroactive the first of January.' [Then] he turned around and walked right on out."

Even though it owned facilities in numerous locales, by contemporary standards Universal was quite small during the Harrison years, when much of the buying was done by partner companies in the field.

Run by the last of the tobacco barons, these companies also served as training grounds for new Universal employees. At a later time, in the years following World War II, buying would shift in the direction of account servicing, but throughout the 1930s Universal's buyers, whether in the partner companies or working from the Richmond office, bought primarily on speculation.

Buying on speculation was relatively simple: the tobacco was purchased and stored, with no guaranteed sale in mind. It would be resold when a customer placed an order that could be filled from storage.

Speculation buying had drawbacks as well as rewards, however. For one thing, space for storage translated directly into time and money. Moreover, such sales often took a great deal of time to consummate because Universal's customers were typically small and geographically dispersed; as a result, salesmen had to make numbers of trips, carrying samples to show prospective customers, then return home to see that the orders were shipped. During the time in question, twenty-five hogsheads was a sizable sale, contrasted with twenty-five hundred or so today. And there was always the danger that tobacco bought on speculation would have to be stored so long that profit would be lost.

But Universal's sales in the 1930s were strong. For the fiscal year ending in June 1930 revenues from sales were $11,500,000. Remaining fairly constant through the worst of the Depression, revenues climbed to almost $13,000,000 by the end of 1935. The following year they rose to $20,000,000. By the end of the decade they were at $21,676,000.

Processing too was far different from what it would become within the next twenty years. Following its purchase at the auction, the tobacco came to the factory where each pile or basket was regraded and any necessary readjustments made. From there some would go to the hanging room, where it was hung on stakes and put through the redrying machine to stabilize moisture content. The remainder would have the central stem removed from the leaf by a workforce of some three hundred to seven hundred women, who accomplished this task by hand. Finally, it was packed in hogsheads ready for shipment.

The workforce was almost entirely black; women performed the picking and stemming tasks and men operated the machines, manning the conveyor belts and dollies used to move the tobacco. The work day began at seven and ended at five, with thirty minutes for lunch. All workers brought their own lunches, which usually consisted of collard greens, fatback, and cornbread, or occasionally fish heads. Hourly wages varied from 7.5 to 15 cents, depending on one's duties. Employees had ten minutes to answer calls of nature; one woman's sole job was to time each person's stay in the lavatory with a Big Ben alarm clock and then wind off a strip of toilet paper and deliver it to the stall. This practice was followed for years in order to prevent malingering and to keep employees from stealing the whole roll.

Workers' days, and for that matter the life of the whole town, were regulated by a series of whistles emanating from the factory. The town, permeated with the odor of tobacco, rose to the 7 A.M. whistle, broke for lunch at the noon one, and finished its workday at the 5 P.M. shriek. Factories were not heated or air-conditioned; the only respite from the choking summer heat of the South was cold water from the melting blocks of ice the delivery man stacked in the communal wooden barrels each day. At the J.P. Taylor Company in Henderson (and perhaps elsewhere as well) factory manager Ralph Thompson allowed employees to sing for a half an hour or so each afternoon after the neighborhood babies had finished their naps. In lyrics that restated dominant themes from three centuries of African-American life, hundreds of voices recalled the slavery era, praised Jesus, and told tales of unrequited love. Outside on the sidewalks, townspeople, white and black alike, gathered to hear the daily chorus.

By today's standards working conditions were substandard and demeaning, but viewed in the context of the times they seem less deserving of censure. This was the era, for example, when farmers in Johnson County, North Carolina, staged a demonstration to protest national economic conditions; the parade featured "Hoover carts," which were the rear halves of automobiles drawn by a mules. Such events, one of which was formally staged in Smithfield on October 7, 1932, included a band and prizes for the most outlandish vehicle. A truck loaded with local unemployed people brought up the rear. These events were staged to send a message to Washington.

This was also the time when complaining workers in businesses across the country were reminded by bosses, who sometimes took them to the factory window to view the line of job seekers below, that someone was waiting to take their place should they find their work too onerous. Often, between two and three hundred people would appear at Universal's factories each morning searching for employment. Lack of labor laws allowed for the practices that Jan Laverge recalled at the Goldsboro plant, where two noted factory hands had worked twenty-four hours a day. "They never quit," he remembered. "They took a nap on a pile of tobacco and kept on working."

As would be expected with such a large workforce, the factories were not without colorful characters and amusing incidents. One such person was Robert Blakely, known only as "Salty Dog" until Social Security laws forced his given name to be carried on company records. Blakely had abandoned the carnival life for one in a tobacco factory, and he got his name from his habit of continually singing the lyrics of a song he had performed on the carnival circuit: "let me be your salty dog 'til your sweet dog comes along."

Buck McCoy, who wore a crudely fashioned artificial leg, was another colorful character. While he was working in the third-floor picking room at the Goldsboro plant, a fire broke out and he found himself trapped by the blaze. His mother, who worked on a lower floor in the stemming room, escaped from the building before him. She spied her frantic son at a third-floor window.

"I'm going to jump!" Buck shouted in desperation.

"Say a prayer first," his mother called.

"I don't know how to pray," he yelled back.

"Say something with God's name in it," she screamed.

McCoy thought for an instant before blurting out his plea for divine protection: "Goddamn—Here I come!" Then he took to the air.

Witnesses reported that his artificial limb dug several inches into the ground, but McCoy, his dubious prayer perhaps answered, escaped with no broken bones.

Unlike many businesses, Universal weathered the times because it had a low overhead operation, because of the constant demand for tobacco, and because of its successes abroad. During much of the 1930s, Universal operated from its modest suite of offices in the Richmond Trust Building at Seventh and Main Streets. There, from a sample room, one other large room and four smaller ones, it oversaw the operations of six wholly owned subsidiaries—the J.P. Taylor Company, Southwestern Tobacco Company, W.H. Winstead Company, State Warehouse Company, Southern States Tobacco Company, and the Universal Leaf Tobacco Company of China. In addition, it was involved in the operations of the Canadian Leaf Tobacco Company, the Norfolk Leaf Tobacco Company, the Kinston Tobacco Company, and seventeen other affiliated companies.

President and director Fred Harrison was often absent from the office and allowed his cousin Pinckney Harrison to care for routine matters. Rounding out the top three executives was Kenneth R. Edwards, the head leaf man. Twelve others made up the managerial force, the total staff numbering about fifty by the end of the decade. As was customary, there were no written contracts. Consequently, most duties revolved around paying for and routing tobacco to customers. Louise Hankins, who went to work for the company in 1927 and left eleven years later to follow K.R. Edwards into his own venture, remembered that a great deal of the business was conducted on the golf course, with cryptic notes being conveyed to her and other secretaries following a game. Often the men were away on the markets, leaving those behind to construct their own routines in their 8:45 to 4:45 work day. Much of the business was conducted by telephone, and few or no written records were kept.

Although it appeared to be a sharp blow at the time, Universal was ultimately to gain when on July 1, 1938, Edwards left the company and opened his own business in Smithfield, North Carolina. Beginning tentatively as a domestic tobacco dealer, he expanded and diversified and ultimately became one of the most important Universal partners.

The Edwards company was later to take on international aspects after the 1953 installation of its new leader A.L. Hobgood. Currently it operates in Mexico, Guatemala, Honduras, Argentina, and Colombia, selling its product to almost all the world's cigarette makers. It remains a key player in the Universal arena.

One of the most important figures in the company during these early days was treasurer Joseph F. Henderson, who joined Universal in the 1920s and soon had all company financial matters under his control. Henderson was neurotically exacting, eccentric, and highly opinionated (He once told Dutch native Jan Laverge never to trust a foreigner: "they're all crooks!") Moreover, he had no interest in anything but money, and he oversaw Universal's finances with conservatism and rectitude. What could have spelled disaster for the company was narrowly averted in 1946 when Henderson failed in a bid as a compromise candidate for the company presidency. He eventually suffered a mental breakdown and lived out his days in a nursing home conducting imaginary transactions with play-money. A childless widower and a millionaire, he accepted the $100 sent to him monthly by a niece who thought him impoverished.

Universal weathered the Depression decade at home and also broadened its horizons by tentative entries into foreign markets. The new business was the result of exploratory trips by Laverge and Warwick to the Mediterranean, Northern Europe, and Central and South America. These jaunts culminated in small gains for the company; more important, they promised greater rewards to come.

In the 1930s Laverge and Warwick could have been described as "floating" employees in Universal's sales department. Both were young and new to the company and both found themselves in a business controlled by firmly entrenched vice presidents who handled the bulk of the sales and regular accounts. Owing to their junior status, the two men were often hard pressed to find new leads and potential accounts to cultivate; as a result, they went after those customers their superiors thought marginal or not worth pursuing. Their accomplishments were significant for the future. For example, in Holland, before the war Laverge sold some four to five hundred hogsheads per year. In 1946, the first full year following the war, the Dutch pipe tobacco industry commission placed orders with Universal for somewhere in the neighborhood of twenty-five to thirty thousand hogsheads. Had it not been for the company's entree there in the thirties, such business may not have been forthcoming. As it was, it foreshadowed the success Universal was to have on the world tobacco market.

.The two main foreign arms of the Universal body in the years immediately prior to World War II were Canada and China, the former being the smaller of the two.

The Canadian operation in the 1930s saw sales fluctuating from year to year and customers, most buying limited supplies of tobacco, varying on an annual basis. About half of the business in Canada was with domestic accounts; Macdonald Tobacco Company was the largest. The other half was spread throughout a number of countries. A sizable business, however, was being done with England and Germany.

Overshadowing the Canadian operations in the 1930s, however, was the one in China. In many ways, its success offset the Depression in America for Universal. The Chinese operation was a staple in the company until the Japanese invasion of China and the ensuing World War II halted operations there.

When Japan's Admiral Nagumo followed his orders and sent his carrier-based planes to attack Pearl Harbor on December 7, 1941, the great global war was immediately in full swing. The United States, and along with it Universal Leaf Tobacco Company, was about to change.

For Universal, the most drastic effect of the war revolved around the loss of the China company. The Japanese invasion of China was, of course, more than a military venture. On the heels of the army came Japanese businessmen, who confiscated foreign interests held in China, including those of Universal. When A.I. McOwan, the last remaining staff member, was incarcerated, the China branch was written off as a complete loss. Moreover, with the Japanese military entrenched in the

Pacific from New Guinea to Okinawa, it was pointless to entertain any notion of expansion in the Far East or Southeast Asia.

The company also had its woes in Europe. The first European problem to surface centered on Spain, which during the mid-1930s erupted in civil war. Suddenly the company found that it was unable to convert pesetas into dollars. Common today, it was virtually unheard of for governments not to allow such conversions at that time. Roughly a half-million dollars of company funds, representing profit and outlay for tobacco, was frozen in a bank in Barcelona.

Laverge made a trip to Barcelona in an attempt to free the funds, but to no avail. Exhausted from fruitless attempts and terrified following all night anti-aircraft fire from the roof of his hotel, he left the country. His life was probably saved by a change of plans. At the last minute he took an Air France plane; the train on which he had originally booked passage was bombed and many of the passengers were killed.

Negotiations with Spain continued, but they ended in frustration. At one point the company even considered bizarre schemes to free its frozen pesetas. For example, it arranged a test case whereby the company was to buy $4,000 worth of Spanish anchovies, which would be contracted to a New York importer at a cost of approximately 10 percent of the pesetas involved. Spanish approval seemed forthcoming, but on second thought Universal's Finance Committee decided to pursue more conventional channels. Only later did a market in blocked pesetas evolve, but Universal suffered a substantial loss when it finally got its money, a process that dragged on until 1944. The final settlement was for $315,000.

Problems in China and Spain were dwarfed, however, by those brought on by the war itself. When Hitler's forces invaded Poland, almost all Universal's dealings in Europe ground to a halt. Throughout 1939, the company continued to do business in neutral Belgium, Holland, and Denmark, but those nations fell to the Nazis in the spring of 1940. This was the final blow. Universal would sell no tobacco on the continent until the war was over, except for minor amounts in neutral countries and also under the provisions of President Roosevelt's lend-lease program. The company did, however, continue business in Great Britain through the auspices of the American government, which funded British tobacco purchases. Formerly supplied almost exclusively by the Imperial Tobacco Company, Great Britain now got its tobacco from several companies, one of which was Universal.

Another boost for Universal's sales, and one that partly offset the loss of the European market, occurred in the form of the lend-lease program, which was aimed at aiding America's allies. Lend-lease came into effect in March 1941 and lasted until August 1945, when it was terminated on the heels of the surrenders of Germany and Japan. Under its provisions, the president had a free hand in providing U.S. allies with war materiel, under whose broad umbrella tobacco was included. This put Universal in the position of supplying tobacco to countries it might otherwise have lost during the war. The volume was far below that of prewar years, however.

An observer of Universal's foreign losses during the war years might have come to the conclusion that the company was in for hard times or worse. Nothing could have been further from the truth, however, as the annual figures for the years 1942 through 1945 clearly show. For the fiscal year ending June 1942, the last before the beginning of a total war economy, gross revenues totaled $33,688,239.91. The next year it was up to $55,854,263.44. Dollar volume for 1944 reached $57,527,523.31, and for 1945 the figure was a stunning $88,138,514.15. And this with the loss of the China company and European business.

The war years were also good for Universal because of the complex interaction between tobacco consumption and the psychological needs and stresses of the consumers. In times of crisis people tend to smoke more, and during the time in question, the whole nation was involved in the conflict. Some thirteen million people were in the armed forces, and during those times tobacco consumption carried neither social stigma nor health caveats. Combat forces customarily received a package of five cigarettes in their K Rations, and cigarettes came tax free—often entirely free—to military personnel. Tobacco products were supplied by American manufacturers under the auspices of a government eager to aid the troops in any way it could. "You had a home market for every pound you could buy, no matter what it was," Laverge remembered. "You were in a real seller's market."

Like most American businesses, Universal underwent change during the war, but not as much as many companies. Laverge and Pinckney Harrison were the only two members of the company's managerial staff to see military service; the others were too old. The company's factory staffs were severely depleted, however, as young men and women donned uniforms and heeded the call of the bugle. And, incidentally, those leaving Universal for the military had life financially better than many of their fellow volunteers or draftees in the ranks. In a patriotic gesture to aid both the individual and the country, Universal followed a practice during World War II of awarding the difference between military pay and company pay while an employee was in the service. R.W. "Will" Tuggle, for example, while in the Army periodically and candidly notified the company of his advance from private to commissioned officer, knowing that he would receive less money from Richmond. At each point his check reflected his new military status. Meanwhile, in the home office wall posters asked employees to buy bonds, which many did.

Of the Universal personnel who served in the military, Laverge had the most interesting tour of duty. He and his wife became American citizens in 1942, and barely twelve months later Laverge was in uniform and a member of the elite Office of Strategic Services (OSS). Eventually assigned to its Secret Intelligence (SI) division, he was involved in intelligence in England and eventually on the Continent.

Pinckney Harrison also served in Army Intelligence. He was stationed in Washington, D. C., for much of the war and rose to the rank of colonel.

A little known sidelight to the larger history of Universal, and of World War II in general for that matter, involves the use of prisoners of war in the American tobacco factories. During the height of the conflict rumors abounded among the rural residents of Virginia and North Carolina that German spies were infiltrating the U.S. mainland. Indeed, a handful did manage to penetrate North Carolina's sparsely populated coast; but the Axis powers were represented in a more numerous, yet less threatening, way by being leased as prisoners of war to private companies. Their presence set rural countrysides buzzing. More than one farmer employed his mule and plow to cut furrows around the family home in hopes of stopping any forest fire started by German saboteurs. The fires never came, but the Germans (and a few Italians) did, truckloads of them, working under guard in the tobacco factories.

Because tobacco, although important, was not considered a war industry, its workforce was soon depleted by the draft as well as by those who volunteered for the military. About the time the problem became serious, company officials learned that they were eligible to acquire prisoners of war to replace personnel in uniform. Arrangements were made by Universal's Richmond office, and soon the company's plants were operated primarily by prisoners, who were trucked from area prisoner of war camps—a notable one being North Carolina's Camp Buckner—to the factories.

Arriving in groups of fifty or sixty each morning, the prisoners worked a twelve-hour day and were supplied food by the military, brought each noon by trucks. Universal had to pay the government for each prisoner. Recollections of the prisoners' effectiveness vary, but Laverge recalled that the company would not have been able to stay afloat without them. He remembers hearing them described as "good workers." Pete Walker, a highly respected supervisor, concurs, adding only that they required close scrutiny. Some worked as far afield in the company system as the Maryland and Kentucky plants.

Although most welcomed the opportunity to get away from their compounds, the incarcerated Germans were not always model employees. Sometimes fights erupted and work stopped until they were quelled. Also, as prisoners of war, they were subject to the military code—they were honor-bound to look for ways to escape and to cause as many problems for their captors as possible. Thus they had to be closely monitored, with armed soldiers acting as guards. Problems of sabotage occasionally arose. At Winston Leaf Tobacco Company, Universal's partner in Winston-Salem, prisoners employed nuisance sabotage techniques. W.A. Goodson Jr. recalls that prisoners there somehow acquired small explosive devices about the size of pens. They would place them in boxcars loaded with tobacco, where they would explode, necessitating assistance from fire-fighting crews. In all, however, Goodson remembers the prisoners as an integral part of the company's operations during the early 1940s: "without these people we would have had to shut down part of the plant for lack of labor."

Although in 1946 few if any people in the company could have foreseen it, Universal was on the eve of major expansion, which would be brought about primarily, but not entirely, by the war. On the home front, tobacco tastes were changing, evidenced both literally and symbolically by a 1945 court decision to remove cuspidors from the country's federal buildings. Clearly the cigarette had become the tobacco of choice. Moreover, as Universal was soon to discover, Europe was in need of tobacco.

Fresh from war experiences, Laverge undertook in 1946 a trip of exploration throughout much of western Europe. Specifically, he wanted to learn the conditions of the tobacco markets in various countries and hoped to reestablish Universal's presence on the Continent. He visited some seven countries and learned that a significant market existed and that tobacco stocks were almost entirely depleted. Prior to the 1946 crop, Universal had sold little more than a hundred hogsheads to any European company; in 1946 it began to sell by the thousands. Laverge's trip, which would lead to even greater sales, reestablished the basis of Universal's trade with western Europe. Moreover, the U.S. government stood ready to help in the form of the Marshall Plan, which was designed to get Europe back on its feet.

Because of its 1930s ventures into overseas markets, Universal was in 1946 positioned to garner a huge share of this new market. In turn, the company used the experience and contacts gained in post-World War II Europe to begin global explorations that would lead it to enormous success in the closing decades of the century. Moreover, the company was entering a new phase because of the appearance of technological advances within its vast factory system, as well as within the business community at large. Soon the world would be smaller and easier to cover. Finally, the company was changing directions because a new generation of people was moving into managerial ranks, and the current president was about to retire.

Mr. Fred gave no inkling to stockholders or colleagues before tendering his resignation on May 31, 1946. The previous year, W.A. Willingham, chairman of the board and a company founder, had died, and now Mr. Fred's departure (although he would remain active in company affairs for another twenty years) paved the way for new leadership from Herbert Jackson.

The change of command following Harrison's resignation was not a particularly smooth one, however. There were several contenders for the position of president, and one influential person in particular—Covington—was opposed to Jackson's bid. Covington's faction wanted Pinckney Harrison in the position but Jackson argued that he had been in the military so long that he was out of touch with the day-to-day operations of the company. The real reason was more likely that Pinckney and Jackson had apparently previously rubbed each other the wrong way, most likely during the period when the former often called the shots. When Covington brought the matter of what role Pinckney should play in the Jackson administration to a head, Jackson flatly refused to be forced. In a late-night telephone conversation with Mr. Fred, who still backed Pinckney's cause, Jackson said crisply, "If you press me any further, I'll resign." The proud Pinckney Harrison subsequently refused the position of vice president. Personalities aside, however, the stage was set for the emergence of a new chapter in Universal's history.

Fred Harrison was born in 1887, and after his death on June 18, 1972, he was eulogized in the lead editorial of the Richmond *Times-Dispatch* in effusive terms. This tribute was written by Virginius Dabney, himself a preeminent figure in the twentieth-century history of the Commonwealth. Dabney hailed Harrison's philanthropy and his personal generosity and also noted his knighthood, about which Harrison never spoke, by the King of Sweden. Dabney called his subject "a great human being," and ended by writing, "There are few like him in any generation."

The eulogy, of course, reflected the public Mr. Fred, but it was the private one who held the helm at Universal. It was probably Fred Harrison more than anyone else who defined—both by actions and attitude—the kind of business Universal would become and remain to the present day. He saw Universal certainly as a business, but he also saw it as a family whose members had the same moral and ethical obligations to each other as they had to their private families. Patriotic in his leadership at the company during the war years and solicitous of his employees who were in the military, he was quiet, unassuming, and known by the nickname "the Peacemaker." He was content to work from behind the scenes, overseeing and approving the company's moves while leaving much of the day-to-day management chores to the more flamboyant Pinckney Harrison. By the standards of the 1990s Fred Harrison might be considered a quaint and reticent Victorian gentleman, but the values he espoused and attempted to instill in those who worked for him continue to shape operations at Universal.

7

Postwar Growth at Home

When Herbert W. Jackson Jr. assumed the presidency of Universal Leaf Tobacco Company in 1946, the country was moving from war to the uncertainties of demobilization. Having conquered the combined forces of Germany and Japan, the United States emerged from combat with strong feelings of solidarity and pride. Demand for tobacco soared to record heights, and Jackson, who always considered tobacco to be one of life's harmless but pleasant diversions, was to have a major influence in helping meet this unprecedented demand.

A heavy-set man with a ruddy complexion, Jackson drove to work each morning in his Cadillac, which he called "the hearse," through a Richmond undergoing change similar to that of the rest of the nation in the late 1940s. Its West End neighborhood was rapidly being developed as a major suburban area, and new roads and subdivisions were being built. New businesses were also coming to the city on the James River that had been host to English colonists, the Revolutionary and Civil wars, and Reconstruction.

Jackson had been first attracted to tobacco warehouse work because of its physical demands. The idea of jockeying hogsheads about, just as had been done in the business since the seventeenth century, doubtless appealed to him as a twenty-two-year-old man recently out of the army just after World War I. Thus, on New Year's Day 1919, he began working for Richmond's J.P. Taylor Tobacco Company, a Universal subsidiary. Rising rapidly through the ranks, Jackson did a seven-year stint in Chatham, Ontario, where he set up operations for the new Canadian Leaf Tobacco Company. Following his return to Richmond in 1934, he was made a vice president. Twelve years later he became president.

By nature Herbert Jackson was a mild-mannered, self-effacing person who shunned the public eye—he said he had "a passion for anonymity"—as ardently as he sought perfection in spoken and written English. His memos, reports, and letters were often stylistic gems, reflecting his admiration for the prose of Winston Churchill. So careful was Jackson in his use of words that he often openly admonished others for misusing them. Once during an automobile trip from the

Chatham, Ontario, plant to the one at Tillsonburg, a distance of about a hundred miles, he was engaged in conversation with Ed Allen, who eventually headed up Universal's Canadian company. Toward the end of the trip, Jackson said, "Ed, it's been a very interesting chat. Do you realize how many times you've cursed since we left Chatham?"

"No, sir, I don't," was the abashed reply.

"Fifty-nine times," said Jackson.

"I'll be damned!" came the spontaneous but immediately embarrassing rejoinder.

"Sixty," said Jackson.

In college, Jackson picked up the nickname "Stony." Doubtless, the person who bestowed it on him had in mind an oblique reference to the famous Confederate general Thomas Jonathan ("Stonewall") Jackson. The name stuck with Jackson for the rest of his life, but was never after college used to his face. Like his namesake, to whom he bore no relation, Herbert Jackson was a committed son of the South, a devout Presbyterian, and an ardent taskmaster. He reflected well the work ethic and individualism of the era in which he was born and raised.

As a leader of Universal, for which he sought the same anonymity that he did for himself, Jackson was known for his conservative stance on all issues. His philosophy was simple: the company's money should be invested only in tobacco because that alone brought the financial return that all connected with the business expected. "Bricks and mortar," a term he often used to describe Universal's physical facilities, were in his view like a carpenter's hammer, merely a tool. Tools gave their user no return; only what they produced could do that. Many Universal people approached Herbert Jackson's desk, which was flanked by twin cuspidors that he regularly used, with ideas that were never implemented because to do so would have cost money. And rare is the Universal employee of long standing who has not heard and repeated the story of Jackson's eliminating one foot from the proposed new corporate headquarters in an attempt to deal with an impending cost overrun. Some fifteen years following Jackson's unexpected death of a heart attack in 1966, a former colleague reflected that "he was the most conservative man I ever knew."

Although Jackson's conservatism may at times have bordered on parsimony, there is no doubt that he was an important force behind the Universal Corporation of today. He was capable of holding disparate groups within the Universal family together by allowing them freedom to pursue their jobs as they thought best, a method of leadership upon which the company still prides itself. This was particularly important where the partners were concerned.

Since its founding, Universal had brought a number of partners under its umbrella. Chief among them was the K.R. Edwards Company. Others included Kinston Tobacco Company, R.P. Watson, W.B. Lea, W.H. Winstead, Winston Leaf, Virginia Tobacco, W.A. Adams, W.L. Robinson, and other smaller ones. Wholly owned companies existed in the form of the J.P. Taylor Company and Southwestern Tobacco Company.

Jackson's theory of governing the partners was basically one of laissez faire, concluding that they would produce best if they enjoyed autonomy. He knew the characters of the men who ran these operations, men often called "popes" or "barons" because of their autocratic managerial styles. Universal always owned 51 percent of these companies but gave them a free hand regarding routine operating matters. Sometimes personnel would be transferred briefly between the Richmond office and one of the partner companies, either in this country or abroad. When an employee went for a stint to a partner company he would answer to management there.

In addition to retaining a good working relationship with the partners, social interactions made the partners feel part of the Universal family. The Lancaster Leaf operation in Pennsylvania provides a case in point. Largely omitted from Universal's main flow, it functioned in isolation until the mid-1950s, when Wallace Chandler arranged to have the annual company golf tournament held at nearby Hershey. The event drew Lancaster Leaf closer to the company. With the advent of super plants, discussed below, and the parallel decline in the partner system, such interactions with the partners changed, however.

Jackson's heyday was during the era of the partner system, and his skills made it work. Often these companies had been formed by the fathers, sometimes grandfathers, of the men currently running them, men who were not accustomed to having their word challenged or even questioned. Only a diplomat as skilled as Jackson could soothe egos on the one hand without compromising good business sense on the other. Although some in the organization thought some partners took advantage of their autonomy, Jackson was able to placate the personalities that made up Universal Leaf Tobacco Company.

Jackson's success with the partners reflected also his ability to communicate with people. "Tremendously capable man, a very affable man," Chairman and Chief Executive Officer Gordon L. Crenshaw recalled from the vantage point of the early 1980s, "the kind of fellow that made you feel you were the greatest thing he had seen that day."

Despite Jackson's leadership, it was four years into his presidency before gross sales volume reached what it had been for the fiscal year ending June 30, 1945. In that year, revenues were more than $82 million. For 1946, the first full year of world peace, they dropped to $76.9 million. The year 1947 saw a further decrease to $73.6 million, while 1948 saw a four-year low of $58.2 million. Higher tobacco prices helped push gross revenue to $79.6 million for 1949, but it was slightly off—to $75 million—for 1950. In 1951, however, for the first time in company history, dollar volume exceeded $100 million, rising to $108,910,396.65.

In his first report to stockholders on September 5, 1946, Jackson observed that several Universal plants were involved in union negotiations and that one of the affiliates had been closed by a strike at the outset of the flue-cured season—the worst possible time. Simultaneously, other affiliates were being pressured to negotiate with the unions, who in the 1940s were making an effort to organize the South. Jackson further noted that a worldwide shortage of dollar exchange made it difficult for foreign countries to obtain the dollars necessary to procure American goods. Also, he later reported unusually high building costs for physical facilities and expressed a fear of what would take place on the termination of the U.S.-financed Marshall Plan.

As Jackson's tenure continued, sales began to grow; although the end of 1952 proved disappointing. The physical volume of tobacco handled was the same as the previous year, but sales revenues slipped to a disappointing $78 million. For 1953, they were back at a healthy $96 million. A milestone was reached in 1956 when dollar volume increased to just over $119 million, never again to fall below the $100 million mark. By the end of the decade the gross revenues were up to $143 million, the largest in the firm's history. For 1965, the last full year of Jackson's presidency, Universal's gross dollar volume stood at $309,924,507. Painful though it was to many, Jackson's conservative approach brought rewards, although there are still those at Universal who argue that the company could have done even better with a more aggressive approach.

Further indications of Universal's growth during the Jackson years are also evidenced from the annual stockholders' reports. Collectively the reports show important trends over time. In 1947, the first year that Jackson delivered his own report, almost a quarter of a million dollars was earmarked for special construction, while a stock dividend of 300 percent was proposed. The next year, additional money was set aside to build two new packing plants and to update others. In 1949 a small packing plant was opened in Nyasaland, in East Africa. In 1953, Eastern Leaf Tobacco Company and Universal Leaf Tobacco Company of China became wholly owned subsidiaries, while the following year an additional two hundred thousand was budgeted for plant renovation. In 1961 experiments that would lead to the inauguration of the super plants were being conducted in Goldsboro. The super plants were huge processing facilities, the size and efficiency of which to that time had not been seen in the tobacco business. Automated and highly organized, they brought processing into the modern technological world. The following year saw another new plant in service, while in 1964 Universal ventured into Greece and reported that an enlargement of the home office in Richmond was also needed.

With the inauguration of the super plants, the early 1960s saw such growth that in 1965, the last year Jackson delivered the annual report, net earnings (after providing for dividends on the preferred stock) were $6,721,458—a marked increase from the $1,492,414 he had reported in 1946 at the start of his tenure.

An important event during the Jackson era was the construction of a new corporate headquarters. For a number of years the company had operated from offices at the Richmond Trust Building, but by the early 1950s it was apparent that additional space was needed.

During this time, the face of downtown Richmond was being drastically altered. On street after street the wrecker's ball was in action, clearing away the old to make room for the new. One of the spots that was razed for business use was the once-fashionable Gamble's Hill area. Situated on a promontory that originally had enjoyed a commanding view of downtown Richmond to the east and the winding James River and Manchester (once a town in its own right) to the south, the area had escaped the ravages of the evacuation fire that destroyed much of the city when the Union forces entered it in April 1865. But by the end of World War II, the stately antebellum houses were run-down. Most were rooming houses, while others were being converted to commercial uses. In at least one, prostitutes did a thriving business. It was to this area, at 201 South Third Street, that Universal moved in 1954.

For the first time in its history, the company had the opportunity to construct a state-of-the-art home office, but such was not to be the case. Before the emergence of a strong executive committee, all major decisions at Universal were made by the president, who may or may not have asked for advice from associates. Accordingly, Jackson asked an architect friend at the well-known local Baskervill firm to draw plans for a building on company property at Third and Canal Streets. Figures for the structure came in at approximately four hundred thousand dollars—fifty thousand dollars more than Jackson was willing to pay. He decided to keep the plans but to decrease the size of the facilities by one foot. "As a result, it was a beehive instead of an office building," Jan Laverge recalled. "It was awful." In his 1954 annual report, Jackson noted that the facility, into which the company had moved in April of that year, had cost "approximately $350 thousand." Not until an additional wing was added several years later, however, did the building become completely functional.

The new headquarters were barely occupied when problems began, one of the first centering on J. Pinckney Harrison, the strong contender for the presidency when Jackson had prevailed in 1946. Harrison, upset because his quarters were so spartan, installed himself in the board room; he acquiesced, however, to having the board room table carried in and out for meetings. James E. Covington, citing claustrophobia, insisted that the wall between two offices be taken out so that he could have more space, the result being that his quarters were the same size as Harrison's and Jackson's.

To make matters worse, about the time that the move was completed someone discovered that a brothel was in operation nearby, so close in fact that the women there had watched with interest as the new Universal building was being built. Former president Fred N. Harrison, no longer active on a day-to-day basis in company matters but nevertheless concerned about its image, heard of the illegal operation. Rather than file a complaint with the police or consult anyone at Universal, he took unilateral action: he personally bought the house and shut down the business. He remains Universal's sole recorded negotiator for such an establishment.

During the two decades that Jackson directed Universal, the company was governed by a strong president who was advised by a board constituted solely of insiders. This system worked adequately until the post-World War II era, when growth and expansion into foreign markets made apparent the need for an executive committee (as well as for other committees to aid management and to function below the board level). As early as the beginning of the 1950s, Laverge, Humphreys, and Warwick had begun pushing for the establishment of an informal executive committee; each noted that Jackson alone was making the major decisions.

In time the board would become a diverse and dynamic force. Made up of people with disparate business backgrounds, it now gives advice to top management; however, in the Jackson era it was quite different. During his day it was comprised of men who had shared lifetimes of intimate collegiality, a situation that fostered a relaxed and informal approach to matters. With rare exceptions, board members were partners and top officers in the company, thus making their collective vision somewhat parochial because it lacked the broader view of the business world outside tobacco. Unfortunately, the effectiveness of the board was also sometimes marred by members who, although effective in their prime, were no longer as energetic as they once had been.

When the Executive Committee first came into being it met only sporadically. Jackson still preferred to call in a few trusted people and informally ask their advice. The stock purchase plan, according to some the most important development pertaining to personnel during the Jackson years, was created in the late 1950s when Jackson worked out a pension system for Universal with the Life Insurance Company of Virginia. Based on a percentage of the employee's pay, the plan had a maximum benefit of six thousand dollars per year. Several years later, rather than increase the maximum, Universal's leaders hit upon the idea of a stock purchase plan whereby each employee was permitted to have 5 percent of his total compensation deducted from his pay and put into the plan, at which point the company would match the funds. Although Jackson had misgivings about matching the contributions dollar-for-dollar, he approved the plan—but with one stipulation: employees could not take out monies they had put in until the fifth year; he believed that such regulation would bind the employee to the company.

Although other lower level committees also evolved, since its inception the company has preferred as few bureaucratic encumbrances as possible. Thomas R. Towers, retired president and vice chairman, explained it this way: "rather than having layers of committees, we want it so that when a decision has to be made, then the people who can make a contribution to that can quickly come together. In our business, if you don't act immediately, you could well lose the opportunity."

Apart from its corporate structure, the uniqueness of the tobacco business becomes readily apparent in leaf purchasing. Despite modern laboratory techniques, the only method of learning tobacco is by working on the markets and in a factory. Jackson once noted that it took a person about seven years to learn tobacco. By that time a buyer should be able to walk on the auction floor with orders for several hundred grades of tobacco, recognize them (see Appendix 3), and be ready to bid in a split second. He would have learned from years of experience what grade would be right for which customer. It is easy therefore to understand that grading tobacco is a subjective process, fundamentally unaltered by science, technology, or automation.

The buyers are perhaps the most glamorous people in the tobacco business, men who play for high-dollar stakes in instantaneous deals and who cherish the freedom to pursue their jobs—which have changed little over the decades—in a less structured, less supervised way than many others in the company. Jackson knew this and prudently did not seek to implement constricting rules upon them or, for that matter, on the company's officer-salesmen. These men, known as account executives, sell the tobacco that the buyers acquire.

No activity in the tobacco business is more interesting and colorful than the auction sale, the focal point of buyers' day-to-day activities. Held in a multitude of Southern towns—from northern Florida to Virginia for the flue-cured crop; in Virginia, Kentucky, and Tennessee for the burley and dark-fired tobaccos; and in Maryland for "Maryland tobacco"—these sales dramatize what to the public's mind is the tobacco business.

When the crop is ready for market it is brought by the farmer to a warehouse in one of the many towns in tobacco-growing areas and turned over to the warehouse. Prior to that, the farmer has separated his crop into rough grades. Unscrupulous farmers sometimes are not averse to hiding inferior tobacco inside piles of tobacco of a higher grade. This practice, called "nesting," might also be done by warehouse people. No matter which, scores of unsuspecting buyers, especially beginners, have been victimized by buying inferior goods. So the buyers always tried to inspect as much of the tobacco as possible before the sale. "It was nothing to go on the floor," said William (who bore the double nicknames of "Billy" and "The Senator") Pritchard, one of Universal's legendary buyers, "and have 250 to 300 grades. You expected to use them all."

Attending each sale are people from various companies. Usually the group consists of from eight to ten buyers, an auctioneer, a ticket marker, and the warehouse operators. The buyers are usually assigned to an individual market. The markets start as soon as enough tobacco has been harvested in a sale area to keep the sale going. Their openings follow typical weather patterns. Consequently, Georgia and Florida start first and northern North Carolina, Virginia, and Maryland, respectively, open last.

Buyers, understandably, are under pressure. As far back as fifty years ago they would spend as much as a quarter of a million dollars of the company's money in one day; for some, the pressure was unbearable. Pritchard reported that he and colleague Charles ("Charlie") Martin bought 13 million pounds in one season in Henderson, North Carolina; and in Lexington, Kentucky, he and a fellow buyer bought more than five hundred thousand pounds in one day.

In addition to the pressures that go with handling large sums of the company's money, living conditions for these members of the business were often at best provincial, although they have changed markedly over the years—especially since the advent of air conditioning and the rise in popularity of motels. Early recollections in the business abound with tales of dirty rooming houses, bad food, and inadequate facilities. Veteran Universal officer John Leavell, recounting the days when he first started buying, tells the story of being sent on short notice to Carthage, Tennessee, "to follow sale," as is the term in the business. Arriving late at night at a shabby hotel, he was informed by the woman in charge that all rooms had a bath. While looking over his prospective quarters, however, he was unable to locate his. The woman then led him to a back window through which she pointed to the Cumberland River. She informed him that it served every room in the house!

Coupled with the pressure of buying was the pressure of having to work under the scrutiny of supervisors who were taskmasters of the first order. Supervisors would routinely pull buyers from the line for an on-the-spot consultation, and public admonitions were not unusual. Thomas R. Towers recalled, for example, standing with his fellow buyers and being handed a sample of tobacco he had bought. He was then told by his supervisor Ches Waddell, "Take that tobacco back to your motel; every night when you say your prayers say 'Oh Lord, please don't let me buy anything as heavy as this again!'" Occasionally customers showed up at the markets and were given the red carpet treatment, making the activities more tense for the buyers. Work days, which usually began at 7 A.M., were for the buyers more often than not followed by evenings back at the warehouse regrading what had been purchased during the day. In the flue-cured market warehouses in Georgia, summertime temperatures would sometimes reach 130 degrees Fahrenheit. Twenty-one below zero has been reported during a sale on the burley market in Lexington, Kentucky.

When work was over for the day, or if the day was Sunday, buyers would often attend impromptu parties at which they would talk tobacco until the early hours of the morning. Towers nostalgically recalled these get-togethers as reminiscent of his military time, when men of like minds and duties shared each other's company following the work of the day.

Recreation often consisted of the a motion picture or a night of drinking. The use of alcohol, alone or with the group, has long been a problem for tobacco men. The story still circulates about the buyer who appeared late one night stark naked in the lobby of his hotel, thus ending several days of sobriety that he had vowed to maintain during that year's season.

Then there were women. Local females who were willing to trade sex for a few days of what they considered the good life of new cars, good food, and some fancy clothes could be found. Professional prostitutes would also follow the tobacco sales, offering their services to the tobacco men, or to the farmers, who were separated from wives and families and were largely anonymous in the late summer in the dusty towns across the South.

To the uninitiated, the auction is begun and concluded so quickly that one is not aware of what has taken place. As buyers and auctioneers walk the aisles of tobacco, they communicate with the auctioneer by a series of actions and gestures known to them alone. Some buyers prefer to stand behind the tobacco, others in front of it. Some face their competitors, and others turn their backs to them. Sometimes a wink, a nod, a movement of the lips, or a subtle forefinger salute indicates that a bid is being offered. John Leavell reported that he once stood close enough to the auctioneer to be able to bid by briefly tapping the auctioneer's hand without attracting the attention of any of the other buyers, who must have wondered how the sale was moving. Another buyer remembered working with an auctioneer who used the prearranged signal of picking his nose to convey information to a favored buyer.

Auctioneers offered their wares in a singsong monologue unintelligible to outsiders. A typical offer would sound something like "Sixty-fie, oh, sevn, sevn, eight an' nine, ten, an' ten, lookin' ten, fo' 'leven, lemme see twelve, twelve. Gone!" The foregoing transaction would take place in as few as six or seven seconds, with as many as eight or so buyers having made bids!

Sometimes tempers would flare if bids were missed or ignored, or if the auctioneer seemed to favor one buyer. Occasionally a brief scuffle would break out. Leavell reported that once in the 1940s he saw a buyer in Goldsboro knock an auctioneer over two rows of tobacco. On another occasion, in Louisville, an irate farmer pulled a shotgun on a group of buyers. Seeking higher prices for his crop, the farmer backed down when the warehouse man stuck a pistol in his back and shouted, "You get your ass out of here!" Neither guns nor fights are part of the auction scene today, but rumors of farmers bringing guns to sales existed into the late 1970s.

Before the mid-twentieth century, tobacco was handled almost entirely by hand. Brought by the farmers to the auction centers, it was purchased, tagged, and taken from the floor by the purchaser, who transported it to his processing plants by either railroad or truck. When received at the factory, tobacco was taken from its transporter by "duckbills," hand-operated two-wheel dollies that lifted and carried a small amount, which the operator took to the scales. There it was weighed, regraded, and arranged in rows by the new grade, following which each grade would be hauled manually to the stemming room on four-wheel dollies, called "jacks." Laborers pulled the jacks with metal hooks. Next, the tobacco would pass through the "ordering machine," which infused it with roughly a 30 percent moisture content, then it would be moved to the stemming room.

Before the advent of the 409 stemming machine—the first really revolutionary piece of equipment in the business—all stemming was done by hand. The tobacco would proceed from the ordering machine on a conveyor belt, its destination a large room in which from two hundred to six hundred people, mostly black women, performed the stemming duties. Varying in numbers according to the factory, the women were paid by the amount of stems they removed, pay being ten cents per pound. Each woman kept the stems in a small canvas bag. Often the women would pour water in the bag to increase weight. With the introduction of the stemming machine, however, hand stemmers were put out of work. This machine, one of the earliest to go into regular service in the factories, had grippers that picked up the tobacco and knocked it free from the stem.

Following the stemming process, the tobacco went to the redrying machines, where its moisture content was reduced to about 12 percent, 10 if it was going to England. Next it would go into a hogshead, which was made on the premises, for the transport. The tobacco was then pressed ("prized") as compactly as possible and the lid ("head") nailed in place. Each hogshead was then stenciled and either stored or shipped. The hogsheads, each weighing about a thousand pounds and measuring about four by four feet in size, were rolled by hand. But the advent of the super plants, whose introduction to the tobacco business was just around the corner at mid-century, changed all that.

Another change took place in 1958 with the introduction of a laboratory, at which time Universal became one of the first companies in the American tobacco business to submit tobacco to scientific analysis. Bernard S. ("Skip") Holt Jr., formerly in the research department of the American Tobacco Company, was hired to organize and direct the lab. Located in Richmond in what was once a mid-Victorian house, the lab was difficult to work in because its facilities were spread out over several floors. Although inconvenient, the lab was so well installed in the Pulliam house, as the structure was known, that it received an award from the Association for the Preservation of Viriginia Antiquities for the conversion of a historic building.

The era of the super plants was getting under way during this time. Long a dominant figure in leaf procurement and processing, Edwin W. Humphreys became the father of them. With a reputation for angering some, alienating many, and bullying those who would take it, he revolutionized Universal.

A native Kentuckian, Humphreys, who was born in 1910, graduated from the University of Kentucky with a degree in metallurgical engineering at the height of the Great Depression. He never worked at the profession for which he was trained, however. He entered the tobacco business in 1934 as a foreman for the R.P. Watson Company in Wilson, North Carolina, and soon returned to Kentucky, where he worked for Southwestern, a member-firm of the Universal family. During World War II he was a buyer for Southwestern, where he became a vice president in 1946. Ultimately he became the leading leaf man at Universal, supervising purchasing and processing.

To the present day, stories at Universal are legion about Humphreys's public tongue-lashings of high-ranking subordinates. "He had a certain tolerance for you," one former Humphreys subordinate recalled. "He would listen to a certain extent and then you could see his face begin to tighten, and he would look at you with those steely blue eyes. His jaw would begin to quiver, and you knew at that time he had heard enough and you'd better back off." One colleague remembers Humphreys as "a man that made up his mind, right or wrong, and would stick with it through hell and high water, and never vary from it; and even after he found out he was wrong, he would think of ways to justify that he wasn't really wrong." But on the other hand, there were those who liked him. John Leavell, a lifelong friend and associate of Humphreys, recalled that "Ed Humphreys was one of the finest men I've ever known. In every respect, he was a great businessman and he was tough, and he got the nickname 'rattler' because everybody said he was just like a rattlesnake, he'd bite you before you knew it. But Ed could be one of the nicest people there was."

Nevertheless, the fear that Humphreys instilled in his subordinates was legendary; the best example was perhaps what happened following an altercation between Humphreys and one of his people in the Lexington, Kentucky, office. Following the exchange, the employee would come to work in the mornings, climb a flight of stairs, go through the accounting department, and descend again to the first floor on the other side of the building in order to get to his office. Circuitous though the path may have been, it afforded him the security of knowing that he was avoiding a potential encounter by not walking past Humphreys' office door.

That Humphreys must have enjoyed his reputation is evident by the fact that his personal automobile license plate bore the numbers "007." To a generation of Americans this signified the code name for the fictional spy James Bond, made popular by novelist Ian Fleming. In a group of novels and motion pictures made when Humphreys was at his height, Fleming's "007" was wily and calculating, tenacious and lethal . . . and his enemies never knew where he would strike next.

All in all, however, Humphreys was the right man at the right time for Universal. Countering Jackson's conservatism, he saw the potential offered by the modern, state-of-the-art, super plant. Because of his position of power, he was able to implement his wishes, and he often deliberately underestimated the cost of an idea in order to sell it. He knew that he had a chance of getting a low figure by Jackson and the committees and concluded—dangerous though such thinking might have been—that he would find the necessary money when the time arose; he was always able to do so. Prior to World War II, and for most of the 1950s, Universal's tobacco processing had been carried on in antiquated plants constructed decades earlier. As customers' needs changed, the company realized that its factories must also change.

Although Universal never manufactured its own processing machines, early on it began installing and experimenting with those made by other companies that specialized in servicing the tobacco industry. Some of this machinery, although viewed with skepticism by Jackson, looked as if it might produce favorable results, but its implementation caused problems at first. Buildings in which the new drying, stemming, and threshing machines were installed and tested had been constructed originally to handle tobacco by hand and were thus not suited to a modern, production-line operation.

Following a study of costs, future usefulness, and financial return, the decision was made, largely at the urging of Humphreys, to turn the Goldsboro plant into a large-scale experiment that ultimately led to the super plants. A.W. ("Pete") Walker, the plant manager at Goldsboro, and his staff installed the new machinery with the assistance of the company that made the machines. Assistance also came from Richmond in the persons of engineers C.H. Hinnant Jr. and M. Deane Cheatham Jr. The experiments, which centered on the way the tobacco was threshed, showed immediate promise. Prior to this Goldsboro venture, a typical factory could turn out about 360 hogsheads of tobacco per day; afterward the average was one thousand.

The millions of dollars expended on the super plants that grew from the Goldsboro experiment were counterbalanced by reductions in labor costs. Under the old system, it took four hundred to six hundred employees to operate a plant; under the new, fewer than one hundred. The increased capacity, coupled with reduced labor requirements, gave Universal a competitive edge. Following the 1960 experiments at Goldsboro, the first super plant was put into operation at Henderson, North Carolina, in 1961, the next one at the K.R. Edwards Company at Smithfield, North Carolina, in 1962, followed in the same year by Canadian Leaf Tobacco Company in Tillsonburg, Ontario. Other super plants soon in operation included Tobacco Processors in Wilson, North Carolina, and Southern Processors in Danville, Virginia. Gigantic and highly automated, they changed forever the way tobacco was processed.

Goldsboro may have been chosen as the experimental plant because of the leadership there. Long recognized as a weak link in the Universal chain, it had been placed under the direction of Pete Walker, a crusty hard-swearing tobacco veteran, and one of the few men who had the temerity to take on Humphreys. "I never had any trouble with Ed," Walker recalled following his retirement, "because he knew that I wasn't going to stand for anything out of line whatever. If he blasted me, I blasted right back at him." Walker remembered the Goldsboro plant as "raggedy-assed . . . no discipline, no order, no nothing. I got all the people together and I said, 'Look, this place has a bad name. The only way we can change that is that we're going to do a hell of a job here. . . . I'm going to work and every one of you are going to work, and you're going to tend to your own business. . . . I'm the hub of the wheel and the rest of you are the spokes. Now let's get going!'" Obviously, Humphreys and Walker were men of similar mind, and Humphreys probably turned to Goldsboro because it was being run as he would have run it had he been in Walker's shoes.

Not only the factory system, but the sales system was changing during this time. Over the twenty years that comprise the Jackson era, Universal's sales grew tremendously. As has always been the system at Universal, the most promising people in the immediately lower echelons were promoted into sales, "bringing them along," as the saying is in the company. Another feature of Universal's business is that, although a salesman may move into the executive ranks of the company, he still retains the sales accounts with which he had previously been working. Therefore, Universal's top-level executives continue to retain and service accounts. Put another way, top Universal officers are nearly all active salesmen.

During the Jackson years the sales department underwent a transition in personnel. Senior officers—Jackson, Pinckney, and Fred Harrison—remained stewards of long-standing accounts, while Jim Covington, back for good from China, developed new clients, especially R.J. Reynolds and Benson and Hedges. But the cadres of a newly emerging sales force were already present in the persons of Jan Laverge and Pierre Warwick. In time these men would be supported by a cast of rising people: Gordon Crenshaw, James H. Abernathy, Walter Robertson, Thomas Towers, Cliff Sutherland, and John Leavell.

Laverge and Warwick had worked together in foreign sales since the 1930s, but with the taste in tobacco after World War II evolving to favor American leaf, they ushered in a new era for the company. Part of the reason for the success enjoyed by the two men probably lay in the fact that they had markedly different personalities and thus complemented each other; another is that they shared the goal of garnering as much foreign business as possible. A colleague used a hunting image to describe the cooperation between the two: "the two of them were just like two bird dogs in a field, working together beautifully."

A native of Amsterdam, Laverge, born in 1909, was a member of a Huguenot family that had fled France for Holland in 1681. For many generations the Laverge men had been Protestant ministers in Holland, but Laverge's grandfather had abandoned the ministry in the late nineteenth century in favor of the tobacco business.

Laverge graduated from college during the depths of the Depression with a degree in mechanical engineering and, with jobs scarce, joined his father in the tobacco business. He came to Universal in 1934 following his father's death. Despite his prior knowledge of tobacco, like everyone else Laverge paid his dues in the hot and dusty factories in North Carolina, and for a beginning salary of $100 per month. He was soon moved to the Richmond office, where his ascendancy began.

Because of his background, Laverge brought a new enthusiasm to Universal's international sales efforts. He was fluent in English, German, and French, which made him a natural choice as the company's chief European representative. Careful, deliberate, and demanding of his subordinates, he came to conclusions methodically and with logical precision.

Warwick, on the other hand, was more of a dreamer, albeit one whose dreams often produced results. A native of Norfolk, Virginia, and a product of schools there, he attended the University of Virginia for three years. He left Charlottesville in 1927 without a degree after his family suffered financial reverses in the lumber business in Florida. Warwick was injured accidentally by a self-inflicted shotgun wound when he was a teenager, and during his interview at Universal he was called on to prove that the absence of three fingers represented no real debility. He won the job, and the contest, when he challenged his interviewer to a race at tying shoelaces. Taking the usual route of a newcomer to the business—four years on the markets from North Carolina to Kentucky—he was assigned to the sales department.

What made Warwick temperamentally suited to represent Universal in the Mediterranean and South and Central America was his love of complex, even chaotic, bargaining. He enjoyed the dickering, the subterfuge, the contrived delays, and the feigned outrage at inconsequential obstacles that often accompany business transactions in those areas. Once, for example, during negotiations in a Middle Eastern country, he and Towers, at that time his assistant, were rebuffed for a number of days before the prospective customer announced that he would not buy at all because Universal's prices were too high. Next came a week of negotiations, which seemed fruitless to the young Towers, who favored returning home. "Patience is the most important thing of all," Warwick counseled. "If we have to, we're going to stay here for a month." After two more weeks of negotiations they concluded a sale that the customer thought he had manipulated to his advantage, and Warwick and Towers headed home with a comfortable profit.

When Covington returned permanently from China, there was some question of what to do with him. Not waiting for an answer, however, Covey went to work developing new business and soon made himself indispensable as a member of the sales force. Energetic, self-motivated, and possessing an ability to win difficult clients, he became one of Universal's top salesmen. He was known for his punctuality, meticulousness of dress, and devotion to a personal code that demanded as much of others as of himself. "If someone welshed on a dollar bet on golf, the devil with them, he just wrote them off," his son James Jr. recalled. "He didn't care about playing golf with them, didn't care about doing business with them, or anything else." Given to occasional outbursts of temper that humiliated more than one waiter, sometimes even marred a dinner party, he was nevertheless a trusting and loyal friend who kept his close allies for life. So close were his friendships that some were kept alive by his children twenty years after their father stopped doing business. In his later years, but before his retirement to Florida, he owned imported horses and enjoyed fox hunting at Virginia's Deep Run Hunt Club where he rode to the hounds. Covington had long before learned the pleasures of country club amenities and had developed a lifelong love of giving lavish parties, the expenses of which still cause eyes to roll for those who remember them. "There used to be a joke around the office," colleaegue M. Norton Howe remembered, "that Covington had an unlimited expense account and he exceeded even that!" Over time, Covington's customers included some of the most important to the company.

In the late 1920s one of the most important relationships between Universal and one of its major customers began. In those years, Richmond's Continental Tobacco Company was a cigarette and pipe tobacco manufacturer, with a plant on Twentieth Street between Main and Cary Streets. One of this small company's directors was Wirt Hatcher, one of whose duties was tobacco purchasing. Hatcher and Universal's Pinckney Harrison were close friends; both of them were avid outdoorsmen and hunters, passionate bridge players, and, above all, businessmen. Although Continental's leaf tobacco needs were small, whenever possible Harrison was given the first opportunity to supply them. Thus began the Universal-Philip Morris connection, which was to become significant to both companies.

In 1929 a small New York business calling itself Philip Morris and Company purchased Continental Tobacco. Although maintaining a New York office headed by sales and advertising director O.H. Chalkley, the company's business activity was centered in Richmond at the Twentieth Street plant, which was run by Hatcher, Edward Dinwiddie, and Clark Ames. In the mid-thirties they were joined by Jehu Archbell, who for many years had been president of the American Tobacco Company of the Orient (headquartered in Turkey). These four men shared two small offices in the concrete factory building on Twentieth Street.

Of the four, Hatcher, the driving force, was mainly responsible for the early success of the fledgling company. Looking for ways to increase business during the Depression, he blended and marketed in 1933 what was to be called the "Philip Morris English blend." In addition to supplying Philip Morris's leaf tobacco, Universal also financed its tobacco purchases. Although the company may not have been underfinanced at the time, Philip Morris was expanding so rapidly that it needed all the credit it could muster. When it bought Continental in 1929 it manufactured 24 million cigarettes for the year. Ten years later it was manufacturing over 12 billion.

Another change in the relationship between Universal and Philip Morris had its origin in a cigarette company called Benson and Hedges. Like Philip Morris, it was located in New York. This small firm, which produced a limited amount of specialty cigarettes, (including Parliament, America's first filtered brand), came under control of the Cullmans during World War II. In earlier years, Joseph F. Cullman Sr. had been a member of Universal's board. Joseph Jr., the second generation of this famous tobacco family, was president of the holding company, Tobacco and Allied Stocks, which had acquired the controlling interest in Benson and Hedges.

Expanding slowly following World War II, Benson and Hedges relied on Universal as its leaf supplier. In time, Jim Covington and Cullman became close friends, and the two of them became a familiar sight on the tobacco markets.

Tobacco and Allied sold its interest in Benson and Hedges to Philip Morris in 1954, Philip Morris thus acquiring Parliament at the time when the demand for filter cigarettes began to rise. Although he died within a year, Joe Cullman Jr. became chairman of Philip Morris's Executive Committee. Many credit him with the unbelievable success the Philip Morris Company enjoys today. From modest beginnings, it developed into a diversified international conglomerate and the largest cigarette manufacturer in the United States. Universal continues to function as its principal tobacco supplier.

Initiated through the mutual confidence between Philip Morris and Universal at a time when the former did not think it could afford its own leaf department, the relationship continues as one of the most unusual in the tobacco business. As recently as 1990 Joe Cullman III observed, "I think [the relationship is a reflection] of the quality of the leadership . . . of Universal."

Universal's sales organization during this period consisted of President Jackson, who was centrally involved with the Gallaher and the

American Tobacco Company accounts and Pinckney Harrison, who was primarily responsible for Philip Morris, on which he was succeeded by Humphreys. Covington managed the accounts for Reynolds Tobacco Company and for Benson and Hedges. On the foreign scene, Warwick had Central and South America and most of the Mediterranean countries. Laverge had Europe, except England and the Iberian Peninsula. These senior figures were assisted by Crenshaw, Abernathy, Leavell, Christian, Robertson, Towers, and Sutherland, who was responsible for the Far East.

In the early postwar years most nations in western Europe were devoid of any tobacco inventory. Attempting to deal with this shortage, European countries where monopolies did not control the tobacco business, most notably Denmark and the Netherlands, created government buying agencies. In 1946, the year of the first major postwar crop, representatives of these agencies went to various tobacco-producing countries, especially the United States. Enormous quantities of tobacco of almost any usable type were ordered. To illustrate the size of this business, Theodorus Niemeyer, who headed the buying committee for the Dutch tobacco interests, arrived in the United States in November of 1946 to advise Universal that his company wished to increase its order for the 1946 crop by 16 million pounds. The order was successfully filled. The Danish order was placed mainly with British American Tobacco Company's leaf buying organization, Export Leaf.

In the later 1940s Japan, Germany, and Austria also sent representatives to the U.S. in an attempt to secure leaf. The Austrian monopoly's delegation consisted of Ludwig von Hurter and Hans Dorrek, who visited Universal first because of its strength in the dealer business. The Austrian monopoly had no dollars available but asked for a limited supply of leaf tobacco on credit. Following extended discussion, Treasurer Henderson agreed to a credit of twenty-five thousand dollars. From Richmond, the Austrians proceeded to visit other firms, the next being K.R. Edwards Company, one of Universal's partners, who promptly offered the monopoly a credit of fifty thousand dollars, obviously without consulting Henderson. As a result, Edwards has had the major part of the Austrian business ever since.

After a year or two, the practice of "order sales" began to emerge. Prior to the war, and indeed for some time afterward, Universal bought tobacco, packed it, and offered it for sale to manufacturers on the basis of samples, sales being often assisted by local agents. Although this system still exists in isolated places, it became more and more usual and

acceptable for a foreign manufacturer to discuss prospective needs with
the Universal executive and to develop a buying program that would be
executed when the tobacco became available. This type of buying obviously demanded great confidence by the manufacturer in the Universal organization. Furthermore, postwar improvements in transportation and communications permitted customers to come to the U.S. to
see their orders executed and to have close contact not only with
Universal's buyers but with the support personnel connected with the
transactions.

Among the first foreign companies to entrust this type of business
to Universal were Gallaher in England, Scandinavian Tobacco Company in Denmark, and Reemtsma in Germany, as well as a number of
the monopolies in Japan, Sweden, Austria, France, and other nations.
The exception was the Italian monopoly, who, although they became
important customers, nevertheless continued to buy on the old system
of samples and offers.

One of the most important events in the history of Universal's sales
occurred in 1954 with the unannounced appearance one Friday afternoon of a South African tobacconist, at that time unknown to anyone at
Universal. Dr. Anton Rupert, who had formerly been in the wine business and had recently entered cigarette manufacturing in South Africa
in a modest way, came calling to announce that he had just acquired the
Rothman company, a small family-owned tobacco manufacturer in
London. "He said that he intended to grow his company into a much
larger one," Crenshaw recalled, "and to go into many other countries,
and he would like to give us all his business. Mr. Jackson and I looked
at each other and we thought that it was likely that we were being offered 100 percent of virtually nothing."

As it developed, both Jackson and Crenshaw were wrong. No one
could have foreseen the growth and success of Rupert's company or the
future importance of this business to Universal. Beginning both cautiously and tentatively, Universal began financing Rupert's needs as he
bought the English firm of Carreras. Next came successful ventures in
Australia, New Zealand, and Malaya, to be followed by Canada, Belgium, Germany and other European countries. Today, Rupert heads
not only one of the world's largest cigarette manufacturing companies
but a network of disparate businesses that stretches around the globe. A
man with a keen sense of loyalty to those who aided him along the way,
he still gives public recognition to Universal (for whom he remains a
key customer) for being willing to listen and then make a commitment
to him on that Friday afternoon in 1954.

Like so many American businesses, tobacco came of age following World War II. At Universal, Jackson guided the company to heights that its original founders would not have been able to foresee. Machinery, automation, laboratories, and super plants in the United States all played vital roles as the company began moving into larger areas of activity.

For a time after the demise of its China company as a consequence of the Communist takeover in 1949, Universal's sole foreign subsidiary was its long established company in Canada. Under Jackson, the initial postwar move abroad was made with the expansion of operations in Rhodesia. The company's forays into countries throughout the world and its growth into an international organization were still to come. After Jackson's untimely death, they were brought to fruition under his successor, Gordon L. Crenshaw.

8

Postwar Growth Abroad

From its inception in 1918, Universal Leaf Tobacco Company had as one of its goals the development of a worldwide operation, an aspiration that first began bearing fruit in the Chinese and Canadian ventures. The Canadian one, the smaller of the two, grew smoothly from the beginning, but the one in China was fraught with problems brought on by World War II and the Japanese occupation of China. Further difficulties came with the 1949 Communist takeover. Halfway around the world, the war also brought a halt to operations in Rhodesia.

The Japanese surrender on board the USS *Missouri* in Tokyo Bay in 1945 ushered in a new, if short-lived, era of prosperity for Universal's China operations. During the war, Universal's A.I. McOwan had been interned by the Japanese. McOwan (along with other American and British subjects) was transported across the Whangpoo River and incarcerated in a British American Tobacco Company cigarette factory at Pootung. Underfed, the group whiled away time growing a vegetable garden and listening to news of the war on a radio they kept hidden. When liberated in August 1945, the emaciated McOwan, clothed in filthy rags and wearing rubber strips for shoes, walked a great distance until he reached the old company headquarters at the famous Shanghai address of Number One, The Bund. Forcing his way into the office, he found in a crisis meeting no doubt the same Japanese businessmen who had taken the company from him in early 1942.

McOwan's language and message were direct: he had come to take over in the name of Universal Leaf, and he wanted a full accounting of all property and inventory, in triplicate and in English, within seventy-two hours. If the Japanese cooperated, he continued, he would try to see that they were treated better than they had treated him. McOwan recovered at least $1 million in tobacco, reestablished Universal in China, and held on until relief arrived in early 1946. Veteran China tobacconist George Macon characterized McOwan's actions succinctly: "Mac was a tough number."

Shortly after the war, Covington, still the liaison between Richmond and China, asked George Macon to assume the presidency there. Also,

George Arbogast, who had been the number one man in China until the Japanese seizure, returned.

The job facing Universal's China people was not an easy one because the company's physical facilities had been damaged by the Japanese during the war. Eventually, however, most of the equipment was recovered and repaired and the China arm of Universal was soon functioning—but not the way it had before the war. The difficulties arose from changes in the way Chinese tobacco was handled.

The changes in the China operation were twofold. First, all new sales of American leaf were to the Chinese manufacturers, roughly the same as in the prewar era, but the buying, processing, and selling of Chinese leaf had come to a virtual standstill because of the civil war that was unfolding. None of the Chinese leaf was being exported, and Universal was unable to sell it abroad, as it had done prior to the war. Second, Universal's operations in China following the war declined because of inflation. Before the war, the exchange rate was about five to one. In the postwar era, however, it soared to 20 million to one, making Chinese currency virtually worthless. George Macon recalled that in the late summer of 1949, just before the Communist takeover, his wife and her friends would go shopping one day, return home to get money from the bank, and pick up the goods the following day. Macon remembered that he would write his personal check, then have his servant go to the bank and pick up the cash. "He would go to the bank, come back with the rickshaw piled sky-high with money, and my wife would get in over the money, get back in the rickshaw and go to these shops. As they drove from shop to shop, she would call out and say, 'Look, I need 10 million,' or whatever the exact amount. The money was bundled up in bundles with say, 10 million, 5 million."

When conditions in China deteriorated to the point that collapse of the government was inevitable, American authorities advised all women, children, and unnecessary people to get out. Macon remained until February 1950. After briefly visiting the United States, he returned to the Orient, this time to Hong Kong, where he resumed control—albeit at a distance—of Universal Leaf Tobacco Company of China. Business was confined, however, to the Philippines, Indonesia, Thailand, and India. As they had been prior to World War II, Universal's properties in China were once again written off as a loss.

Although China figured prominently in a government suit brought against Universal, it was, as far as the company was concerned, little more than a large area on the world map between 1949 and 1972. In that year, following President Richard M. Nixon's tour of China, Norton Howe made a tentative visit that was to lead to Universal's reestablishing ties with the tobacco interests on the Chinese mainland.

A country not beset by the vicissitudes of political and military upheaval that have affected so much of the rest of the world, Canada has long been the site of one of Universal's most stable bases of operations. When Jackson assumed control of Universal in 1946, the Canadian Leaf Tobacco Company was in good shape, as it had been since he himself had headed it decades earlier, and the Canadian tobacco industry had not changed much. Under the existing buying system, each buyer (who had a territory consisting of 100 to 150 farms) called on each grower. Buyers recorded the varieties of tobaccos being planted and the number of acres under cultivation, thus garnering knowledge of the year's prospective crop volume. As the tobacco grew, the buyers—almost always knowledgeable in all aspects of growing, curing, processing, and final product preparation—would give advice to the farmers. Following curing, the tobacco was graded and brought to market. After the sale, the farmer was responsible for getting the tobacco to the factories.

This system changed in 1957, however, with the introduction of the Dutch clock auction, which had originated at the flower auctions in Holland. Unlike other tobacco auctions (where prices are bid up and the highest bidder wins), under this system the beginning price is high and the clock runs backwards. The tobacco is brought to auction on flats of from one to twelve bales, then is graded and priced by the buyers, who in turn pass the lists of the prices to their colleagues in the "clock room." As the clock runs back toward the price evaluated by the buyer, a button is pushed and the clock stops; the tobacco is sold to the bidder who has stopped the clock. At first Universal did not favor the new system, but as time passed, it was accepted as an efficient way to market crops.

An important development in the Canadian operation took place in 1959, when the leading company in Anton Rupert's group, Carreras Ltd. in England, abandoned its leaf-buying and processing operations in both Canada and Rhodesia. These two operations, Leamington Sales in Canada and the Lytton Tobacco Company in Rhodesia, were offered to Universal as a package and were subsequently purchased. In Rhodesia, Lytton was integrated into Rhodesian Leaf Tobacco Company as a second processing facility, but in Canada a separate unit, Simcoe Leaf Tobacco Company, which would operate independently of Canadian Leaf, was formed. Promoted mainly by Warwick, this move proved to be a wise one. From 1959 on, Universal operated two separate companies in Canada.

A further development involving the Canadian operation during the Jackson years came about as a result of the 1960 purchase of thirty acres of land in Tillsonburg, which over the next two years saw the construction of Canada's first tobacco super plant. Based on a group decision of E.D. Allen, Ira Huff, C.W. ("Charlie") Thomas Jr., William ("Bill") Burroughs, and Herbert Jackson, the new plant was modeled on the one just completed in Henderson, North Carolina. The new facility further changed Universal's competitive position and was financed 100 percent by the Canadian branch of Universal. As soon as the new plant was operative, the old one at Chatham was phased out. At the same time, Allen became president of the Canadian Leaf Tobacco Company, a position he had held de facto for many years but whose title, until 1962, officially referred to Herbert Jackson.

Despite the abilities that Warwick and Laverge brought to the fledgling foreign sales force, the moves that Universal made beyond China and Canada into other countries were not always smooth ones. The first obstacle centered on the necessity of convincing the ever-cautious Jackson of the financial reward of any new venture.

As Jackson was working into his position of company leader in the late 1940s he was reluctant to become further involved in the African arena, but he was finally willing to do so minimally if the expansion could be handled through Universal's Canadian operation. Jackson sent George Cheatham and Ed Allen from Canada to Rhodesia, where they began laying groundwork for what was to become the Canadian Leaf Tobacco Company of Rhodesia. In the beginning they operated as tobacco brokers only, and from shabby offices in a blighted neighborhood. The initial venture was no more than a minimal one.

To assess the business more closely, a number of Universal's people traveled to Rhodesia. Warwick went in 1951 and was followed the next year by leaf expert William "Bill" Saunders and Howard Woodson, a top accountant. Warwick strengthened the organization there with the hiring of Jack Last for sales and Charles Kemp as the chief accountant. What little amount of tobacco that was bought was packed through a small dealer, the Kileff Company. A further decision was made to send two Universal buyers to Salisbury. In April 1953, Stuart Christian, who chose Thomas Towers to accompany him as assistant, went out. This trip, one of many from the 1960s through the 1980s, began Christian's long association with Africa as Richmond's liaison officer. He had joined Universal in the late 1930s as a temporary summer employee only, but by this time had found himself responsible for coordinating the company's entire African interests.

In 1953 another important step was made for the African operation when Jackson himself made a trip there, followed later the same year by Laverge. Immediately realizing the potential that lay in the African market (as did Harrison, Warwick, Humphreys, Christian and—by that time—Jackson), Laverge argued that Universal should either get in deeply or abandon the venture. When asked by Laverge if Rhodesian tobacco had a future in the world market, Christian replied, "You couldn't miss with a missing machine." Laverge advocated that the Rhodesian company be completely severed from the Canadian one and placed under the direct control of Richmond. Thus was the Rhodesian Leaf Tobacco Company formed, absorbing the Canadian company's personnel with the exception of manager George Cheatham, who left Universal to establish his own operation in Salisbury. In 1954 a new manager, Enoch Haley, was sent from the United States.

A South Boston, Virginia, native, Haley did well in a market previously dominated by long-established English firms. His major contribution to Rhodesian Leaf's eventual success was his suggestion to combine with a small company, R.W. Noakes, owned and directed by R.A. ("Bindy") Noakes, who had emigrated to Rhodesia with Donald "Don" Bell and George Hinds in 1948. This trio had a small and simple processing facility that had developed some excellent customers. In the mid-1950s Laverge returned to Rhodesia and organized the purchase of the Noakes company by Rhodesian Leaf, an action that proved to be decisive in Universal's success in Rhodesia. Haley then returned to the U.S., while Noakes became managing director.

A native of Liverpool, Noakes, along with other family members, had been in the leaf tobacco business in England for a number of years when his father made a trip to Northern Rhodesia in 1935 in an attempt to collect on bad debts. In the course of the trip Noakes' mother was killed when the car her husband was driving was involved in an accident. Noakes' father never returned to England; instead he remained in the tobacco business in Northern Rhodesia.

Following a brief stint in the Army during World War II, the younger Noakes migrated to Salisbury, Rhodesia, where he opened an arm of the family business in 1945 and another in Nyasaland two years later. At first he sold heavy-bodied tobacco, especially favored by the

Imperial Tobacco company at the time. With the advent of an intensified research project in the business, many types of tobaccos soon became available that were more attractive or suitable to the export market.

Noakes had met Herbert Jackson before the war when he had purchased Canadian tobacco from Canadian Leaf. Later, in the mid-1950s, he began making small purchases for Universal, during which he met Laverge and other Universal representatives. Following these explorations, Noakes sold the company to Universal. He remained with the company until his retirement.

At the time, the optimistic forecast was that Rhodesian Leaf Tobacco Company would be able to buy and sell 30 million pounds—approximately 10 percent—of the colony's tobacco crop within four years. The forecast, however, actually turned out to be conservative: in 1964 Rhodesian Leaf bought and sold 100 million pounds, one-third of the crop. In 1960, the company built a new processing factory, including an office complex. All went well until 1965 when the Rhodesian government renounced allegiance to the British crown and declared the African country independent. This step was the result of fears on the part of Rhodesia's ruling white minority that British authorities planned to give control to the colony's black population.

Following a series of acrimonious confrontations, the United Nations, at the behest of Great Britain, entered the fray, and imposed economic sanctions in 1966. Among the Rhodesian exports proscribed by the international embargo was tobacco. At the time sanctions were imposed, Europe and the United Kingdom were the largest consumers of Rhodesian tobacco. According to veteran African tobacco man William ("Billy") Hunt, sales were cut almost by half, at which point the Rhodesian government entered the picture and formed the Tobacco Corporation, whose representatives traveled the world, especially Asia, attempting to find new markets.

Further exacerbating matters, Rhodesia soon found itself embroiled in civil disturbances in the form of black nationalist guerrilla incursions from the north. These forays ceased with the advent of black majority rule in 1979, but tobacco farmers had to be protected by the system called "bright-lighting," whereby circuit-riding guards protected farms and farm families at night.

Problematical also was the fact that Universal's assets, including ongoing earnings, were frozen in Rhodesia, leaving diversification the most practical way of dealing with the problem. The company soon invested in apartment buildings, company-owned farms, and a business that made hogsheads, cases, and other items used in tobacco transport. Headed by Derek Edwards, who was in charge of Rhodesian diversification, the new ventures worked as a stop-gap measure until sanctions were lifted and business operations could resume.

Potentially devastating though the short-term loss of Rhodesian business could have been, it did have its positive side. Because Universal was temporarily out of the tobacco business in southern Africa, searches for other growths of tobacco seemed the likely way to deal with the problem. Such activities, however, still left a number of tobacco people idle. The time was obviously ripe to focus attention on other geographical locales. Under the direction primarily of Towers, the African tobacconists took their expertise to Southeast Asia—the Philippines and especially Korea. This operation proved enormously successful when Korean tobacco was found to be of an excellent quality. Universal soon began looking to other markets on the African continent, one of the most important being the revitalization of an older business that had earlier failed.

When George Cheatham arrived to begin the African branch of the Canadian Leaf Tobacco Company, one of his first tasks had been to form an operation in Nyasa (now called Malawi) that specialized in dark-fired tobacco. Plagued by mismanagement from the beginning— one of the indigenous managers thought he was successful if he simply moved the tobacco by selling it at cost!— the operation was soon abandoned. Nevertheless, Rhodesian Leaf continued to keep buyers on the Malawi markets, and their purchases were packed by Imperial Tobacco Company in Limbe. By this time, Malawi had begun to produce both flue-cured and burley, which soon found acceptance on the world markets.

The implementation of U.N. sanctions against Rhodesia gave a boost to the demand for Malawi tobacco and vastly stimulated that country's production and sales. In addition, Malawi produced another small crop, an Oriental-type tobacco, which the newly formed Limbe Leaf Tobacco Company contracted to buy and sell. To accommodate this business the company erected a small packing shed in Lilongwe, prospective capital city of the soon-to-be independent Malawi. Also in the 1960s Universal purchased a small firm owned by Jack Stevens, who soon became the managing director of Limbe Leaf.

In the mid-1970s the Malawi government asked Universal to allot them an equity interest of 40 percent in Limbe Leaf, a request that was reluctantly agreed to but one that later paid large dividends. By the late 1970s a substantial expansion of packing facilities became necessary and a plant, similar to Universal's super plants in the U.S., was designed and built in Lilongwe.

Following its tribulations in Rhodesia and its success in Malawi, Universal began expanding into other African countries. Buyers from Malawi made contact with the Ugandan government and initiated a small trading business, but they soon were hampered by officials working under the too-close scrutiny of dictator Idi Amin. Uganda sold dark-fired tobacco to Malawi. This tobacco ultimately went to English customers. A different situation existed in regard to Tanzania, however.

Bordering on Malawi to the south and Kenya to the north, Tanzania is a long country running up the east coast of Africa on the shores of the Indian Ocean. The country chose a socialist form of government in 1961 and has been a one-party state since 1965, with the Tanganyika African National Union dominating the political scene. Tanzania produces two tobacco crops, flue-cured and dark-fired. Although the quantities are small, the quality is good and Universal has done a lucrative business in both types.

Zambia, the former Northern Rhodesia, until recently an autocratic regime dominated by Kenneth Kaunda, also produced good quality tobacco, some of the best flue-cured in Africa. Following independence, tobacco auctions were begun in the capital of Lusaka, where a modern processing plant was built with foreign aid. Universal operated for some time in Lusaka using personnel from Malawi, but both quality and quantity of the crop decreased and the operation was abandoned.

The problems associated with Universal's functioning in African countries can perhaps best be illustrated by looking ahead to what happened in Angola. Like many African countries seeking to shed vestiges of European colonialism, Angola received its independence, in this case from Portugal, in 1966, only to suffer the pangs of revolution and eventual Marxist rule. While under Portuguese control, its tobacco interests with Universal fell under the care first of Warwick, then of his successor, Towers. Ultimately the Angola tobacco operation was a complete failure because the revolution forced suspension of Universal business there.

Following the highly successful undertaking in Rhodesia and lesser ones in other African countries, Universal looked to other latitudes to further its interests. The next venture centered on Greece, where in

1964 Laverge was able to gain a toehold for the company in a somewhat circuitous way.

During the mid-1960s the Dutch company of Deli-Maatschappij was, like Universal, seeking to expand. For many years involved only in the growing of cigar-wrapper tobacco in Sumatra, Deli began experiencing difficulties following World War II. After Indonesia became independent and expelled the Dutch, the directors of Deli-Maatschappij recognized the need to diversify. Establishing offices in New York, they invested in a number of nontobacco businesses, some eventually highly profitable.

Through friends, Laverge discovered that Deli-Maatschappij was looking for a partner to put together a tobacco deal in Greece. He, and later Crenshaw, met with the two leading Deli officials and learned that the venture was to be modest and would require a Universal investment of approximately $250,000. At a board meeting in Richmond, Jackson and others endorsed the undertaking. Jackson, who believed in hedging his bets, always preferred to start new ventures as partnerships. That way, if anything went wrong, the company lost only 50 percent of the total investment. As it turned out, the business prospered, if only in a limited way.

Greece has been a major producer of Oriental tobacco for hundreds of years, but the purpose of the new partnership (Gretoba SA) was the purchase, packing, and sale of burley, the production of which had just begun in the Salonica area. A small processing facility was built in Salonica headed by an experienced Greek tobacconist named Ioannides. Sales were handled by Ludwig von Hurter, who was retired from the Austrian Tobacco Monopoly and was now an employee of Deli-Maatschappij in charge of its off-shore tobacco operations, mainly in Italy and Greece. A modest but successful operation followed when, owing to von Hurter's efforts and backed by Universal's worldwide connections, orders were secured from such important customers as the Japanese Tobacco Monopoly, Philip Morris, Reemtsma, and others. One mistake, however, was the decision to engage also in buying and packing Greek Oriental tobacco, for which a warehouse in Kavala was equipped. The idea behind this move was that, after the burley crop was bought and packed, the packing of Oriental could follow. Difficulties soon arose in several forms, and the venture was abandoned the following year.

Following a trip to Greece in 1965 by Humphreys and Laverge, the decision was made to expand the Salonica factory by adding a second redrying machine and some threshing equipment. Then, in the 1970s, Ioannides was replaced as general manager by George Darmi. Following Darmi's premature death, the Greek operation came under the joint leadership of leaf manager Raul Manas and the company's chief accountant, Vafeas. Although small, the Greek operation remains an important part of Universal. It has about a half dozen accounts servicing European manufacturers, the Japanese Monopoly, and Philip Morris. More important, perhaps, Greece served as the stepping stone to other European ventures for Universal. Laverge, because of his relationship with the Deli Maatschappij, nursed this company for many years. He was followed by Lucius Cary and, after Cary's death, by Henry Harrell.

While Universal was searching in the post-World War II years for ways to increase its foreign enterprises, it also happened upon an innovation that revolutionized the cigar industry. Called the "Microflake" process, it originated with Jan Laverge and the Dutch connections he had maintained since his youth.

When the young Laverge lost his job with the American Tobacco Company and accepted an offer to come to work for Universal in 1934, he turned down a similar offer extended in his native Holland by Koch and Company, a cigar tobacco dealer started by Laverge's grandfather. Run in the 1930s by Laverge's uncles and cousins, the company later merged with Scheltema to form Koch Scheltema, of which Laverge's younger brother August Theodoor ("Chris") was director. This company was ultimately purchased by Deli-Maatschappij; August subsequently became president of the combined corporation.

Born in 1920, Chris was trained as a lawyer before he entered the tobacco business following World War II. During the war he had served in the Dutch forces and had been assigned to the Eighty-second Airborne Division of the U.S. Army. Severely wounded in a glider crash that killed his three American companions during the invasion of the Netherlands in September 1944, he later served as one of two Dutch prosecutors at the war crimes trials in Japan. He was involved in the case that culminated in the hanging of Japan's wartime prime minister General Hideki Tojo. While in Japan, August married an American. When he returned to his homeland in 1948, he reentered the tobacco business following a training period on the American markets in the Universal system.

Meanwhile, the American Machine and Foundry Company (AMF) was having trouble marketing their new machine designed to make cigar binder. As noted previously, cigars are made of three principal parts:

filler, binder, and wrapper; wrapper and binder are made of the full tobacco leaf. One leaf usually could be made into wrapper or binder for only two cigars, and the rest was wasted. AMF's machine would take the cigar leaf scrap, grind it into a fine dust, and convert it into sheets. At substantial savings, the sheet could then be used as binder. Virtually all binder today is made this way.

As early as 1957 Laverge and his brother had discussed the possibility of combining resources to make sheet tobacco. They became seriously interested in the venture about the time AMF began searching in Europe for possible investors. AMF was unable to raise sufficient funds, and the Laverges began meeting once a month in New York to lay groundwork for producing sheet tobacco using technology purchased from AMF.

August located a German cigar leaf dealer who was interested in joining the enterprise, sufficient stockholders were identified, and the sheet operation became a reality. The Microflake factory in Schifferstadt, Germany was formed; Universal and Koch Scheltema were the principal stockholders. The business was exceedingly profitable at first, declaring roughly 100 percent of capital dividends. Ultimately, however, the worldwide energy crisis of the 1970s and the advent of rival techniques for producing sheet helped bring about the liquidation of Microflake. More important to its demise, however, was the changing public taste for tobacco. At the time that Microflake was liquidated, cigar consumption was dropping at an annual rate of about 10 percent. "It was a sad thing to see," Laverge noted, but keeping the factory would have resulted in over-production of cigar sheet.

An interested observer looking at Universal Leaf Tobacco Company during the twenty-year period encompassing the Jackson era finds a company guided by dynamic and complex people and forces. Jackson—elder statesman, primary leader, and final authority—managed the entire Universal system. He held together the partners—numbered at roughly fifteen in Virginia and North Carolina alone—and governed a diverse and intricate business. Perhaps because of his strong religious beliefs and his logical and systematic world view, he applied easy but steady force to Universal between 1946 and 1966. Calm, compassionate, and able to cope with a host of personal problems that continually haunted him, he, like Mr. Fred before him, saw himself as the father of the modern Universal family. Will Tuggle noted years later that, during Jackson's term, "the company got a reputation as absolutely solid, dependable, financially strong. It was a period of growth, solid growth."

During Jackson's era the company was also greatly influenced by trends in the tobacco industry at large. The first was the rising demand abroad for American leaf, the second a consolidation of manufacturers as scores of old firms disappeared or were incorporated into larger ones. Consolidation also led to greater sophistication of buying on order. In this time of change, Universal showed again one of its primary qualities, one that would give it a competitive edge and would guarantee a hold on the future.

Most businesses, especially those that are publicly incorporated, feel intense pressure to generate maximum earnings for each annual statement and are not inclined to spend large sums for distant gains. In many ways, however, Universal defied this conventional wisdom by its willingness to invest in science and technology and by its willingness to develop accounts that competitors considered inconsequential.

In addition to its financial strength, Universal was known during the Jackson years as a company for which accuracy was a consuming passion. Doubtless Jackson, with his mathematical training and logical approach to problems, instilled in all the company's employees the need for precision and exact performance. After all, millions of dollars were at stake. "I think we did better than a lot of people. I really do," Will Tuggle said. "I would not accept any mistake as being inevitable. I remember when IBM told me, 'This system is going to be 99 percent accurate.' I said, 'That's not acceptable.' It wasn't acceptable really. We didn't accept mistakes." This was another Jackson legacy.

Yet Tuggle and others in the company would agree that Universal had been too conservative in the two decades following World War II. But if Jackson had been overly cautious, this trait was offset by the more aggressive satellite figures who played a part in shaping the company during the time.

Humphreys's role in the growth of the company is almost as important as Jackson's. He oversaw all purchasing and processing of the leaf, and he was the chief mover behind the super plants. A man less certain of himself might have been reluctant to gamble with millions of the corporation's dollars, especially in the presence of a company president known to be indifferent to "bricks and mortar." Humphreys—along with Laverge and Warwick—was one of the people who recognized that the partner system, although once a necessity, was beginning to outlive its usefulness. Irascible, at times even demeaning, Humphreys knew exactly what he wanted, and as it happened what he wanted was good for Universal.

Then there were Laverge and Warwick. Traditionally, men of the American tobacco business have been Southerners, people wedded to a region and a way of life somewhat divergent from the rest of the nation. European born and bred but acclimating quickly and well to the social and business climate of the South, Laverge was an indispensable player in Universal's expansion. A man not only of financial vision but one with managerial ability, he was the right man at the right time to bring European and African markets into Universal's network. Warwick's talents were also unique. By both temperament and inclination he enjoyed the rough-and-tumble Middle Eastern and South American bargaining, at which he was successful. The creative collaboration of these individuals with such experienced hands as Covington, J.P. Harrison, and others in the home office made Universal unique in the leaf tobacco business in the 1940s, 1950s, and into the 1960s.

By 1965 Gordon Crenshaw had spent nineteen of his forty-three years in the employment of Universal. For a number of months prior to the spring of that year he had been given additional duties and responsibilities, although he did not suppose that he was being singled out in any way. In May, he received a summons from Jackson, who was in Sweden attending to the Swedish tobacco monopoly account. The request asked only that Crenshaw come to Sweden as soon as possible. Upon the younger man's arrival, Jackson invited him to dinner. During the course of the conversation he said simply, "We want you to become president."

In retrospect, Crenshaw, who was junior to several others who might have been candidates for the post, was able to recognize that such an offer had been in the making. Nevertheless, it was a heady experience, especially with such older men as Covington, Laverge, Harrison, Warwick, and Humphreys still on stage. Acting with the advice of other senior members of the organization, Jackson instituted a system whereby he would become Universal's chairman of the board and chief executive officer when Crenshaw was installed as president in October. That way, Jackson could supply the needed advice and guidance as Crenshaw worked his way forward as heir apparent.

During the winter of 1965-66 Jackson often met informally with Crenshaw and offered advice about routine as well as philosophical matters. Such help was useful because the new president now had under him several people for whom he had worked during the entire time he had been with the company. The older man, however, never finished counseling his protégé. On March 26, 1966, Jackson died suddenly of a heart attack at his six-acre estate in Richmond's Chatham Hills. His wife, the former Josephine Mann Rose, had died six years earlier.

"It was an absolute shock," Crenshaw recalled. Barely four months following his promotion, Crenshaw found himself in charge of a corporation with a permanent staff of seven hundred and a seasonal workforce that approximated ten thousand. In addition to its personnel, Universal at the time of Jackson's death was listed as having twenty-two affiliated companies with plants in six foreign countries. It was on record as having done $300 million worth of business the previous year. Although the transition had proved to be a smooth one to date, Crenshaw suddenly realized that he indeed had his work cut out for him. "My reaction," he said, "was that I've got a hell of a job on my hands." Not only had he not had sufficient time to learn all the older man had to teach, but he was soon to take on additional duties of a much larger scale.

Because Jackson's death left a void at the top that needed to be filled immediately, Crenshaw would become the new chief executive officer. Barely had he learned the rudiments of one job before he was cast by circumstance into the next higher one. Although Jackson had not divulged it to anyone, he doubtless had conceived at least some sort of a scenario for easing Crenshaw into the chief executive officer's chair, a plan that would have been executed over the time period he thought appropriate. Such, however, was not to be the case.

9

A Worldwide Company

Under the leadership of Gordon L. Crenshaw, Universal became a worldwide organization. Expansions were made into all parts of the globe, most notably in South America, the Far East, and Southeast Asia. To see the growth of the company during Crenshaw's tenure, one need only look at yearly revenues. In 1966, for example, Crenshaw's first year as company leader, annual revenues were $348 million. Two decades later, in 1987, it had reached the $2 billion mark. Figures reflected in the company's annual reports are not startlingly large for any particular fiscal year; rather, they reflect solid growth: in 1966, $348 million; in 1968, $396 million; in 1971, $463 million; in 1974, $626 million; in 1978, $839 million; in 1981, $1 billion; in 1986, nearly $1.5 billion; and so on.

From the beginning of his tenure, Crenshaw brought a different perspective to top-level management. Although in many ways Crenshaw was cut from the same social and educational cloth as many other Universal officers, a marked difference existed between his business philosophy and that of his predecessors.

A native Richmonder and a graduate of the city's John Marshall High School, where he had been an excellent student, Crenshaw had gone on scholarship to the University of Virginia, where he majored in economics. In both high school and college he had been a leader, first as co-editor of John Marshall's student newspaper, later as editor of the one at the university, where he was also elected to the Raven Society and the leadership fraternity, Omicron Delta Kappa.

Crenshaw, who graduated in 1943, was offered an opportunity reserved for a few military inductees of his generation who showed exceptional promise. Having already committed himself to the Navy, in which he was ultimately commissioned, he was selected by the government to attend Harvard University for further study. Though he was sent there to take military courses, he ended up in what was essentially a graduate business curriculum. After completing his studies, he served on board ship in both the Atlantic and Pacific before returning to Richmond. He briefly taught economics at the University of Richmond before accepting an entry-level job at Universal.

Crenshaw ascended Universal's corporate ladder in the normal way, although he chafed somewhat at having to sweep floors in the South Boston factory after having been a Navy officer. After coming through the sales department under the tutelage of Warwick and Laverge, however, he was thoroughly knowledgeable about the tobacco business and was ready to assume the company's top post. Even so, there were obstacles to overcome and potential problems with which to deal.

For one thing, there was much potential for discord in Universal's upper ranks. Warwick, Laverge, and Humphreys were all senior by a decade or more to Crenshaw, who had had barely four months in the presidency and was now, because of Jackson's death, headed for the position of chief executive officer as well. Any one of these senior people was a logical contender for higher office in the company. In addition, the board of directors, at this time still comprised of tobacco people, had to be satisfied that this new and youthful leader could handle the job. Although Crenshaw was aware that Jackson, Covington, and Pinckney Harrison had been instrumental in his rise to the presidency, he knew also that no one could have foreseen the situation brought on by Jackson's death.

Preparing for the first board meeting in his new job, Crenshaw recognized that he confronted problems of both protocol and policy, ones that if not handled carefully might jeopardize his effectiveness: how could he acknowledge and reward the long-time contributions of the most important people in the Universal system, powerful men who one day were his seniors and the next his subordinates? Crenshaw elevated Warwick, Laverge, and Humphreys to newly created positions as senior vice presidents, in effect extending to them the only recognition and promotion at his disposal. At the same meeting, Towers became a member of the board, partly as a result of the evolutionary process but also at Crenshaw's behest.

Support for Crenshaw, who functioned both as president and chief executive officer until Towers was elevated to the presidency in 1982, came by degrees, but the important thing was it came. The senior officials did not break ranks; continuity was maintained. Universal was still on a firm foundation.

At the time Towers was elevated he was the obvious choice for president. He had been with the company thirty-four years, had been involved with tobacco operations on four continents, and was an affable, easygoing, and highly competent manager. He had come up through the ranks the usual way, following graduation from Richmond's St.

Christopher's school and the University of Virginia. He had also seen
U.S. Navy service as a destroyer navigator in the South Pacific during
World War II. A lifelong history buff who had spent countless hours
under the informal tutelage of the great historian of the Confederacy
Douglas Southall Freeman, Towers brought to the position of president a humanist's view of the world. His tenure was brief, however;
medical problems forced his resignation barely two years into his new
position. In retirement he continues to take an active part in Universal.

Having consolidated his position, Crenshaw began to make his mark
in terms of executive style. Although at the time no one—probably not
even Crenshaw himself—knew it, Universal was on the brink of important changes in spring of 1966; a new team with new ideas was about to
take over.

In the past, the man at the top had essentially done as he wished.
Crenshaw, however, chose to govern more by consensus, asking for
and acting on advice from others. In addition, the Universal board,
long top-heavy with insiders, under Crenshaw became more diverse as
the opportunities arose to bring a broader business perspective to bear
on issues. New programs and benefits, some of which were initiated
under Jackson, were updated and enhanced for Universal's rank-and-
file personnel, while others were introduced. Jackson's informal agenda
for the company was neither canned nor shelved at the start of the
Crenshaw years; it was expanded, modified, modernized, and used to
set the stage for Crenshaw's own initiatives.

The push toward implementation of new technology at Universal
had begun in a systematic way when Herbert Jackson was president.
Under Crenshaw, however, the most significant advances began, particularly in the area of processing. Although the super plant era began
five years before Jackson's death, under Crenshaw the super plants came
to full fruition; facilities were updated every few years. For example,
the Henderson, North Carolina, super plant, fully operational in 1961,
by 1982 was outmoded. That year the old threshing and separating
systems were replaced. This $6 million expenditure is representative
of the periodic updating required to keep the super plants in state-of-
the-art effectiveness.

In 1977 Universal's first extrusion plant was put into operation in
Lumberton, North Carolina. On the green tobacco markets the company had traditionally packed tobacco in hogsheads. Under this system, called "green prizing," the tobacco was taken from the auction
floor to a power pressing machine, run up a conveyor and pressed into

barrels, then taken by truck to the factories. With the more efficient extrusion method, the tobacco was blown through a tube, compacted into cubes, and baled. Following success at Lumberton, other extrusion plants were constructed at Rocky Mount, North Carolina; Danville, Virginia; Greenville, Tennessee; and Lexington, Kentucky.

In 1979, a further advance was made when electronic programmers were first introduced at the Simcoe plant in Ontario, Canada. Electro-mechanical devices were replaced with purely electrical ones. Smaller and more reliable, they could be programmed to almost any degree of sophistication. The simplest are no more than sequencing apparatuses, but the more sophisticated have a memory and the capability to analyze data, ultimately making decisions and controlling machinery. At first viewed with skepticism, they were soon accepted by employees. The company moved fully into the electronic age in the 1970s.

Other innovations also came about during these crucial years. Business volume had grown to the point that something had to be done about the antiquated billing system. The process was automated. Another problem that surfaced was that of coordinating the movement of tobacco to and from the factories. Charles ("Charlie") Beard was appointed clearinghouse coordinator and given an office in Wilson, North Carolina. His job was to keep track of newly purchased tobacco by telephone and to route it to the factories. To do this efficiently, he took advantage of technology.

By the mid-1970s Universal was handling so much tobacco that a better way of controlling it had to be implemented. At that point the "congestion report" was devised. The report, based on data that formerly came to the Richmond office, was soon computerized and is now issued each morning. It lists the status of all tobaccos in the entire Universal domestic system.

Another procedural innovation introduced during these years was a statement of quality control guidelines. Comprised of some of the first written instructions given to factory superintendents, they included requirements for scrap removal, tipping lengths, packaging instructions, and so on.

As the worldwide need for better information about nicotine and tar content of tobacco arose, Universal resurrected an industry system to provide the information. In 1980, the company introduced blending silos. These were enclosed metal bins about forty feet long, ten feet wide, and ten feet high. At one end was a mechanism that looked like a series of egg beaters. Each silo held about thirty thousand pounds of tobacco, which would be mixed for about half an hour in order to blend it evenly—after which a reading of its mean content and average constituents could be obtained. New to Universal but not to the tobacco industry, blending silos came into being because of requests from customers legally required to post nicotine and tar data on cigarette packages. Silo blending ensured that everything from one load would have identical numbers regarding content. Three of the silos were in use in Danville, Virginia, and three more in Smithfield, North Carolina. Within months, six additional ones were installed in Henderson and in Wilson (both in North Carolina), continuing a trend that has spread to other factories.

Universal in the 1970s also continued experimentation in its threshing system in an attempt to make larger pieces of tobacco while keeping stem content within an acceptable size. To do this, machinery had to be continuously upgraded and replaced. The Richmond office also supplied help—technological and otherwise—to many of its foreign affiliates in the 1970s. Among them were Italy, Zimbabwe, Mexico, Brazil, Korea, Thailand, the Philippines, and Malawi.

As volume increased and the operation became more detailed and scientific, the need for more sophisticated communications became obvious. Prior to Crenshaw's rise to the top post, Holt had been reassigned by Jackson from the laboratory to R.W. ("Will") Tuggle's department. Tuggle, whose primary duties centered on traffic, shipping, and storage, was feeling the pressures from the increase in the volume the company was handling. He was also becoming more involved with liaison work between Universal and the government.

A new system, called Customer Services and Product Coordination, evolved under Tuggle that reduced the day-to-day operations in the factories to a set of information sheets, which at a glance would tell the status of any order in the Universal system. Holt prepared instructions that were circulated to the domestic factories. At first the instructions were rejected, but it soon became obvious that having all information about orders together in one place was necessary.

Today, instructions involve what tobaccos are being processed, how they are being blended, percentages and restrictions regarding blends, the quantity and yield to be derived, how the tobaccos are marked and packaged, and what is to appear on the package. Additional information includes what weight and moisture the package must contain, and how by-products that have been generated are to be handled. Further, there are instructions as to how tobacco is to be handled following processing: where is it to be stored, what its destination is, how is it to be sampled, how it is to be inspected, and whether it is to be chemically analyzed. Other required information centers on the salesman and the customer, with Holt's staff gathering data to help identify the particular order. Questions on the form also solicit data concerning which factory will process the order, the daily volume produced by that factory, the changes in status, how much has been received and processed, and how much has already been bought. Collected daily and forwarded to Richmond by computer, these reports provide the base information for weekly meetings in Richmond.

The partner system, which served Universal from the 1920s through the 1950s, was starting to present problems well before the end of Herbert Jackson's tenure. Humphreys was primary among the critics of the system; he (along with others) argued that liquidation of these smaller entities in favor of consolidation into super plants was more cost-effective. As Crenshaw became more comfortable in his job he began examining the partner system and eventually he oversaw its demise.

During the late 1960s and the 1970s the tobacco industry worldwide saw a consolidation of manufacturers and major purchasers that—because of changes in technology—wanted to buy tobacco from one central source rather than from a group of dealers, even though those dealers might be associated with a large parent organization such as Universal. For example, the Carreras group in Great Britain normally purchased tobacco from about ten U.S. suppliers. Once the firm was combined with Rothmans, however, the parent company wanted to deal with only one supplier.

The partner system was also causing problems in other ways. As time passed it became more and more difficult to control these affiliates because many partners had accumulated sufficient wealth to last them for life and it mattered little to them whether their factories were state-of-the-art facilities.

Another consideration of those who argued for dismantling the system centered on freight costs. It was less expensive to send tobacco to a single super plant than to operate several small factories because such factories were located in major markets. Finally, there was the generational factor. In many cases when the older men who controlled the partner factories retired or died, there was no one to take their places.

Thus the partner system was phased out. Longtime employees were reassigned or cared for as companies such as Person-Garrett, R.P. Watson, W.B. Lea, and L.B. Jenkins disappeared. With them disappeared the cumbersome system of funding each partner roughly $1 million to finance each annual tobacco crop (or an occasional three hundred thousand dollars or so for new stemming equipment or the like). As the partners' facilities were abandoned, they became storage locations or packing points. Such were the final dispositions of properties owned by J.P. Taylor and Southwestern, and the K.R. Edwards Company. Occasionally the properties were sold, in one case given to a local church. It was apparent that the partner system, although once workable, had become an anachronism. (However, a few strong virtually wholly owned affiliates remained, such as Lancaster Leaf and the K.R. Edwards Company.)

Construction and updating the super plants plus the dismantling of the partner system had two immediate effects. First, by making the commitment to super plants, the company placed itself ahead of the competition. Consequently, unlike so much of American industry in the 1970s and 1980s, Universal began the fourth quarter of the twentieth century in fiscal good health. In addition, because the partner system had been dissolved, corporate energies could be devoted to seeking other tobacco markets and also eventually to moving toward diversification. Spurred by Crenshaw's urging, Universal began exploring the entire world market and extending its interests around the globe. China, Canada, and Rhodesia had long been satellites in Universal's sphere, but now a new thrust, pushed by the rising cost of U.S. tobacco, began to extend further.

Roughly one month after Crenshaw's rise to the presidency, Rhodesia, at that time the site of the company's most significant overseas affiliate, was drastically affected by the imposition of U.N. sanctions. As explained previously, the loss to Universal was substantial, and new foreign initiatives became imperative.

Changes also manifested themselves in a new relationship with the government. In a way, Universal and the federal government may be said to have grown up together. When the company began operating in 1918, the government was rarely involved in the day-to-day affairs of American businesses. That condition changed, however, especially for companies that were involved in worldwide commerce.

Following World War II, Universal's contact with the government revolved around supplying tobacco to Europe under the Marshall Plan, which, after its technical expiration in 1952, was continued under Public Law 480. At the time the Marshall Plan was implemented in 1948, the government also determined a need to regulate tobacco prices, a precedent it had set in 1933 when, under the Agricultural Adjustment Act, tobacco farmers were encouraged to take money for allowing fields to lie fallow.

The program, which is still functioning in the mid-nineties, limits tobacco production to stabilize farm income. Quotas are placed on the quantity of tobacco that can be marketed. An average price is calculated annually by the Department of Agriculture according to a congressionally mandated formula. Tobacco that fails to bring the support price is purchased by stabilizing cooperatives called pools. The pools are actually farmer cooperatives and are funded by and operated under contract with the Commodity Credit Corporation. Funds borrowed by the pools must be repaid with interest from the sale of pool inventories. Over time, Universal's Jim Abernathy and others became experts in this part of the business and acquired a good deal of pool tobacco for resale by the company.

Universal also dealt with the government on "barter deals." Begun in the late 1940s as a method of providing economic aid, primarily to Third World countries, the barter deals were trades of strategic materials for commodities. High profits could be made in such materials, but they could not be brought into the United States unless the importer could find an American exporter willing to supply a needed commodity, such as tobacco, to the country in question. Inevitably, there was risk, especially when third and sometimes fourth parties became involved. Sometimes these deals, handled by Tuggle, would require the commitment of as much as $10 million of company money. Stressful though such dealings were, they often paid well. For example, profits, which came in the form of discounts that Universal shared with customers involved in the deals, amounted to $650,000 for the first year. Tuggle estimated that he handled more than one hundred such deals while the barter system was in place.

Tuggle was further involved in federal government activities on Universal's behalf with his work in the European Common Market, with its system of internal free trade coupled with common tariffs on imports from countries outside the community. For some time Universal's leaders had thought the tariff against American tobacco was too high. Finally it became Tuggle's job to do something about it. He began by making personal contacts in Washington, particularly in the departments of Agriculture, Commerce, and State. As a consequence, he and representatives from other tobacco interests were appointed to government advisory committees. The end result was that the tariff was lowered to a more acceptable level.

During the Crenshaw years the government also imposed more and more duties and controls on American businesses. One of the most difficult regulations for the company to deal with in recent times has been the Foreign Corrupt Practices Act. Implemented in 1977 primarily for the purpose of eliminating under-the-table deals, the act brought under scrutiny companies such as Universal that did a large volume of international business. Because the company conducts annual audits, it was easy to perform an immediate check to determine if foreign business was being transacted in accordance with the new law. The audits confirmed that it was; nevertheless, company officials still complain that the law is too severe. They have also found it useful to prepare a pamphlet on business ethics, which is distributed through the company's worldwide system.

One aspect of government relations that played a large part in U.S. businesses with worldwide connections for many years centered on the Central Intelligence Agency. It was common practice for Universal personnel returning from abroad to be contacted by representatives of the CIA to get their impressions of countries they had recently visited. As it did for the Internal Revenue Service, Universal supplied facilities for the CIA interviewers. In recent years, popular sentiment has turned against such information gathering techniques, and the practice has been discontinued.

Another important event during these years was the company's move to a new corporate headquarters. By the late 1960s Richmond was in need of an expressway system to carry commuters from its West End suburbs to the downtown area of the city. In the mid-1960s planning was begun for the construction of what came to be known locally as the Downtown Expressway. As plans neared the final phase, engineers decided to run the roadway so close to the Universal building that its addition, originally constructed to alleviate crowding, would have to be removed. The company was forced to relocate not only by space constraints but by the increase in worldwide business and the rise in regular visits from foreign partners and clients, many of whom needed temporary office space.

Following inspections of available buildings in the downtown area, none of which was suitable, the company purchased a lot adjacent to the Virginia War Memorial on Belvidere Street on which it planned to build. In the meantime, however, an existing building came on the market. One visit to the building, located at the corner of Hamilton and Broad Streets, convinced Universal's officers that it would suit them if it was remodeled. They purchased it for $750,000 and spent an equal amount converting it. Universal moved into its new quarters in the summer of 1968. Over the years the building has been expanded twice. In 1974 a two-story wing was added on the east side adjacent to the Downtown Expressway. Covering 13,500 square feet, the new space was used to house green leaf accounting and general accounting. In 1988 another wing was joined to the one erected fourteen years earlier. This addition, totaling 14,500 square feet, houses the Department of Human Resources, the insurance manager, the corporate relations manager, the corporate director of administration, the internal auditors, some senior officers, and the Department of Processing and Engineering.

With the completion of the new complex, Universal finally had its modern, attractive nerve-center for its worldwide operation. The sample room was built to take advantage of northern light to accurately judge tobacco; the executive offices were spacious; and there was ample parking. Moreover, the company paid attention to esthetics in furnishing and decorating. Not only were there rules about decorations for private offices, but care was taken in selecting art for the lobby. Put in charge of that aspect of the move, Jan Laverge sought original works by local artists and also borrowed from local museums—the Valentine Museum and the Virginia Museum of Fine Arts—works that complemented the furnishings. In some cases artifacts from the history of tobacco, from Dutch urns to American cigar store Indians of the nineteenth century, were displayed.

In its early years, Universal was a loosely run organization, one that relied on the strengths of people who were given a great deal of autonomy. Early on Crenshaw realized that this casual attitude had to be modified. The company was growing so rapidly that more order had to be imposed.

The man who contributed most in this vital area was Wallace Chandler, whose tenure with the company spans both the Jackson and Crenshaw years. Born in 1926 into a rural family in South Boston, Virginia, Chandler was raised on a six hundred-acre tobacco farm. He entered the army at age seventeen and soon found himself in officer's candidate school, and became a commissioned lieutenant at age eighteen. He was soon to be a company commander in combat.

Following his release from service and subsequent graduation from

Elon College in 1949, Chandler was literally forced into Universal. He was headed for law school when a family friend, R.E. ("Bob") Clark, a Universal vice president, intervened. Against Chandler's wishes, Clark sent a chauffeured car for him, with instructions to the driver to stay in front of the house until the young man agreed to go to Richmond. Chandler acquiesced and learned during his interview that Universal would pay his way through law school if he gave them two years of service; he rethought his position and joined the company. In time he rose to become vice chairman as well as the architect of many operational and administrative changes in the Universal system before his retirement in 1991.

Assisted by W.A. ("Billy") Winfree, treasurer; Elijah Roark, controller; and Leroy Owen, assistant secretary of Universal, Chandler oversaw the company's administrative procedures. When he was named assistant secretary in the early 1950s, the administration consisted of old-time officers, a few department heads, and assorted bookkeepers and record-keepers. Informally structured, it was overshadowed by the flamboyant men in the sales and leaf departments.

When Chandler came to the Richmond office following a stint in the factories and the completion of law school, he assumed the duties of company attorney. The first area he overhauled and modernized was payroll. Next came the Finance Department, followed by Data Processing. In time, Chandler was also involved in setting up the company's Accounting, Communications, Auditing, and Legal departments. A determined man who did his work behind the scenes, Chandler played a central role in the company's modern history, first as a tax man, later an officer, then secretary and general counsel.

Having grown up in the tobacco world, Chandler knew it well. But he also mastered administration and was willing to assume the burden for it at Universal, thus freeing other senior officers to devote their energies directly to tobacco.

Wirt L. Grubbs Jr. was also an instrumental figure in office changes. A former tobacco buyer, affable and outgoing, he became the company's personnel officer and subsequently its first director of human resources.

The Crenshaw years saw more than Universal's growth to a worldwide business, however. While company officials were exploring global possibilities, changes were taking place in the headquarters at Hamilton and Broad Streets. Most of these were the result of Crenshaw's concept of how a large business should run.

Not until the beginning of the twentieth century did the American business world begin moving toward objective standards by which it could measure itself. Prior to that time businesses were likely to be run by the owner, or the strongest person he could find to put in charge. Crenshaw was on the forefront of a new concept when he began moving Universal into the arena that one might call modern corporate professionalism.

While at Harvard, Crenshaw was struck by the way faculty approached the study of the business world. He later observed that before that time he had as a student been accustomed to learning the contents of books and of professors' lectures. At Harvard, however, he was introduced to a system in which students were presented with hypothetical circumstances that gave rise to a problem. They were then asked to provide ways to solve the problem. Called the "case system," it taught Crenshaw that business issues are best solved when experts pool knowledge rather than when one person makes unilateral decisions.

One of the most important changes Crenshaw made was revamping the board of directors. Early on, he established himself as a leader who, as one colleague said, was "consultative." His method was to get the facts and consider all sides of the question, then have each point of view debated before reaching a decision. Sometimes his decisions went against the advice; nevertheless, he chose to have the advice before acting.

Crenshaw proposed board members with varied business interests because they could bring a broader base of experience. Under Crenshaw, the board, which meets five times each year, has the responsibility of following the affairs of the company in a general way and of serving specifically on committees that are also advisory. If there are special problems the board may be asked to meet more often.

Chosen because of their expertise in their own businesses, directors provide an objective point of view. "When a board is comprised of inside members completely or largely," Crenshaw noted, "from the outside it is perceived that the chief executive officer is controlling the board. The real value is to have a board that is dominated by people on the outside who are not beholden to the chief executive officer. The chief executive officer is beholden to them."

New names began appearing in the annual reports as members of Universal's board. Included among them were Fielding L. Williams, from the law firm of Williams, Mullen and Christian; T. Justin Moore, a lawyer and CEO of Virginia Electric and Power Company; Joseph A. Jennings, chairman of United Virginia Bank; Lawrence A. Blanchard Jr., vice chairman of Ethyl Corporation; A. Paul Funkhouser, president of the CSX Corporation; Ronald E. Carrier, president of James Madison University; State Senator Elmon T. Gray, president of Gray Lumber Company; and—of particular significance—Fred G. Pollard, a lawyer and longtime public servant, who had served a stint as lieutenant governor of Virginia. Like his colleague Fielding Williams, Pollard was affiliated with the law firm of Williams, Mullen and Christian, long associated with Universal.

Emanating from the board are several committees: the Audit Committee, the Executive Compensation Committee, the Finance Committee, and the Executive Committee, the most important one in the system. Other committees are responsible for in-house matters.

Tracing its origin to the early years of the Jackson era, when it had little power and convened sporadically, the Executive Committee soon was meeting every Monday morning from one to three hours. It worked from a prepared agenda and took care of matters requiring ongoing attention, such as capital expenditures, liquidations, formation of new subsidiaries, and decisions having to do with employee benefits. In addition, liaison officers responsible for large territories presented periodic reports to the committee. In a general sense, this was the committee that kept Universal running on a day-to-day basis.

Under Crenshaw, Universal instituted in the mid-1970s a new form of compensation for both officers and rank-and-file employees. As far back as the 1920s the company had had a system of paying a regular salary and awarding an annual bonus. Bonuses varied in amount, and the only year one was not forthcoming was 1932. Under the system, one junior officer sardonically remembered, "they just got a great big goddamn hogshead full of silver dollars and turned it over in the middle of the sample room, and Mr. Jackson got a scoop shovel and the vice presidents each had a spade and some of us had knives; and you went in and got what you could out of the goddamn thing, and the fellow with a knife didn't have much of a chance against a guy with a scoop shovel; I'll tell you that!"

Earlier, a stock purchase plan had been implemented by Jackson, who saw it as a way of bonding employees to the company because they would lose if they quit, but it was not until the 1970s that the Management Performance Share Plan came into being. Based on merit and awarded by the Executive Compensation Committee with the concurrence of the chairman of the board, this plan offers additional compensation to company executives.

In earlier days, Universal hired young men, sent them to the factories, and all too often forgot they were there. The result was that promising candidates for promotion left the business for other jobs where opportunities seemed greater. Crenshaw recognized this problem and set about to rectify it. Remembering his own case as a former Navy officer and Harvard graduate student who started at Universal sweeping factory floors, he knew that some way must be found to let those at the bottom know what rewards awaited them at the top.

To solve the problem, the company started a monitoring plan, which began the day the new employee was recruited. Two kinds of recruitment evolved: a few were recruited because they happened to be friends of those in high positions at Universal and were known to be good workers. More often, however, recruitment began formally on college campuses but was limited, however, to Virginia and North Carolina. Recruiters sought young men and women with degrees in varied fields and considered primarily their grades, evidence of leadership qualities, and evidence that the candidate could get along with others. When hired, the young person would be sent to the rigors of factory work but would be monitored by a senior staff member in Richmond. This way, more recruits knew they could look forward to rewards of a high order. Using this method to the present, Universal has been able to attract and hold almost all of its more promising employees, both male and female. "There is very little movement in our company, either departures or entries from the outside," Crenshaw noted.

By the end of Crenshaw's first decade as CEO, Universal was in strong financial condition. Its modern corporate structure was in place; its overseas ventures had been successful; and the company had an excess of working capital. Net earnings steadily increased through the 1960s, the end of which saw the company operating in fifteen countries outside the United States.

At the decade's end Universal's annual report to stockholders contained for the first time information about a new kind of venture. The company had acquired, in its initial move toward diversification, controlling shares of a business outside of tobacco called Inta-Roto, which produced machines used in packaging and other fields, made designs for industrial use, and produced cylinders used to make imprints on packing materials.

Herbert Jackson had always considered moves into foreign tobacco markets to be diversification. He believed that Universal should be in the tobacco business only. However, the company's excess of capital, coupled with a far-reaching federal government report, made the company start thinking otherwise.

In 1964, the tobacco industry began undergoing its most profound and long-lasting change, when the surgeon general issued a report on the relationship of tobacco use to health. It garnered support and gathered momentum, finally reaching into the highest echelons of government when, in the late 1970s, the secretary of Health, Education, and Welfare under the Carter administration announced a federal campaign against the use of tobacco. The campaign continued into the 1980s, becoming even more vocal and sharply focused in the 1990s. To put teeth in its resolve, the government increased the cigarette tax.

Antismoking campaigns were not new to the tobacco industry. However, never before had the effects of one been so far-reaching. Partly as a precautionary measure and partly because of its robust financial health, Universal began a tentative program of diversification, to be discussed later. Since 1968 the company has moved into various fields, such as fertilizer, modular homes, land development, agriproducts, title insurance, and others. In 1988, as a holding company, it changed its name to Universal Corporation. This was the same year that Crenshaw retired, and Henry Harrell became his successor.

10
Modern Foreign Operations

When Gordon Crenshaw assumed the presidency, the company's Canadian and Rhodesian branches were solidly based, moves had been made into Malawi, Uganda, and Zambia, and another was planned for Angola. Greek tobacco interests had been developed, but Germany, briefly the site of the Microflake venture, would become a casualty of the business climate of the 1970s. Universal had for years been steadily growing, but greater enterprises were yet to come.

By 1966, most if not all of Universal's top executives had had experience in foreign countries. One man in particular, however, was to be of major importance in the years immediately following Crenshaw's assumption of control. Reminiscent of Buck Duke's entry into China earlier in the century, Jan Laverge saw more than anyone the potential for foreign operations.

Although long an American citizen, he had kept close ties with European friends and family members. Laverge, who was at home on any continent, had been a key player in Universal's success in Rhodesia, had nurtured the fledgling company interest in Greece, and, with his brother Chris, had paved the way for the Microflake undertaking. But that was only the beginning.

After Universal struck a successful deal with Deli-Maatschappij to operate a joint venture in Greece, Laverge began looking westward toward Italy and soon learned that all exports of Italian tobacco were in the hands of one man in Milan. He discovered that the country's entire tobacco business was under the control of the Italian Tobacco Monopoly headed by Dr. Pietro Cova, who later would figure in Universal's entry into Mexico. Those who wanted to raise tobacco could do so only if they had a concession from the monopoly.

Ludwig von Hurter, who had previously assisted in establishing Universal's participation in Deli-Maatchappij's Greek enterprise, Gretoba, was also in charge of Deli's interests in Italy. Secretive by nature, von Hurter was reluctant to talk about the Italian part of Deli's operation until he and Universal had struck the deal in Greece. Deli-Maatschappij had entered the Italian market earlier by buying out a local tobacconist named Giointella, who had held the flue-cured concession in Umbria before he was overtaken by financial difficulties. After von Hurter concluded the deal for Deli and had named the new venture Deltafina, he selected Guy Norton as his successor. Norton too would later play a prominent role in Universal.

Laverge began moving toward an agreement with von Hurter, resulting in a meeting in Rome in 1966 between Laverge, assisted and supported by Chandler and Winfree, and his brother August, who with von Hurter, represented Deli. As a result, Universal bought into the Italian market by acquiring 50 percent of the Deli-owned Deltafina for just over a million dollars, but problems surfaced immediately. Although Universal officers had scrutinized Deltafina's operations on-site before entering the partnership, they could not have known that within the first nine months the company would lose half a million dollars.

Troubled by such losses, Laverge called a meeting in New York the following year. Attended by the two Laverges, Guy Norton, and Deli-Maatschappij's Carol Goldschmidt, it began on a tense note when Jan Laverge pointed out that Deltafina's earlier projection of a half million dollar profit—which in reality had turned into a half million dollar loss—bordered on being unacceptable to Universal. However, the meeting ended on an amicable compromise that had far-reaching effects for the company. It centered not on an exchange of cash or stocks but on the seed used in raising the Italian tobacco crop.

Four years prior to Universal's entering into partnership with Deltafina, more than two-thirds of the Italian tobacco crop had been destroyed by blue mold. Following this turn of events, Deli-Maatschappij engaged a team of agronomists to develop a tobacco seed that was resistant to the blight. The team developed a hybrid, which Deli-Maatschappij immediately patented. In order to produce the hybrid, a male and a female strain had to be used. And to keep the patent from being stolen in Italy, the female strain was kept in Bastia, Italy, the male in Heemstede, Holland. The pollen was gathered in Holland and flown to Italy, each female plant being fertilized individually. The compromise reached in 1966 allowed Deltafina to buy the seed at a discount, which, as the Italian demand for tobacco increased, brought handsome profits from the sale of the seed.

Universal's Italian holdings were further augmented by its entry into sales of burley, which was soon to become popular in Italy. Working out a deal with Roberto Memmo, who held burley concessions from the monopoly, Universal was now well established in Italy. Guy Norton oversaw the business while Memmo, through his connections, dealt with Italian officials. Eventually, Universal and Deli bought Memmo out. Today, following the construction of new factories in 1972 in Francolise and in 1982 in Assisi, the Italian company handles a total of about 40 million kilos of flue-cured, dark-fired, and burley annually.

In addition to being quite successful financially, the Rome office is in many ways the showpiece of Universal's foreign operations. Its main quarters were once owned by a motion picture company that lavished both money and attention on the structure and its gardens. Magnificently furnished, and used for social occasions as well as work, the facility looks more like a private villa than a business office. Farther south, in Africa, Universal entered the Angolan tobacco market in 1966, mostly as a result of work by Donald F. Bell and Pierre Warwick, who later turned it over to Towers.

Like so many other tobacconists worldwide, Bell came into the business almost by accident. Born in 1924 in England, he served in the British army during World War II, returning in 1947 to what he remembered as "a very depressed England with a Socialist government who were imposing all sorts of inhibitions." Young and willing to relocate, he interviewed with the Liverpool office of the R.W. Noakes Tobacco Company of Rhodesia. The interviewer, Bell recalled, said that "I was the 'nearest bloodybloke to Liverpool.'" So he got the first interview and the job offer, which he accepted. He afterward discovered there had been about fifty applicants for the position.

In time Bell became a central force behind Universal's African ventures, which revolved around the Rhodesian Leaf Tobacco Company. He rose to the rank of senior vice president and liaison to Europe and Africa with Universal but was killed in1987 when a family-owned plane piloted by his son struck an antelope and crashed while attempting a landing at Bumi Hills near Lake Kariba, Zimbabwe. Perhaps Towers best expressed Bell's efforts for Universal when he described him simply as the man "who so capably looks after Africa."

Bell placed business in Angola under G.J. ("Gaby") Kremer, whose adventures in Angola could well be the script for an action-packed movie. A native Hungarian who had suffered in World War II concentration camps, Kremer immigrated to Rhodesia in 1948 when he was twelve years old. He learned English and prospered in his adopted country, and eventually acquired a thousand-acre farm on which, among other things, he raised tobacco. Relocating to Angola, he joined the Universal family as head of the local company, SETA, whose customers included Portugal, England, Germany, and Japan. Relying on Kremer's knowledge of the Angolan government, the company departed from its usual way of doing business. For the first time, it became involved in the raising not only of tobacco but of other crops and livestock.

Attempting to widen its base, Universal acquired through the work of Towers and Kremer vast land holdings from the Angolan government, the only stipulation being that they be fenced and put into production. Two tracts, totaling some twenty-five thousand acres, were soon the sites of farms, complete with houses and dependencies for the overseers, who with their families migrated from Rhodesia. The venture looked promising, with two hundred acres of tobacco being grown the first year, five hundred the second, and one thousand in the third.

The Angolan enterprise was, Towers remembers, "the perfect combination," in that Universal was growing, buying, and processing tobacco simultaneously. Moreover, operations there broadened with the introduction of corn crops, grown because tobacco badly depletes the soil and rotation is required. Next came the introduction of African cows bred to Rhodesian bulls. Disaster was lurking in the wings, however, in the form of an impending nationalist revolution followed by the collapse of the government.

By the time political problems began fragmenting Angola in the mid-1970s, Kremer was married, the father of three, and the pilot of his own airplane. He also had in his employ or under contract a number of local tobacco farmers.

As political conditions worsened, the factory, which Kremer described as the best in Angola, came under siege from revolutionaries. Universal had been instrumental in constructing the new facility, using its staff from Rhodesia. On several occasions subjected to harrowing searches and mob intimidation, Kremer soon found himself in the middle of a revolution, in which rival factions, one with strong backing from Moscow, were vying to wrest the country from Portugal. A socialist government, Kremer feared, was only a matter of time.

Kremer was forced to confront the gravity of the situation in May of 1974. Arriving at the office one morning, he was handed a message that had come in by mistake overnight on the telex. Addressed to a local official, it was from Moscow, requesting passports for ten Russians scheduled to come to Angola to lend assistance. Kremer could well guess what lay ahead.

During the remainder of 1974 all semblance of order began disappearing as the factions fought each other with increasing bitterness.

Many of Kremer's farm workers were successful in escaping the country by automobile, despite arriving at their destinations in bullet-riddled vehicles.

As the fighting got closer to Benguela, the small town in which the Kremers lived, conditions worsened. Up to this time the fray, although violent, was not such that Kremer could not keep the business operating. Moreover, he thought the strife would soon cease. Because he was on friendly terms with members of opposing forces, he even found himself in the position of amateur military strategist when he convinced warring factions to engage in combat in an area that would not affect his business!

As hostilities increased and more guerrillas drew nearer, however, the family spent a harrowing night huddled under the hallway staircase while the house was being heavily damaged by mortar fire. The next incident occurred when six partially intoxicated guerrillas—grenades on their belts and automatic weapons at the ready—arrived to search the house for military firearms. Their leader carried a sawed-off shotgun. Bragging that they had been trained in Russia, they held the women and children hostage while they searched. Tense moments occurred when weapons were pointed and grenade pins almost pulled. Finding only hunting rifles and a handgun that one of the guerrillas tried unsuccessfully to steal, they calmed down and asked for a drink.

"So when this was all finished," Kremer later recounted, "we ended up drinking Scotch with these guys. They weren't fighting an enemy in us, but they really didn't know what they were doing. They were just power crazy, and they had guns in their hands, and they had been sent out to do something."

Following this incident, Kremer knew it was time to act. Gathering together his family and any employees who wanted to get out of the country, he and colleague Tom Phillips began some half dozen evacuation flights in two small planes. Flying at treetop level to avoid small arms fire from the ground, they refueled from caches of previously hidden aviation fuel. All who wanted to made it to safety, never to return. "My wife and children have never set foot in Angola from that day," Kremer reported. "And they thought they were going away for a couple of weeks until that thing blew over." Kremer worked for Universal for many years and today is headquartered in Switzerland. Company interests in Angola have been terminated.

Towers observed in retrospect that he, Bell, and Kremer misjudged the political situation in Angola. Additionally, they underestimated logistical problems caused by Universal's being an absentee landlord of a series of farms. Owning farms, on which the farmer, his family, and often even his children's education ultimately become company business, proved too problematical.

Because Angola had long been racially integrated and politically quiescent, all three men erroneously thought it was one of the most stable countries in Africa. "We said that Angola would be the last place to fall," Towers ironically recalled. "And so that is why we kept throwing money back into it." When Universal's Rhodesian interests were curtailed because of the sanctions, the company once again looked for other markets. What came immediately to mind were Oriental countries other than China, which had been closed to the West since 1949. The Rhodesian failure also contributed to Asian initiatives by making additional personnel available, some of whom spearheaded movements into such countries as Thailand, Korea, and the Philippine Islands. The man chosen for the job of tapping the Orient was John Pinks.

Born in 1930, Pinks early left home in England and, at age seventeen, joined the Imperial Tobacco Company in Salisbury, Southern Rhodesia. Switching to Universal, he was in the perfect position for the Far Eastern assignment. At age thirty-six, Pinks headed for a new challenge, carrying with him, he recalled years later, only three things: his personal luggage, a briefcase, and a faint heart. His assignment was to survey the Far East, particularly the Philippines, and to set up two flue-cured packing operations—one in the Philippines, the other in Korea. "It was, of course," he recalled with understatement, "a great challenge," even though he had prior experience in the area as a salesman for the Rhodesian Leaf Tobacco Company.

Arriving in Manila, Pinks found his assignment even greater than he had thought because the tobacco market had already been organized and was under the control of one Harry Stonehill, an American ex-G.I. who had served in the Philippines, recognized the opportunities there, and returned following military service. Moreover, Stonehill had enlisted the aid of the Philippine government, which had extended enormous privileges to him. Thus Pinks faced what amounted to an informal monopoly. "They didn't want to become involved with us," he remembered.

Pinks reasoned there was only one thing to do. He had to get to the farmer, the source of the tobacco. Requesting assistance, which arrived in the form of Jim Southern, who had had experience in Rhodesian tobacco, the two began mapping a strategy. Before one could be planned and implemented, however, the whole matter assumed the character of a Saturday night crapshoot.

"We were sitting in the office one day," Pinks recalled some twenty years after the event, "talking as to how we could start this thing. . . . We had no idea really how we could get into it because we didn't have enough contacts, but as we were talking, two young Chinese fellows came into the office, one being Tom Santiago, and the other one being Vicente Yang, and they told us they thought they could help us buy tobacco in the provinces if we were interested. When I think about it, it was hair-raising. They told us that we would have to advance them 50,000 pesos, about 2,500 U.S. dollars. We would just have to give them the cash, and they would go out and buy the tobacco for us and bring it back."

Men of less daring might have balked at such a risky arrangement in a country they little understood. After investigation and discussion, however, Pinks and Southern agreed to take the gamble. "We decided not to tell Universal about it," Pinks recalled from the safety of retirement, "because I think they would have died of heart failure. Anyway, [Santiago and Yang] went off, and a few weeks later the first truck loads arrived. To our relief, it was quite nice tobacco."

As the Philippine business progressed, Santiago and Yang became Universal's main buyers. At the same time, Pinks and Southern began traveling to the provinces to monitor purchases. It was a job that produced little result but much danger. "One incident I remember very vividly," Pinks said, "I was coming back from the Ilocos Norte region traveling south back to San Fernando, one of the larger towns in the area to stay the night. My driver appeared to be putting his foot down and going faster and faster, and I said to him, 'Why are you going so fast?' He said, 'Listen Boss, I have got to get through the next town before four o'clock; otherwise all the gun shooting starts.'"

"So," Pinks continued, "I said, 'Okay. You just keep going, and don't stop 'til we get home.' The town we were talking about was notorious as a center for one of the Philippine political factions, and they used to have a gun fight every night, and a lot of people got killed."

On another occasion, Southern was attacked by a mob and then jailed for his own protection; he learned later that an automobile in his entourage had accidentally struck and injured a child in one of the provinces. Luckily, Southern was carrying a satchel of money to buy tobacco. Following payments to the jailers, and the attention of one official's wife who prepared special meals for him, Southern was allowed to go free. At the time of his departure the whole village gathered to see him off, wishing him well and inviting him to return. "So you can see, it was not an easy job," Pinks said. "There were quite a few dangers involved in it."

Within four years the Philippine business was running smoothly, with the aid of such other personnel as H.P. ("Chief") Parrish, Robin Carver, and Thomas ("Tommy") Meyer. Pinks and Southern rented a plant at Agoo, La Union, and installed machinery that enabled them to turn out a better product. Today, Orient Leaf, as the Philippine branch is called, buys, processes and sells primarily flue-cured tobacco. Its main market is Western Europe, East Asia, and the Middle East.

Next Universal sought entry into Korea.

At Universal, executives keep apprised of activities in the entire tobacco world. So it was that Towers, soon to be instrumental in the company's Korean endeavor, learned that the Gallaher group was buying substantial tobacco there. Following consultation with Laverge who, although he never made a trip to the Far East, was concerned with all foreign operations, Towers suggested that Pinks go to Korea to assess the operation.

Arriving on a cold February day in 1966, Pinks made contact with the Taiyang Trading Company and, with an interpreter, visited the provinces. Facing a government monopoly like the one in Italy, Pinks bought an initial five hundred tons of tobacco, which had to be guarded around the clock until it went aboard ship for transport.

Pinks also brought samples of Korean tobacco back to the Richmond office, where all who graded it were astonished at its superior quality. Clearly, there was the prospect of an excellent business in the country. The Korean venture quickly flourished, and soon Peter Osborne, Joseph Hines, and Maurice Bronley, all old Rhodesia hands, were on the scene. Osborne, a young man of twenty-three at the time, would later play a large role in Korea, where he married a Korean and settled.

Ironically, the country in which some of the best tobacco is grown was also one of the hardest workstations in the Universal sphere. Moreover, Korea has harsh winters and hot, humid summers. When the company set up shop there, Korea was still suffering the effects of the bitter and divisive war that had ended in 1953. Roads were barely passable, accommodations sparse, and food strange-tasting to the Western palate (although Pinks noted that the local cuisine was never a problem for him). Bedrooms were small compartments used for living during the day, and beds were rice-mat floors on which bed clothes were laid. The rooms were unheated.

That conditions for Westerners in the provinces were difficult is clearly evident from a story of what happened to Towers during a lunch break with a factory manager and Pinks. "I will never forget it," Towers recalled. "Lunch time came and the factory manager gave us a bowl of stew and two hard-boiled eggs and a spoon. John turned to me and said, 'Unless you like dog, I wouldn't eat that stew.' He said, 'It's dog stew,' and put it down. He and I ate our two eggs, and the factory manager ate all three bowls of stew."

But Universal stayed and prospered. After ironing out problems in redrying, especially for the exacting English market, the Korean part of the business began to grow. In 1976 Universal and the Taiyang Trading Company formed Oriental Processors and Exporters of Korea (OPEK), which purchased the Jochiwon factory from the Office of Monopoly in 1977. After renovating the building, it installed modern processing equipment.

The quantity of flue-cured and burley available in Korea is determined annually by the Monopoly and is based on supply and demand. Historically, the total crop has varied between 100 million and 110 million kilos. OPEK is the largest exporter in the Republic of Korea.

Although it now holds its own, Thailand, under the direction first of Warwick, then C.S. "Studie" Carr, and later Henry Harrell, has been the most problematical of Universal's ventures in the Orient.

Universal originally entered the Thai market with Y.K. Hsu, the oldest son of Mohan Zee, who had long been instrumental in the China branch. Under the direction of Henry H. Morton, who followed Y.K. Hsu as manager, the company also buys tobacco farther north, near Laos and Burma. Thai Am Tobacco was established in Chiengmai in 1973 to grow, cure, buy, process, and export flue-cured tobacco. A 1973 merger with Opat Lertpruk formed a company that operated ten curing stations with 333 barns and dealt with some thirteen thousand farmers each season. Since 1981 Thai Am has also purchased burley for export.

Despite these evidences of progress, the Thailand operation has been plagued by difficulties. The Monopoly often changed orders drastically, having to make up for inaccurate estimates later in the season. Moreover, Universal has never been satisfied with the profit margin it maintains there.

Another event occurred in the 1970s that deserves mention: the reentry of Universal into China. Lucrative though it was, particularly in the 1920s and 1930s, China had been a problem child in the Universal family because of its unstable political situation. The company had to abandon operations there in 1941 with the coming of war and again when the communist takeover in 1949 forced the expulsion of Western interests.

After President Nixon's 1972 Shanghai communiqué, it became legal for U.S. citizens to travel to mainland China. In the spring of 1973 Norton Howe went there to make an informal survey. Howe reopened a door that had been shut since 1949 when he bought a small quantity of tobacco from the Chinese. He returned the following year with samples, and was able, through the Fritz Otto Lorje Company, to start trading in Chinese leaf. Before his retirement in 1989, Howe made some ten trips to China, not only for the purpose of dealing in tobacco but also, with the aid of Universal personnel, for the purpose of assisting the Chinese in the growth and production of their tobacco.

By 1970, Universal had expanded as far as possible in the Far East. An operation in Indonesia proved unsuccessful and had been abandoned; entry into Taiwan, which had been growing tobacco since the nineteenth century, proved impossible because of the opposition mounted by those in local markets. Universal also has a toe-hold in Guntur, the tobacco capital of India, where it supervises the grading and packing of tobacco for export, principally to Western Europe. India exports flue-cured, burley, dark-fired, and several native types.

Beginning in the late 1940s, Pierre Warwick took charge of sales throughout Central and South America and soon was selling substantial amounts of tobacco in Argentina, Peru, Bolivia, and the Dominican Republic. By the 1950s, however, approaching the end of his career, Warwick turned over sales in South American countries to Roulhac Ruffin, who in turn began sharing responsibilities with Walter Robertson, grandson of Universal's founder, J.P. Taylor.

By the early 1960s, Central and South American flue-cured and burley increased to the point that the production covered most of the local needs. At roughly the same time these growths began being accepted by world manufacturers. An excellent judge of tobacco, Robertson took the lead in buying small quantities of the best South American growths for use in Universal's blended strip exports. Cautious at first, he began with a modest fifty tons of Argentine flue-cured; however, he was soon buying several hundred tons in individual purchases.

By this time, Universal had expanded its European operations by joint enterprises in Germany, Greece, and Italy with the Deli-Maatschappij, whose cigar leaf branch, Koch Scheltema, was a substantial dealer in northern Brazilian tobaccos. Koch Scheltema had been in the Bahia area as early as the 1920s, but by the late 1960s its interests had moved south to the Blumenau/Rio Grande provinces, in which flue-cured was starting to be produced. It was in this area that it purchased a family-owned firm called Tabacos Blumenau.

Because Jan Laverge's brother Chris was president of Deli-Maatschappij, Universal was privy to Koch Scheltema's expansion. Moreover, Universal soon learned that although the South American flue-cured was being moved at a competitive price, Koch lacked sales contacts and customers to take full advantage of the situation. By consent of the Deli and Universal, Robertson was sent to visit Koch in the spring of 1969. He immediately saw the potential of the new growth, evidenced by his purchase of five hundred tons of tobacco, which replaced Universal's Argentine imports. Additionally, Robertson reported that the Deli seemed favorable to cooperation in the area. In late 1969 a three-man delegation went from Universal to assess the situation. The delegation's report was mixed, and over the winter the company mulled over what to do. Should it try to go it alone in a new country or should it combine forces with Deli?

Universal decided that it did not have the personnel to start a new enterprise in an unknown country. The decision was thus made in the spring of 1970 to approach the Deli-Maatschappij with a proposal to buy half its interest in southern Brazil, first the company in Blumenau, to be followed by participating in the purchase of Tabacos Tatsch in Santa Cruz. Santa Cruz was eight hundred miles south of Blumenau and was the center of a rapidly developing flue-cured area, in which Deli was negotiating. On his annual trip to Europe, Laverge and his brother struck a deal whereby Universal would buy 50 percent of Blumenau and Tatsch for just under one million dollars.

The new Brazilian tobaccos caught on, with exports and production showing a steady rise. Soon, an upgrading of facilities was needed, all the more so because the decade of the 1970s was also the period of consolidation of the cigarette manufacturing industry in Europe and of increasing demand by the manufacturers for the raw material to be delivered in "ready to manufacture" strips. The decision was made in 1974 to install threshing machinery in the old Tatsch building in Santa Cruz, the first dealer threshing facility in Brazil.

The South American business got an additional boost when in 1974 Philip Morris opened a cigarette manufacturing facility in Curitiba,

Brazil, not far from Blumenau, and asked Universal to be its leaf supplier. Although near retirement, Laverge agreed to represent the company for negotiations in South America, as did his brother August. At the time, the two companies' total production was four thousand tons annually, but the Laverges soon learned that Philip Morris wanted a whopping three thousand for the first year alone! Expansion of all facilities was of the highest priority. From a production of four thousand tons in 1974, Universal's Brazilian enterprise, now called Tabacos Brasileiros, produces and sells over sixty thousand tons annually. The production of flue-cured in Brazil currently exceeds that of Zimbabwe and is second only to China and the United States. Brazil's operation is now another independent and successful part of Universal, the largest outside the United States and today one of the training grounds for young tobacconists in the Universal system.

The story of Universal's entry into Mexico is prefigured by a tale of intrigue and subterfuge that was played out on the international stage even before the company became involved. During World War II, a U.S. Army officer by name of Philip Betette, who was a member of the occupation forces in Rome, met the director of the Italian tobacco monopoly, Dr. Pietro Cova, who persuaded him to go to Mexico to grow tobacco. Italy's tobacco had just suffered a severe blue mold epidemic, and he was anxious to find other supply sources. Betette set up shop in the early 1960s in the town of Tepic in the western state of Nayarit. Although he knew nothing about tobacco, assuming it was all the same and simply had to be grown and packed, Betette made contracts with local farmers and in time built a processing plant. Soon he was making regular shipments to Italy.

All went well until the Italian government discovered that the Mexican tobacco, which was burley, was being marketed under the guise that it was a native Italian product. A number of Italians were arrested and charged with importing tobacco under falsified documents. Betette was left in Mexico with no export market.

Now the sole man in control, Betette approached the K.R. Edwards arm of Universal, forming a working relationship with A.L. Hobgood, W.E. Parham, Louis Flowers, and Edward Dinnsen Jr. In time Betette duplicated his earlier efforts for Edwards, for whom he again negotiated with farmers and built a factory before he sold his interests to the company and settled in Rome.

Known since 1972 as Casa Export, the Mexican facility was soon supplying about one-third of the export market for Mexican burley, a tobacco readily accepted by cigarette manufacturers in Western Europe, the Far East, and North America. Increased domestic consumption of cigarette-type tobaccos in turn led to periodic shortages, prompting Casa to look for additional sources of burley. Programs were started in 1972 when Flowers and Dinnsen toured Central America, performing taste tests on tobaccos in Panama, Costa Rica, Honduras, Guatemala, El Salvador, Nicaragua, and Belize. The K.R. Edwards Company, working with Stuart Christian as liaison, decided to invest in Guatemala and continue expansion in Mexico. Following the identification of target growing areas, farmers were induced to try tobacco along with their traditional crops.

As Universal's global sales of tobacco, procured from twenty or more countries, grew, coordination in sales efforts became increasingly important. Each of its overseas operations has retained autonomy in its sales effort, for the practical reason that customers prefer to deal directly with the people "on the spot." However, it was also necessary that Richmond be informed of each overseas affiliate's sales activities. Hence, the system of information flow to Richmond and in turn the dissemination of information from Richmond to the various affiliates was strengthened. Although not directly involved in each affiliate's sales, the responsible officers in Richmond continue to provide coordination and guidance for a more effective worldwide sales program.

At the same time, the company began holding international sales conferences to bring together annually all foreign managers for the exchange of information and a better coordination of its global sales effort.

One conference, typical of such meetings, was held in Richmond in November of 1986. On that occasion members of Universal international operations in Canada, Brazil, Italy, Greece, the Philippines, Thailand, Zimbabwe, Malawi, Mexico, the U.K., and Holland gathered to devise ways to improve sales. Such problems as global oversupply of leaf tobacco and contract-buying directly from farmers were discussed. Information was also disseminated about barter, counter trade, and finance techniques on various markets. At the same time, salesmen learned of the upgrading of the London office in order to better coordinate efforts at international sales and to strengthen customer service.

11

A Changing Industry

By 1966 Universal had gained the level of technical proficiency with which it continues to operate today. Its partner companies were fading, some having been dissolved, others disappearing by attrition. Complete with all the technology that modern science could provide, the era of the super plant had arrived. Sales had become international in scope, and the change from selling with samples to servicing preexisting accounts was firmly established.

In earlier times, life on the markets was often a hectic catch-as-catch-can existence. Transportation was by train and automobile, and amenities such as air-conditioning and rooms with private bathrooms were usually little more than wished-for luxuries. Since 1966 that has changed, however, as reflected in the seasonal activities of the late Billy ("Senator") Pritchard, a native of Vance County, North Carolina, and a familiar and for many years a colorful Universal representative on the tobacco markets.

One of Universal's top buyers from the 1950s until his death in 1987, Pritchard led a typical tobacco buyer's life in the mid- to late twentieth century. Following a stint in the Army Air Corps, he entered the tobacco business by way of the J.P. Taylor Company in Henderson, North Carolina, and was soon sent to Greenville, Tennessee, where he ran the factory. Like other young tobacco men before him, he learned to grade tobacco by working on the hanging line, a job free from the pressures of buying but nevertheless a demanding one because the tobacco had to be graded precisely so that each bundle would be identical.

Pritchard wanted to get into the buying side of the business and took every opportunity to "follow a line" during a sale. Often he would arrange to do so by asking a regular buyer to let him substitute for a row or two. "I tried to make myself as likable as possible," Pritchard remembered, "because I knew I needed some help when I started." Soon he was in Georgia serving as a driver and "relief man" for a regular buyer.

Although Pritchard learned tobacco quickly and ultimately became a company legend, in the beginning he was subjected to the same initiation as all the others. Humorous only in retrospect, one anecdote centers on Pritchard's purchase of unsatisfactory tobacco when he was working for Ches Waddell. Waddell sent a regular buyer to relieve Pritchard, who was ordered to report to his superior. "Mr. Waddell was sitting on a pile of tobacco and had his head in his hands, and I thought he had become physically ill," Pritchard remembered. "I walked up and said, 'Mr. Waddell, what's wrong?' He said, 'Don't say anything to me right now. You've made me so sick that I just can't stand it!'"

Pritchard mastered his trade, however, eventually buying on the flue-cured markets before moving on to the burley in Kentucky, then back to Maryland, where he had begun years before. The Lexington market, on which Pritchard also bought, has long been considered the most prestigious of all. Pritchard's responsibilities were increased when he was tapped to go to Thailand in an effort to straighten out internal problems there. He moved later to the Japanese account, on which he spent the remainder of his career.

Pritchard's tenure spanned the times when tobacco buying changed markedly, even though the auction system itself did not. He began under the old system, when a buyer left home to follow the markets had little more than sparse communication with the head office during the season. In that era, an individual farmer might grow less tobacco than the farmers of today but he had a greater concern for quality. In that time, also, tobacco was "pulled" more frequently than currently—meaning the leaves were removed from the plant at different stages of maturity in order to produce different kinds and qualities of tobacco. In addition, farmers often grew tobacco as one of many crops, whereas in modern times the majority of a farmer's acreage may be in tobacco. The farmer's emphasis now is on speed, which translates into profit, but this change necessitates careful buying, grading, and regrading once the crop is on the market.

Because tobacco comes to the warehouse in fewer grades, the modern buyer must think in terms of what grades he is buying and also how they can be modified in the factory by the regraders and those on the blending line. The task might seem simple to an outsider, but often each client demands a different blend or consistency. Each buyer—and often as many as ten or twelve follow the same sale—must keep in mind what account he is buying for: domestic, Japanese, British, Australian, and so on. Additional pressure arises from having to buy while under the scrutiny of customers. More than ever before, customers from around the world show up on the markets to observe their tobacco being bought and processed.

Although a modern buyer faces fewer grades of tobacco and fewer bidders than in the old days, he still has to worry about the problem of "nesting"; now, however, the farmer is more often the culprit, whereas in the past it might have been the warehouse manager or someone working for him. The modern buyer also still has to know tobacco intimately and be willing to assert that knowledge in a split second, often working in front of an international audience that formerly would not have been there.

Other changes in buyers' lives have also come about. Transportation is more rapid, and air-conditioned motel rooms now bring a welcome end to a day in warehouses where the temperature routinely hovers above one hundred degrees. In the old days the buyer would come home in the evening after a sweltering day to an equally sweltering hotel or boardinghouse room, his only relief being an electric fan—if, indeed, he had brought one.

The auction itself, however, which is the heart of the tobacco buying system in the United States, is still performed by auctioneers whose buyers communicate their bids, with occasional flares of temper, in gestures known only in this closely knit fraternity. It is an age-old system carried on in colorful but uncomfortable warehouses in which, if it were not for the sounds of automobiles outside and jet aircraft overhead, one could imagine himself a visitor to an earlier century.

Although the market system has changed little since the 1960s, Universal's Leaf Purchasing department has undergone a substantial transformation. Initially reorganized and brought under the control of Humphreys, it subsequently passed to his tough-minded successor, John Rose, of Henderson, North Carolina.

Rose's association with tobacco began in 1938, when he joined the J.P. Taylor Company in Henderson as a foreman. Following Army service during World War II, he returned to the business and in 1970 was elected a vice president of Universal and was made responsible for all leaf purchasing and processing in the United States. During his rise, Rose had learned his trade from Humphreys.

In some ways Rose was similar to Humphreys, although his dealings with subordinates were not as harsh as the Kentuckian's. By some accounts, Rose was not interested in fine distinctions in grades of tobacco. He was known sometimes to buy for volume rather than quality, and he would brook no challenge to his decisions. W.C. "Bill" Lacy remembered that for Rose there were no shades of grey: everything was either black or white. Also, he was known by those who worked for and with him as being cut from the same cloth as Humphreys. "He was jumpy. He was quick. [But] he was a little closer to ordinary people than Humphreys was," Will Tuggle remembered.

Under Rose, Universal continued its aggressive buying; "Rose was a student of the dollar," as one associate remembered. Like Humphreys, he favored buyers who were assertive. During his tenure the company handled the most tobacco in the United States. At the time of his untimely death from a heart attack in 1978, Rose was touted as having contributed significantly to Universal's growth not only through aggressive buying but, more important, through the concept of processing centers as profit centers as well as customer service centers. Reflecting the significance of his work, his position was split and given to two people shortly after his death. Lucius F. Cary III took over leaf processing (and also the job of Philip Morris market liaison) while Lacy assumed the duties as head of leaf buying.

Lacy, who was already in the wings before Rose's death, brought a new theory of administration and leadership to the leaf department. A native of South Boston, Virginia, he had attended Davidson College before doing a stint in the Coast Guard. Following his discharge he came to Universal, where he had worked briefly as a weekly employee before being sent to the markets. He served as a foreman, relief buyer, buyer, supervisor, and district supervisor before assuming the top position in the leaf department.

Lacy was receptive to new ideas about how modern businesses should function—one of the hallmarks of the Crenshaw years—and he brought a refreshing openness to leaf purchasing. Soon he was supervising a part of the company that early on began to witness more and more involvement by other members of his department; formerly the top man had made all the decisions. Lacy admitted that often his job was to act as a moderator and coordinator. The autocratic hand of a Humphreys—or even of a Rose for that matter—was no longer at the helm in the leaf department. From the beginning, Lacy made it clear that he valued others' ideas and theories.

First on Lacy's agenda was allowing people under him more authority. J. Lee Rogers became responsible for Area A, Florida and Georgia. R.F. ("Tiny") Angel took over the duties in Area B, the South Carolina and Border Belt. Ralph Garrett supervised Area C, encompassing North Carolina and the lower part of the Middle Belt. Bill Jordan was in charge of Area D—the Northern Middle Belt, the traditional Old Belt, and Maryland. These people oversaw a total of sixty-six buyers who were also responsible for shipping in their areas.

Each Friday morning a leaf meeting was held in the Richmond headquarters to summarize the week's activity; attendance was mandatory for those in charge of each area. By the conclusion of the meeting, each area supervisor knew how much tobacco his buyers were expected to acquire for each account during the following week, along with the prices they were to pay. As was customary, Lacy would also talk daily with supervisors, passing the information from these telephone conversations along to Towers, Crenshaw, or other account managers. By the early 1980s, when Universal was fully computerized, most of this information was available the next morning in the Richmond office.

Also by then a formal program was put in place in the leaf department to train young men to be managers and, perhaps, ultimately company officers. Meanwhile, in processing other changes were taking place.

Since the 1960s, the decade that saw the introduction of the super plants, changes in processing have been more of degree than kind. Hundreds of workers have been replaced by automation, and the company has increasingly sought to provide customers with a more uniform product, aided by more accurate regrading and blending. In order to do this though, major modifications of existing facilities and installation of new ones had to be carried out.

By the 1970s and 1980s processing to exact specifications for each customer had become the largest segment of the company's operations, which in 1991 encompassed six states and twenty-three foreign countries. Although the company is worldwide, its main processing facilities still center in North Carolina. Great advances and major expenditures, however, have been made in facilities in Canada, Brazil, Italy, Zimbabwe, Malawi, Korea, the Philippines, Thailand, Mexico, and Turkey.

After Rose's death, Lucius F. Cary III was the dominant figure in Universal's American leaf processing from 1978 to 1983, when his own career was cut short by death. One of the company's rising stars, he was forty-three at the time of his death. He was succeeded by Robert C. ("Bob") Covington.

Born in 1931, Covington was raised on a tobacco farm in Southside Virginia that had been owned by several generations of his family. Educated in local rural schools, and later at Richmond's Virginia Commonwealth University, he early set his sights beyond the family farm. As a youth working in the tobacco fields, he had often envied the affluent tobacco men whose chauffeured cars regularly plied the area. "I was harvesting tobacco and they were riding around, and I thought that was the job for me," he recalled years later.

Following a tour of Army duty, Covington entered the tobacco business in 1954 with the J.P. Taylor Company in South Boston and worked his way through various factory positions during the next few years. Unlike his predecessors, however, Covington had a career change when the company's first laboratory outside the Richmond headquarters was built in the South Boston plant and he was appointed manager. This event marked the beginning of a lifelong interest in quality control, one that led to a number of changes in the company's factories.

In 1969 Covington joined forces with Skip Holt in the Richmond laboratory. Trading ideas with such early quality control proponents as Enoch Haley, factory manager at South Boston, and Robert ("Bob") Bostic, a Kentuckian who worked in various Virginia and North Carolina factories, Covington found himself more and more interested in how to produce a better product. Working under John Rose, and later Lucius Cary, he was soon traveling the worldwide company circuit. Covington increasingly focused his attention on machinery and equipment used in processing. By 1983, when he was put in charge of processing, he and Frank G. Tedder had already taken steps to standardize quality control in both domestic and foreign factories. Quality control involves, among other things, constant experimentation and introduction of new technology, the hallmarks of Covington's tenure. Covington cites his early partnership with Tedder as instrumental in changing the way Universal approaches processing worldwide. Currently Covington's title is senior vice president and processing director.

When Covington stepped into the newly created position of processing director, he brought to it the same kind of openness as did Lacy to the leaf department. Operating on the theory that the worker whose voice is heard and heeded is the worker most dedicated to the company, Covington early began encouraging subordinates to be candid in their dealings with management and, insofar as possible, to approach their jobs in the ways they thought best. "If you can persuade people to do things on their own," he noted, "or make them willing to do things, you're better off," an observation he characterized as being at the center of his management theory.

When Lucius Cary was named head of processing, Universal began making strides in adapting the technology of the 1980s to the tobacco business. Cary combined energy with compassion and was also a person who had the natural ability to elicit the best from those working under him. He had briefly attended the University of Richmond before he entered Universal and started at the bottom in the factories. At the time of his death he had achieved the rank of executive vice president.

Company engineers saw in their new boss a man who was ready to listen. John Coleman, corporate director of engineering, remembers Cary as a superior who would give support to any new idea provided the initiator had conducted an examination of what he was proposing and was committed to the success of the project. This was indeed a new and refreshing atmosphere, far different from the days when C.H. Hinnant, Universal's first engineer, was told by a plant manager that his operation had never had an engineer, did not need an engineer, and never anticipated needing one!

One of the first improvements to come from the engineering department during Cary's tenure was the Vertical Lift Separator, the forerunner of a new machine called the Counterflow. When Cary ordered the company's engineers to evaluate existing machinery in the factories, they found that the performance of these threshers needed upgrading. Coleman modified Hinnant's original idea and came up with a device that could perform three separations of the tobacco in one machine. Following testing, the Counterflow was perfected and put into use. Universal has a patent on the machine, which is under license in five countries and marketed around the world. Over 350 of them have been sold, and royalties have been substantial.

Engineering played a role in 1983 when the new Universal plant in Petersburg, Virginia, began operating with total computer control, all functions being performed with a screen and keyboard. Setting a standard for the industry, it was the prototype of similar systems now in all company plants.

M. Dean Cheatham, another force in Universal's engineering department, best summed up the engineering contribution to the company in the last two or three decades. "Awareness in this company that engineering had a place," he noted, "was brought about by the change in where the profits would come from. In the old days they put their money into buying tobacco and putting it on the shelf and speculating on selling it for profit later. But stabilization came in and killed speculation. Then we had to concentrate on being a service organization. That led to better factories, and more machinery and more mechanization. All this caused engineering to take on more importance."

Universal's commitment to technology is perhaps best exhibited by the Research and Development facility in Wilson, North Carolina, which was in full operation by 1990. Designed as a kind of think-tank where ideas are generated and put into at least experimental practice, it is staffed by a mechanical engineer and an electronics specialist who originate techniques to aid in the production of a better product. The company also works with foreign companies on prototype technology.

In addition to the new streamlined methods used in processing, Universal's tobacco in the modern age has become increasingly subjected to scientific analysis. During Jackson's presidency Universal had recognized the importance of such studies and the need to gather information about the chemical properties of tobacco and had opened a laboratory. Of prime importance was the moisture content in tobacco shipped to the English customer Gallaher. In addition, German customers, Reemtsma for example, began requesting scientific data regarding sugar, nicotine levels, and tar content in their purchases from Universal partner, K.R. Edwards Company. Also during this era, cigarettes were changing from the nonfilter to the filter type. As a result, changes in blends were needed.

Today the Universal laboratory also has the responsibility of setting standards for the size of residual stem and of measuring sand content, which has long been a problem in the tobacco business. It also develops methods of insect control and is studying the problem of blue mold, which for years has been the scourge of the tobacco business. (The 1980 outbreak, which devastated Cuba's crop, infested the United States by way of the prevailing summer winds and finally ended up destroying 75 million pounds of tobacco as far north as Canada. Earlier, in 1962, it wiped out the entire Italian crop.) The lab augments by scientific study what until the late 1950s had been left to the subjective eye of the buyer. Although small, the laboratory in the Richmond headquarters provides an important function in modern Universal operations with its continual study of the properties of the leaf.

Some people in the factories, where satellite laboratories were soon established, at first resented the activities of the lab personnel. Early on, when representatives of the Richmond lab arrived at some of the factories they often found themselves isolated, sometimes even shunned, and a few managers even initially refused to cooperate with them. Ultimately, processing personnel and buyers generally accepted the new scientific methods when they realized they could augment, but not replace, subjective evaluations of tobacco.

In earlier days, ending gradually during the 1950s, company factories were run by what Covington candidly described as "straw-boss thinking," a system centering on the dictum of, "You do what I say, or else."

That era has passed. Gone are the times when a manager could control his large workforce by firing half a dozen people on a whim, knowing that there were perhaps two dozen or more waiting at the factory door to take the jobs and probably perform them with fewer complaints. Gone also are the days when white men alone could expect favored treatment, or when hourly workers could not look forward to advancement and therefore had little incentive to improve performance.

In Universal's factories of the last two decades or so both the salaried and the hourly employees are better educated—although many hourly workers still lack high school diplomas—and an attempt has been made to make them more knowledgeable about (and committed to) their workplace. For example, employees' views on such topics as methods for improving working conditions and increasing productivity are sought at all levels. Retirement benefits are offered, and a seniority system serves as an incentive for workers to remain.

Of ever greater importance is the system of cross-training. Because tobacco factory work is seasonal, employees in the past had only annual layoffs to look forward to following the processing of the yearly crop. Under the modern system supervisory personnel (and permanent hourly personnel) are cross-trained so that, in addition to seasonal duties, they also remain employed during the off-season.

This system was put in place when Bob Covington determined that multiple tasks could be done by the same factory people instead of by outsiders who were hired for short-term tasks. Thus, factory upgrades, changes in machinery, maintenance, and light construction jobs are performed by those who during the regular tobacco season are involved solely in processing. Covington's theory is that cross-training engenders loyalty from workers because they can see that their needs and ideas are taken seriously. Many hourly employees, however, still prefer to work only during the processing season. Some return to seasonal jobs such as farming; others are women who prefer to stay at home; still others live during the off-season on unemployment benefits.

For many years the company has made an effort to promote women and minorities into supervisory positions in domestic factories. For example, at Tobacco Processors in Wilson, North Carolina, Kenneth Pittman is assistant plant superintendent. An African American with a bachelor's degree in business management, he works a racially mixed staff of roughly one hundred on each shift. He was recruited into the company in 1981 from his former job as a manager/buyer for a retail store. His goal is a company position in public relations or in sales.

Burley tobacco—grown primarily in Kentucky and Tennessee—being offered for sale in a Kentucky warehouse. Buyers often work in sub-zero temperatures. Photo by Pamela Barefoot.

A Thai woman stacks green leaves preparatory to processing.

Stacking tobacco in a Universal facility in India at one of the smaller operations in the Universal family.

Tobacco stacked in the sample room in the company's Richmond headquarters. It is from such samples that manufacturers' representatives worldwide select tobacco to ship around the globe.

Tobacco prepared for human consumption, from the genus *Nicotiana* of the nightshade family *Solanaceae,* comes from tiny seed such as this.

John Rose, shown here in the 1970s, who took charge of company leaf purchasing and processing following Humphrey's retirement, was "a student of the dollar" and a tough taskmaster. During his tenure, Universal continued to handle more leaf tobacco than any other dealer in the United States.

Above, native children play with a bundle of Universal tobacco in Zimbabwe. *Below,* a native poses on his water buffalo in front of a small Universal buying station in the Philippine Islands.

Joseph F. Cullman III (*left*), whose family has long been involved in Philip Morris and associated with Universal for some seventy years, and former Universal president and CEO Gordon Crenshaw in a North Carolina warehouse in the early 1980s. Photo by Howard Walker.

A Universal employee stacks bundles of tobacco in the Philippine Islands.

Allen King became the first president in Universal's history not to rise through the ranks from the factories to the Richmond office when he was promoted to his current post in 1991. Photo by Maurice Duke.

Instrumental in forming the early link between Universal and Philip Morris and also an early and forceful director of the China branch of the company, J. Pinckney Harrison was known for his air of sophistication and studied use of the English language. He was also Fred Harrison's cousin and confidant on business matters.

Always working behind the scenes, Wallace Chandler was instrumental in reorganizing internal operations at the Richmond office.

The Lytton processing plant in Harare, Zimbabwe; Universal operates three processing plants in the country. Africa is among the world's most important sources of tobacco.

Thomas R. Towers and Universal Hong Kong employee Y.C. Hsu atop the Great Wall of China in 1986. Universal executives regularly visit the company's worldwide facilities.

Gretoba SA, the Greek Universal processing plant, which served as the stepping stone for Universal into other European countries, shown here in the early 1970s.

Ready for shipment to manufacturers all over the world, hogsheads of tobacco are stacked six high in Universal's Henderson, North Carolina, warehouse.

Similarly, Alma Lucas, an African-American head picking supervisor in charge of from thirty-five to fifty people in the same plant, came to the company in 1965 expecting to be a seasonal hourly worker. At the K.R. Edwards partner company, Wayne Bagget started in the prizing room in 1978 and rose to be Edwards's first African-American plant supervisor, with roughly sixty workers in his charge. Glenda Davis, a white woman who started in 1974 in the same department as Bagget, worked her way through various jobs to become storage manager supervising twenty-five people. Also, an ever-increasing number of white people are filling the ranks of the hourly employees, who in the past were exclusively African Americans. Workers may still punch the time-clock at 7 A.M., but they know they will finish work on time or receive overtime pay. In the event there is insufficient work for the entire force, each person knows that he or she will receive three hours pay for appearing for work on time. In four company factories—Danville, Henderson, Smithfield, and Petersburg—employees have unions to represent their interests. There have, however, been no prolonged strikes or protracted negotiations between the unions and management.

Another change in the new factories is the presence of specialists. Formerly, the factory manager was a leaf specialist first and a manager second, his managerial abilities often questionable. Today, in addition to the general manager, there is a production manager, a leaf specialist, a laboratory manager, and an engineer. No longer are there people milling about waiting for orders. Each factory is leaner and schedules are more closely planned. Men such as Thomas B. ("Red") Bennett, a former University of North Carolina basketball player and one of the first factory managers to hold a college degree, Frank Tedder, Agnew Galloway, and John ("Johnny") Moser were representatives of the new breed.

A young man or woman coming into one of Universal's factories today can expect training in, and orientation about, the various departments. He or she can also expect to find a receptive ear for questions and ideas. Such an introduction to the system is quite different from the era when a person was hired and left largely alone to fend for himself on the theory that only the fittest would survive. No longer does a newcomer have to act as Covington did when he was sent as a young man to a Maryland factory. "I got there," Covington reported, and "the door was locked, so I got a crowbar and broke the lock off. The whole plant was filthy, and I found a hardware store next door and got brooms and cleaned it up and went to work all on my own ingenuity."

One area in which the company thus far is unsuccessful, however, is its inability to attract women who will proceed through the factory and buying apprenticeship. Mildred Wood, Universal's assistant treasurer, believes that the nature of the business itself may be at the center of the problem. Wood, who has given forty years of service to the company, noted the conditions on the markets. "There's a certain sacrifice that these men make that maybe the women haven't wanted to make," she observed. The conditions are "hot, dusty, hours are terrible, . . . and at a moment's notice they might have to pick up and go overseas." But the question of how to attract women to the business remains unanswered and the problem unsolved.

As the volume of tobacco throughout the worldwide company system increased, tighter control was needed. John Meredith was appointed traffic manager in 1947 and ultimately became traffic director. His job was to devise plans whereby tobacco in the Universal system in the U.S. would flow smoothly from the auction to the plant and then on to storage or to the customer.

Entering Universal as a bookkeeper following his graduation from Richmond's John Marshall High School, Meredith soon found himself on the markets as a "pencil and traffic" man. He became responsible for the tobacco as soon as the buyer had purchased it, and his primary task was to get it to the redrying plant. After the tobacco was redried and sold, he invoiced it, arranged for shipment, and executed necessary paper work. Soon he was coordinating activities from the Richmond office, with various traffic personnel, chief among them Swanson Waller, under his control.

With the nationwide decline of the railroad system, Universal turned to independent truckers to carry its product. Faster and easier to load and unload than railroad cars, trucks had only one major drawback: the ease with which they could be hijacked. Tobacco was almost impossible to mark or to identify—at least to the satisfaction of a court of law. Sometimes an independent trucker would lose two, or even three, trucks to thieves during a season. Although the company several times considered doing so, Universal never bought its own truck fleet because of the seasonal nature of the tobacco business. It was cheaper to let independent truckers haul the leaf than for company trucks to sit idle during the off-season.

One innovation that occurred in transportation was the introduction of a safer and more efficient method of handling ship-bound tobacco. Formerly, hogsheads had been loaded into cargo holds—a costly, unwieldy, and dangerous practice; under the new method they were first put into sea containers, then the whole container was hauled aboard ship by a crane. Because of their space-saving characteristics, these cardboard boxes of uniform sizes replaced the more cumbersome hogsheads.

Today, Universal's traffic department is headed by M.S. ("Mac") Walker, who is in charge of a staff of nine. Ships' containers have been standardized, with identically packaged tobacco regularly departing from both East Coast and West Coast ports. Truck hijackings are extremely rare, owing to better markings on bulk tobacco. Transportation has become a major department of the company.

As progress was made in buying, processing, and transportation, Universal's sales department continued to play a major role in the company's success. Following World War II, sales was under the leadership of the senior officers. At that time (and for the most part even now) there was no formal training program. Buyers bought large quantities of tobacco on speculation, the novice buyers learning customers' needs from samples. This experience was acquired in part as the various tobaccos were brought from storage and prepared for viewing.

In the early 1960s, American flue-cured and burley were the dominant tobaccos used in cigarettes worldwide. American manufacturers made relatively little use of "off-shore" tobaccos, whether their products were manufactured for domestic or export sales. Universal's major domestic customer was Philip Morris. In the early days of the Philip Morris/Universal relationship, Pinckney Harrison had been in charge of the account, and he dealt directly with Wirt Hatcher, a senior officer at Philip Morris. In addition to their business relationship the two men were friends and companions at the bridge table and on hunting and fishing trips.

Now one of the world's largest conglomerates, Philip Morris was in the early years exclusively a tobacco manufacturer with only a small percentage of the cigarette market. Perhaps difficult to comprehend in the modern day, Universal was from time to time called upon to finance Philip Morris's tobacco. In many ways, the growth of that company has influenced the growth of Universal.

For more than a decade after World War II, Universal supplied more and more tobacco to Philip Morris. Operating decisions there were still being made by Hatcher, who worked closely with Universal's Pinckney Harrison. Soon George Macon, a longtime Universal employee, moved to Philip Morris and into Hatcher's position in leaf, while at Universal Ed Humphreys replaced Harrison.

Changes other than personnel were also taking place, however. Philip Morris acquired Benson and Hedges, primarily owned by the Cullman family, for whom Universal was already the supplier. With the acquisition the Cullmans became significant stockholders in Philip Morris. Joseph F. Cullman III and his first cousin Hugh became officers of Philip Morris and brought with them key people, among them Clifford Goldsmith and John Cookman, who ultimately rose to top positions. Soon Joe Cullman III, longtime friend of Pinckney Harrison and James Covington, became Philip Morris's chief executive officer.

From the early 1960s until retirement, Humphreys handled the Philip Morris account. In his day-to-day dealings he worked closely with George Macon in Richmond and Joe Cullman in New York. With the dramatic growth of Philip Morris, and because of the importance of the relationship to both companies, the chief executive officer of Universal needed to be closely involved, to the extent of being the senior account executive in the business with Philip Morris. In the late 1960s Gordon Crenshaw assumed this role, working with the senior people at Philip Morris in New York—Joe Cullman, George Weissman, Ross Milhiser, and Hugh Cullman—and with George Macon in Richmond. The principal person in New York with whom Crenshaw conducted business was Clifford Goldsmith, executive vice president in charge of leaf and processing, who became president of Philip Morris. The relationship between the chief executive officers of Universal and Philip Morris continues to this day.

John Rose, who had replaced Humphreys as head of buying and processing, played a role in the handling of this rapidly growing business with Philip Morris. His primary responsibility was to administer and execute Philip Morris's orders. During these years, Howard Cone was also a key man in the Philip Morris/Universal relationship, working with Hugh West, the leaf director of Philip Morris, in supervising the purchase of their tobacco. Cone was known and liked by virtually everyone in the trade. His rapport with farm leaders, warehousemen, and trade association officials proved to be a tremendous asset to both Philip Morris and Universal.

Rose was succeeded by Lucius Cary who, in this capacity, did an effective job until his death, at which time he was followed by John Gregory on the leaf side and Bob Covington in processing. In the meantime, George Macon was succeeded by William Longest and subsequently by Witcher Dudley at Philip Morris.

Traditionally, Universal had bought for Philip Morris virtually all its U.S.-grown tobacco. With the worldwide expansion of both companies, it began supplying the lion's share of the foreign growths purchased by Philip Morris as well. This arrangement continues today.

During the 1970s and 1980s, Philip Morris gradually began entrusting Universal not only with domestic and international buying but also with processing more and more of its tobaccos. Today, the major part of its tobacco is processed by Universal, which in addition renders a variety of other services. For example, the company assists and works on behalf of Philip Morris in relations with the government and the various farm groups. Total services involve many people in Universal in many different departments who work with their counterparts at Philip Morris.

With one brief exception, the business between the two firms has expanded without interruption since its beginning. Following Congoleum's unsuccessful takeover bid for Universal, Philip Morris grew concerned as to what might happen if its principal supplier should fall under the control of people with no knowledge of tobacco and in whom they would have no confidence. As a consequence, Philip Morris began placing its own buyers on the markets and for a few years did in fact purchase tobacco with its own staff. The company finally determined, however, that this was not a prudent practice and discontinued the program, and Universal resumed its position of handling Philip Morris's order business in the United States. It continues to do so today. Since resuming its position of Philip Morris's principal supplier there has been a continuing growth, not only in the volume of purchases, but in processing as well.

Other domestic cigarette companies supplied by the Universal Group are R.J. Reynolds, the American Tobacco Company, P. Lorillard, Brown and Williamson, and Ligget and Myers. Thorpe and Ricks and K.R. Edwards Company, Universal subsidiaries, have been suppliers to these same domestic companies for years. These manufacturers use both U.S. and off-shore flue-cured and burley tobaccos.

Following Jim Covington's retirement, Stuart Carr handled the Reynolds business. He was succeeded by Stuart Christian, who in addition aided K.R. Edwards with its accounts. Some years later, James Starkey worked with all the domestics because of his knowledge of the U.S. tobacco programs gained through his prior position as U.S. deputy undersecretary of agriculture. In addition to the major cigarette manufacturers, Universal has traditionally supplied pipe and chewing tobacco manufacturers such as Pinkerton, Middleton, Lane, and Sutliff.

Although accounts at Universal are theoretically headed by one person, they are not the only ones involved in managing them. During his tenure, Humphreys was in charge of both leaf and processing. He—and everyone working in these two departments—had to make it his business to know the customers and representatives from each of the many companies and to work closely with them. In time Bob Covington, Rose, Cary, and Lacy all played central roles in these activities. Currently, during the six-month growing, buying, and processing season, people from Universal are in constant contact with customers. During the off-season, contact is less frequent, but the company's sales force makes it a point to keep customers informed about the quality and size of the upcoming crop. Such interactions, part business and part social, let the customer know that his business interests and his personal friendship are important to Universal. The company's account executives, who numbered roughly two-thirds more in the early 1990s than in the mid-1960s, continue to follow this method.

During the 1960s and 1970s major changes occurred in the way tobacco was sold worldwide. In earlier times there were small companies whose clientele were primarily local. These companies consisted of manufacturers of all kinds of tobacco: cigarettes, cigars, snuff, pipe tobacco, and chewing tobacco. In order to service them Universal's salesmen regularly made the circuits, carrying samples.

Many smaller manufacturers were bought out by larger groups — Anton Rupert's global holdings being a case in point—and there was a growing interest in American tobaccos on the part of government monopolies. Huge accounts began to evolve, lessening the need for salesmen carrying samples. Although samples and offers remained important, emphasis was increasingly placed on what other services the company could provide. Packaging, quality specifications, coordinated shipping from different world points, and similar activities all became of concern.

Because of the demand for changing services, the function of foreign-based Universal agents also changed. In the early decades of the century such agents were important as liaisons between company salesmen and customers. Often the agent would accompany the Universal man as he visited customers. Because of the growing popularity of air travel, the consolidation of the manufacturers, and the increasingly direct contact between manufacturers and suppliers at the sources, the services of agents grew less important.

The company also had to achieve greater coordination in buying and processing, as well as among the departments in the Richmond office. Sales and traffic had to work together, as did account executives and buyers on the markets. Sales also had to work closely with processing in order to monitor the quality and uniformity of work in progress. Thus the whole company had to be restructured to function as a total (as opposed to a purely sales-oriented) organization, with purchasing, processing, and sales interwoven.

Crenshaw, Towers, and Laverge were instrumental in restructuring the sales department. Stuart Christian's principal responsibility was in domestic sales, but because of his experience in international sales he also had considerable responsibility in this area. James H. Abernathy coordinated sales for the foreign government monopolies, in addition to his responsibility for pool purchases. Experienced younger men, such as Henry Harrell, Lucius Cary, and Norton Howe, were elevated to positions in sales. These changes also involved a restructuring in the Richmond office administration. That task fell to Wallace Chandler.

Despite the changes, the personal element remains important, because the tobacco business is a closely knit fraternity, built on relationships and personal and family friendships of long standing. In addition, younger members of the sales force need to be introduced to customers so that, when the older men step aside, younger ones can manage the accounts.

As sales of non-U.S. tobacco increased, executives in Richmond became aware of and responsible for each customer's worldwide needs. Therefore, the international sales force had to have current information about the world's tobaccos. From the 1960s, sales grew to be the business of many people and departments at Universal—from the account executives to the supervisors in the factories and the buyers on the line, men who knew on what days what customers would arrive to see their tobacco bought and processed. Although some thirty or so company members work in sales, actually almost everyone in Universal's management has a hand in accommodating clients, some in direct contact with the customers, others in leaf, staff services, agronomy, and processing.

Universal found itself privy to information on the customers' requirements and had to inaugurate a system, albeit informally, where each customer's account was handled confidentially. The large manufacturers did not wish to share the strategies they might be pursuing on the market, so account executives, buyers, and factory supervisors protected the integrity of each account by maintaining silence about specifics. This system was called the "Chinese wall." To be sure, information about the tobacco world in general was always shared. What was going on in an individual account, however, was known to only a few within the Universal hierarchy. The sales department, with rising figures such as Randolph ("Randy") Robins, Willem de Vries, and Edward ("Ned") Schaaf, still operates this way today.

The personal relationships between salesmen and clients is typified by an event that occurred in Jordan. While on a business trip from the Richmond headquarters, Jim Abernathy contracted hepatitis and was hospitalized for almost six weeks. Knowing his condition to be serious, Abernathy's wife traveled to Jordan to be with him. Although she had planned to seek public lodgings, one of Abernathy's clients insisted she stay with his family, which she did for the duration of her visit. At a later time, when Abernathy was hospitalized in Richmond, the Jordanian customer requested a fifty-thousand-dollar credit, which Abernathy readily approved from his hospital bed. The debt was repaid before it was due.

With sales assuming an international flavor, some of the younger staff move upward into sales positions where they are given a great deal of autonomy in handling accounts. Each year at its international conference, sales department personnel learn about developments and trends in the worldwide tobacco market. Frequently at these meetings account executives find they can give or receive aid from colleagues with expertise in different countries, thus allowing the company to retain valued customers who otherwise may have sought tobacco outside the Universal network.

The world in which the modern Universal sales executive moves is illustrated by an event that involved Towers while on a trip to Portugal with Pierre Warwick. At a formal dinner at the home of George Mello, a member of one of Europe's most prominent tobacco families, Mello turned to Warwick during a break in the conversation. There were some twenty guests, each with a serving maid behind the guest's chair.

"Pierre, I understand you have been checking on my credit," Mello said.

"That's right. I thought it was the prudent business thing to do," Warwick responded as the young Towers sat in stunned silence.

"I don't mind," Mello said after a pause. "What did you find I was worth?"

"Five hundred million dollars," Warwick responded.

Mello thought for a second and calculatingly ended the conversation when he said, "Pierre, I wouldn't sell for that."

Universal has undergone a host of changes in its worldwide system since the mid-1960s. In the area of purchasing, changes revolved primarily around the way the leaf department was organized. The old "one man as ruler" method disappeared, and those who worked in leaf gradually had more and more to say about how the department was run. At the same time, the department became more efficiently organized, and everyone dealing directly with tobacco knew what was going on in the Universal system and on the world tobacco stage. Although life on the markets changed little, the way tobacco was handled, as well as all dealings revolving around it, did.

In processing, the period since the 1960s has been marked by enormous technological advances, while parallel ones have occurred since then in the sales department, which became more global and more adept at servicing accounts. And Universal's transportation methods changed also in order to accommodate the expansion. In the nineteenth century, there was a saying that the sun never set on the British empire. At the end of the twentieth the same could be said of Universal Leaf Tobacco Company. It is the undisputed leader in its field. All company ventures were not so successful as those dealing with tobacco, however, as the following chapter will indicate.

12

Diversification and Litigation

From its founding to the 1960s, Universal dealt exclusively in the purchase and sale of leaf tobacco. In the middle of that decade, however, a report emanating from the United States surgeon general changed the complexion of the tobacco world. The government's 1964 report on the adverse effects of using tobacco products posed a much more serious challenge for the business than had critics of the past. Formerly, criticism had been focused on arguments based on moralistic grounds. This time, however, concern centered on health, with the surgeon general arguing that tobacco use caused or exacerbated illnesses such as cancer, emphysema, and heart disease. Many tobacconists did not at first believe the report, but faced with a question as to what the future would hold, tobacco companies, particularly those in the United States, began to consider their options, the most logical of which were an expansion of markets abroad and diversification at home.

Although diversification had been talked about in Universal's top offices for some time, it was clear that such a movement would have little or no chance of success so long as Herbert Jackson was president. Believing that his company should deal only in tobacco, he had already stated his official hostility to diversification, although several Universal partner companies had earlier undertaken such ventures on their own. "Our diversification is selling the same product to a lot of different peoples," Jackson had written. "There are some advantages to that too," he had further argued, "arising from the fact that good times and bad times and health scares don't hit all countries the same time or with the same force." Jackson also considered Universal's entry into foreign countries as examples of diversification.

During an earlier era, Jackson's perception would have been correct, but in 1964, the picture was different. "We realized that there were some very, very dark clouds on the horizon confronting the tobacco business and that we ought to think about diversification," Towers recalled.

The movement toward diversification was led largely by Crenshaw, Laverge, Towers, and Chandler and relied on earnings from tobacco.

Hesitant because of their lack of knowledge of other businesses, the men moved cautiously and agreed on certain methods. They would approach small, often family-owned, businesses; they would forswear hostile takeovers; they would seek ventures that were counter-seasonal to tobacco; and (as far as was possible) they would leave in place the established management of any company they bought. They decided not to become involved in businesses that would dilute the company's primary interest, which was tobacco.

Because of this caution and inexperience, Universal's diversification program got off to a slow start. Outside advisers suggested the purchase of two farm equipment companies, but the company declined. Other consultants suggested that it enter the insurance business. Again it declined. As Wallace Chandler observed: "the price was too high, and you worried about what you were getting involved in." Ultimately, Universal relied on the advice of Wheat First Securities, a Richmond-based investment banking firm, but efforts at diversification remained largely in limbo between 1964 and 1968.

When Crenshaw came to the presidency in 1966 he made diversification a priority. Two years later his efforts seemed to pay off with the acquisition of two disparate companies. One was the Richmond-based Inta-Roto. The other was Overton Container Corporation of Smithfield, North Carolina. Inta-Roto was a machine manufacturing company comprised of three divisions: the machinery division, which engineered and built industrial machinery (principally laminators, coaters, and flexographic presses for use in packaging and other fields); the mill roll division, which manufactured engraved steel cylinders used in the making of designs, such as those on some automobile seat covers, leather products, and vinyl coverings; and the engraving division, which produced cylinders used on rotogravure presses to imprint designs and lettering on packing materials. Overton's primary business was supplying containers to the tobacco industry. Universal's diversification program was officially under way.

In 1969 the company, advised by the Stanford Research Institute, acquired 100 percent of the assets of Magnolia Manufacturing Corporation, a South Hill, Virginia, business that specialized in modular home construction. From this acquisition was formed Universal's Unitized Systems Company (USCO), a subsidiary that would manufacture mobile homes and sections for single-family homes. USCO was soon in production in three different plants.

Next Universal joined with one of Richmond's best-known real estate developers and began to negotiate with E. Carlton Wilton, president of E. Carlton Wilton Inc., until late in 1970, after which the two companies made an announcement of the formation of Universal-Wilton, whose immediate goal was to construct a planned community in Richmond's West End. The intention of the new company was to build more than eight thousand housing units and additional facilities on twenty-three hundred acres of land at a site called Tuckahoe Village, involving an expenditure to exceed $150 million. Prior to the announcement Universal had formed Universal Land Use Corporation, a subsidiary that began developing a low-cost housing project on two hundred acres of land near Suffolk, Virginia, and a mobile home park in Currituck, North Carolina.

Also during this time, Universal Woods, a company based in Louisville, Kentucky, that manufactured a product designed to replace high-pressure laminates such as Formica, was gathered under the company umbrella through the K.R. Edwards Company. Offering thirty-five different wood grain patterns in virtually any color, the company's products could be used on kitchen cabinets and on household, hospital, health care, and laboratory furniture.

Perhaps the brightest prospect to appear on Universal's horizon during its early diversification attempts was announced in late December 1978 when it made public its tentative agreement to acquire Unifi, a fibers firm based in Greensboro, North Carolina. Disclosing an acquisitions figure of $25 million, Universal reported that it planned to merge the company, which processed and sold synthetic fibers, into an undisclosed unit of Universal Leaf. At the time Unifi was the nation's second largest synthetic fibers firm. Merger negotiations were halted, however, when the two companies failed to agree on a price.

Five years after the abortive attempt to acquire the synthetic fibers firm, Universal acquired the Blakely Peanut Company of Blakely, Georgia. Blakely, a small satellite in the Universal sphere, bought and produced peanuts for domestic and export edible sales, oil stock sales, and peanut-hull pellet sales for livestock feed and fuel. The company also processed and sold seed peanuts to the retail and wholesale trade. Gross sales were in excess of $30 million for the year preceding the acquisition. Despite the work put into these ventures, Universal's early attempts at diversification were largely unsuccessful.

After almost a decade of struggling with Inta-Roto, in particular trying unsuccessfully to trim its managerial staff, Universal's leaders realized that they could not make the business profitable. Late in December 1977 they sold it to the people who were managing it. The modular home venture (USCO) failed because of a national recession in the home building industry. Universal was unable to rent or sell the units it had constructed and was forced to withdraw from the business.

The relationship with the E. Carlton Wilton company proved most successful, but, because it involved the use of land in the Richmond area only, its life was limited. Universal-Wilton, operating on a fifty-fifty partnership, bought land, obtained zoning permits, constructed external utilities and major roads, then sold the parcels to developers. The group also constructed and retained ownership in apartments and commercial properties that were subsequently sold.

At its height, Universal-Wilton was able to accumulate large tracts of land—as much as thirty-five hundred acres—in one of the most desirable areas of metropolitan Richmond. As planned, most of the sales were made to E. Carlton Wilton, Inc.; however, as the area became more established and real estate values increased, the company began selling to other developers. By 1987 the project was complete and the relationship was terminated.

The first attempt at diversification on a major scale occurred in 1980 when Universal acquired the Royster Company, headquartered in Norfolk, Virginia. Royster was a manufacturer and marketer of phosphate fertilizer materials, mixed fertilizers, and micronutrients. The company also stored fertilizer materials at deep water and inland terminals and sold crop-protection chemicals, seeds, and grain. Organized in 1885 by Sheppard Royster, the company was privately owned until 1975 when the first public offering of stock was made. Still under the control of the Royster and the Burroughs families, who held the major portion of the stock at the time of the merger, Royster was a financially healthy company that operated in a manner similar to Universal: it was a seasonal agricultural business located in the Southeast; it had its business roots firmly planted in three-quarters of a century of experience; the executive and managerial staff was composed of personnel who had begun at the bottom of the company ladder; and it was conservative in its approach to business. When it became a wholly-owned subsidiary of Universal in 1980 it reported earnings for the previous year of $2.9 million on sales of $227.8 million. Indications were that the acquisition would be a mutually satisfactory and profitable one for both companies.

Such, however, was not the case. By 1984 Royster had been sold to Superfos, a Danish company that had a large international fertilizer operation and wanted to expand its position in the United States. An acquisition that had been announced in the 1980 annual report on such a promising note, with four pages of color photographs, a prose description, and pertinent statistics, quietly disappeared from the Universal family.

Seen objectively, the failure of Royster was more a matter of circumstance than an error in judgment. There was no way to foresee that Universal was entering the fertilizer business just as that business (and American agriculture in general) was on the verge of one of its most severe depressions in its history. Through reorganization and improvement in efficiency, Universal was able to achieve a satisfactory level of performance relative to other fertilizer companies; nevertheless, return on investment was not acceptable. Although Universal made no formal attempt to dispose of Royster, when it was approached with a suitable offer, it made the decision to divest. Royster went to the Danish firm for $115 million. Universal had paid $109 million for it four years earlier.

In November of 1984 Universal purchased all outstanding shares of capital stock of Lawyers Title Insurance Corporation and Continental Land Title Company for a cash payment of approximately $115 million. Founded sixty years before in Richmond, Lawyers Title employed just over three thousand people at the time of Universal's acquisition and accounted for approximately 13 percent of title insurance underwriting in the United States. Shortly after this acquisition Continental Land Title Company became a subsidiary of Lawyers Title, followed by the consolidation of several of the two companies' offices. An important part of Lawyers Title was its National Division, comprised of fourteen offices established in major metropolitan areas around the country.

Almost immediately, Universal's insurance operations generated profits, and in 1987 they achieved the largest annual revenues in their sixty-year history, contributing over 50 percent to Universal's bottom line. Adding to this growth were high levels of commercial and industrial activity, increased use of title insurance in residential transactions, a surge of residential refinancings, and the increased use of credit equity lines following passage of a new federal tax law.

Lawyers Title's National Division also made immediate strides following its acquisition by Universal. Several major transactions set the course for its increased performance. Macy's leveraged buy-out of three shopping centers and eighty-eight department stores contributed to the

National Division's growth. At the end of 1986, with a network of more than thirty-seven hundred agency, branch, and subsidiary offices; more than twenty-six thousand approved attorneys; and offices in the nation's metropolitan centers, Lawyers Title was in a strong position. After almost twenty years of trial and error it seemed as if diversification were finally beginning to work. However, the tide turned abruptly in the late 1980s when Lawyers Title began to lose large sums. In June 1991 the board of directors authorized management to proceed with a plan to separate Lawyers Title from Universal Corporation and to distribute all the outstanding shares of a newly organized holding company for Lawyers Title to shareholders in a tax-free spin-off on the basis of one share for each four shares of Universal's common stock.

Capitalizing on negotiations begun years before by Jan Laverge, a far more successful step in diversification took place in April 1986 when Universal acquired NV Deli-Maatschappij, which had operations in tobacco and also in commodity trading. A Dutch company originally engaged only in the leaf tobacco business, Deli had in recent years diversified into international commodities trading. At the time Universal acquired the company it was dealing in coffee, tea, rubber, vegetable oils, sun-flower seeds, and timber. Regarding the tobacco aspect of Deli's operations, the acquisition allowed Universal to gain a larger position in the flue-cured and burley markets of Brazil, Italy, and Greece and also to extend its current dark tobacco operations into several international markets.

The success of the diversification program was reflected in the annual report of 1987. Despite the fact that Brazil had just experienced its worst tobacco crop on record and that the company's U.S. tobacco operations were below those of the preceding year, Universal still recorded improved results. Net income for the year rose from $47,106,000 to $55,973,000. On a per-share basis, earnings rose 51 cents to $3.25. Gross revenues of $2.1 billion showed a sharp increase over the previous year's $1.4 billion. The gains could be traced directly to the success of the new acquisitions of Deli-Maatschappij and more importantly of the title insurance business.

Had it not been for changing attitudes toward tobacco, Universal would probably never have seriously considered diversification. But by the late 1980s and early 1990s it was steadily becoming more than a leaf tobacco dealer. Company officials saw what Thomas Towers had said years earlier when the surgeon general's initial report on tobacco had been issued: there were "dark clouds on the horizon" for tobacco, and diversification seemed the next logical step. Still, however, Universal's attitude was that it would not dilute its tobacco interest in its diversification efforts. Tobacco was still to be the company's chief interest.

Probably nowhere else in the modern corporate world are there people who transact business as do tobacconists, as has been alluded to many times throughout this book. While the world's international super powers operate on the theory of "trust but verify," the world tobacco companies continue to operate essentially on trust alone. "We have a few contracts in our business," says Gordon Crenshaw, "as it relates to sales, but [they are] invariably with governments. The bulk of our business is still done on a man's word or a very informal letter."

How the tobacco business came to be one in which million-dollar transactions are confirmed with a handshake, a cursory note, or the annotation on the back of a matchbook or napkin, no one seems to know. Some in the business argue that the degree of trust has its roots in an idealistic code of ethics originating perhaps in Renaissance England where—according to custom—a man's word was his bond. Others, Will Tuggle for example, approach the phenomenon more pragmatically: "you can't describe tobacco," he notes. "This sample looks like this and you say 'It doesn't look like that to me'—subjective. I think this honor thing grew up because there was no other protection. I think it was very pragmatic rather than idealistic. There's no way that you can define or describe tobacco within the limits that are necessary for a contract."

So respected is the code of mutual trust in the tobacco business that it has even affected some governments. Towers, who was in charge of Universal's Portuguese business at the time of that country's revolution, successfully convinced the Marxist-oriented board that had taken over the Mello family's Tabaqueira Company that unless the board paid the company's past bills its tobacco credit would suffer worldwide damage. Over the six months following that meeting, the board paid the family's outstanding debt of $1 million.

On another occasion, this one closer to home, one of Universal's people accidentally overcharged a customer $3 million. The person at Universal subsequently caught the error and called the customer with an offer to rectify it any way he wanted. The Universal man made several proposals, ending with, "or I can make a counterbalancing mistake over the next couple of weeks and wipe it all out and you'll never know the difference."

"Why don't you do that," came the reply.

With attitudes such as these, it is understandable that tobacco companies have traditionally retained only small legal departments. At Universal, where orders are verbal rather than written, there is little need for a large legal staff. "Ours is not a business run by lawyers and accountants," one senior Universal staff member once proudly confided. Nevertheless, all tobacco business cannot be conducted solely inside the world of tobacco, and like all corporations, Universal has had its days in court.

Universal's first major encounter with the legal system took place on the eve of World War II in Lexington, Kentucky. The Lexington case began in 1940 and ended in the Supreme Court six years later. It centered on the charge that numerous domestic tobacco companies, including Universal, were in collusion to fix prices. Although only technically involved, the company became implicated because it was the buyer for both Philip Morris and Export Leaf of Kentucky.

The Lexington case had its origins in governmental probes into the tobacco industry, which had begun as far back as the 1920s. With the implementation of the New Deal, Department of Justice investigators took a heightened interest in monitoring the nation's businesses. Following a lengthy investigation, Justice charged the tobacco companies with violating the Sherman Anti-Trust Act. This set the stage for a ourt battle.

Held in an area long unhappy about tobacco prices, the trial dragged on through the summer of 1942. Centering their arguments on circumstantial evidence suggesting collusion between the tobacco companies, Justice Department attorneys had a sympathetic ear in a jury whose members were all in some way involved in tobacco. When the jury heard that the president of American Tobacco Company had a personal income of near three-quarters of a million dollars—and this during the Great Depression—it was in no mood for legal niceties. The jury brought in a guilty verdict in October. Subsequently a circuit court upheld the district court, as did the Supreme Court in 1946. The story was reported in the Richmond papers, and the press played upon the local angle and mentioned Universal, who successfully entered a plea of "no contest."

Although the company was not listed as a principal and was not fined, the litigation and public attention stung Universal's president Jackson for two reasons. He was personally an ethical man, and he headed a worldwide enterprise known for its honorable dealings. He thought that both his and his company's integrity had been impugned.

To make matters worse, Universal had to endure public censure as though it had been mentioned as a principal in the suit. Privately, however, Jackson could take some solace in the fact that it had not been. "I don't think we ever thought we belonged in the case," Laverge later noted, "because we were not principals. We were commissioned agents. We do what we're told by our customers to do. . . . We were simply told what to do. I think it was a very strong feeling at the time that we were involved in an unfair way."

Following the Lexington case, Universal found itself embroiled in international legal difficulties when in 1958 it was indicted by the federal government for violating the Trading with the Enemy Act. This was an act instituted to prohibit trade with any country deemed by the government to be a real or oblique enemy of the country.

After China was closed to Western interests in 1949, businesses that represented mainland China but still dealt with the West were based in Hong Kong. Under the direction of Cliff Sutherland, Universal continued to do business with Nanyang Brothers, formerly of Shanghai, which had long been a Universal customer. No one at Universal gave the matter much thought when a shipment of tobacco delivered to Nanyang in Hong Kong ended up in Red China; however, a government agent discovered what had happened and began an investigation, following a paper trail that ultimately led back to Richmond. Technically, Universal was guilty, however unintentionally, of dealing with an enemy regime, as stated in the charges lodged against it by the government.

Wishing to avoid adverse publicity in Richmond, Jackson answered the complaint in a federal court in Norfolk, one hundred miles away. Perhaps the company could have fought the charge, but, as Wallace Chandler pointed out, "It would have cost so much." He also noted that "it was a flat fact that the tobacco did move from the company in Hong Kong to Red China, and it was purely a question of did we know that it was going to happen. In fact, it did happen; so how do you refute it?" Universal was found guilty, with the brunt of responsibility for the sale falling on Sutherland's shoulders because he was the Chinese connection.

The case was concluded when Universal agreed to plead "no contest" and pay a fifty-thousand-dollar fine. The matter, however, was not closed so far as Jackson was concerned. He was so angered over what had happened that twenty-five years later Will Tuggle recalled with vivid detail what took place. "I remember Mr. Jackson called [in] all the officers and maybe managers, I'm not sure. One of the officers was late to the meeting and got one of the worst dressing downs I ever heard, which indicated Mr. Jackson's tension, how strongly he felt about this thing. And Mr. Jackson was angry, and very forceful and there was absolutely no question that he meant nothing like this was ever going to happen again. And that nobody was playing a game with this sort of thing."

John Meredith, the company's traffic manager, who was also present at the meeting, recalls the event this way: Mr. Jackson "had a check for fifty thousand dollars in his hand. He said, 'This fifty thousand dollars is going to be a lesson to all of you. I'm turning it over to the United States government, and I hope I never have to turn another one.' I'll never forget it if live to be a million," Meredith concluded. "You could hear a pin drop in that place."

The next legal problem for the company also began in 1958 when Pierre Warwick became embroiled with the Internal Revenue Service over whether he could have his wife accompany him on business trips abroad and declare her expenses as tax deductible. The contested taxes were collected from the Warwicks in 1958 and 1959. Warwick had taken the position that because of the close interpersonal relationships between agent and client in the tobacco business, his wife was central to his business success. Whether or not the case might have been decided differently had the IRS initiated the litigation is impossible to say. However, it was Warwick who sought the ruling, and the case ended up in the U.S. district court in Richmond. The verdict was rendered in 1964.

Victories in cases of this kind had formerly been won on the basis that the wife was as knowledgeable about a product as was her husband and consequently the two of them functioned as a team. In this instance, however, Warwick, with the blessing of Jackson, took a different tack. It was Warwick's contention that his wife's contribution had nothing to do with her knowledge of tobacco. They argued that she was, as Jackson asserted on the witness stand, a "social lubricant," a spouse who—through personal interest in her husband's clients and their wives—facilitated the sale of tobacco.

The initial verdict was returned against Warwick, but with the aid of Chandler and others he eventually won on appeal when the district court concluded that Sarah Warwick's trips were indeed related to her husband's work: "they were neither pleasure nor vacation trips in any sense of the words." It was a precedent-setting decision, invoked to the present-day as a textbook case.

Another case with important implications for the tobacco business at large centered on an antitrust suit that began in 1974. Involving the tobacco markets of the two Carolinas and Kentucky, it came about when farmers filed a class-action suit charging that the dealers and manufacturers were engaged in price fixing. In this case, Universal joined other dealers and manufacturers to present a joint defense.

The key suit was filed in South Carolina; the judge in Kentucky waited for the announcement of the South Carolina verdict before he entered the case. John Peters, an antitrust expert with the Richmond firm of Williams, Mullen, and Christian, represented Universal's interest. Legal action was halted, however, when the judge dismissed the case without a trial after rendering a decision that there was no class action. The case, Wallace Chandler later noted, "could have created havoc within the industry if [it] had gone the other way, but we felt very comfortable. We felt very confident that we had done nothing wrong, that the system that we had was a system set up by the government, and we were simply doing what the government said do. And we said that over and over. There was really no collusion whatever anywhere. We did everything we were supposed to do, exactly the way we were supposed to do it."

Of all the legal problems that Universal confronted over the years, however, none took so high a toll, both financially and emotionally, as did a major takeover attempt instituted against it. A mild precursor had occurred in the late 1960s shortly after Crenshaw succeeded Jackson. Short and abortive though it was, it paved the way for a much more serious and further reaching takeover attempt a decade later.

In 1966 the New York company of Sun Chemical, whose major product was printing ink, took an interest in Universal. By chance, a broker who knew a member of the Sun organization was also acquainted with Pierre Warwick and approached him with the idea of a merger between the companies. Strategies have now been developed on how to fend off unwanted suitors in proposed merger situations, but at that time business executives were unacquainted with the importance of not dealing directly—at least in the early stages of the often-acrimonious negotiations—with those who sought unsolicited mergers.

The head man at Sun Chemical came to Richmond to discuss the situation and, following a weekend meeting of Universal's board and a dinner at the Commonwealth Club, Crenshaw rebuffed the merger idea. Sun backed off and, following an unaccepted invitation of key Universal executives to visit Sun's New York headquarters, the proposal was dropped; but not, however, without Warwick taking some criticism for having let the matter progress as far as it did.

Although allowing Sun Chemical's people to get a wedge in Universal's corporate door may have been unwise, it produced one positive effect: the company was better prepared when in 1976 it faced its greatest challenge yet in the form of a vicious battle waged by the Milwaukee-based Congoleum Corporation, makers of floor coverings.

On Friday afternoon, October 7, 1976, secretary Esther Garrett, who served Universal for more than fifty years, put through a telephone call to Gordon Crenshaw from the chief executive officer of Congoleum, whose board had met and decided to initiate a takeover bid for Universal. The caller, William D. Kyle Jr., announced that he was coming to Richmond that weekend to meet with Crenshaw, who spurned the overture.

While Kyle waited at Richmond's John Marshall Hotel, trying to make contact with Crenshaw, Universal's board was devising its defensive strategy. Soon, the company was served with the papers from Congoleum's lawyers making a definite offer, which under law the board had to act upon and also give reasons for its actions. James C. Wheat Jr. of Wheat First Securities, and Morgan Stanley, a New York company, provided a letter indicating that Congoleum's offer was too low. Meanwhile, Universal had hired a nationally known legal expert on takeovers, Martin Lipton of New York City, but not before it learned that the other most famous lawyer in the field, Joseph Flom, was on Congoleum's team. Both men were members of firms that specialized in takeover cases and made their services available to clients on an around-the-clock basis seven days a week. The offer, which sought to merge Universal into Congoleum, amounted to approximately $153 million. Universal responded by characterizing Congoleum's offer as "totally unacceptable." Citing a long record of uninterrupted growth, it further added that the company would not "flourish as part of a conglomerate such as Congoleum."

On October 27, Congoleum announced it had filed statements with the U.S. Securities and Exchange Commission and with the Commonwealth of Virginia and that it would tender an offer directly to Universal's stockholders. Universal countered by setting up a roadblock by filing a request for a hearing before the Virginia State Corporation Commission. The company had bought time, just as it did three weeks later when it filed a suit, this time out of state.

Registering its complaint on November 24 in district court in Chicago, Universal targeted the First National Bank of Chicago, which was reportedly heading a group of banks that had agreed to finance Congoleum's takeover bid. The suit alleged that Congoleum did not have a firm financial agreement from the bank group when it announced its proposed tender offer to purchase Universal. Universal further claimed that First National's action would violate the National Banking Act by making an equity investment for its own account in another company. As in the previous federal suit, Universal asked for at least $50 million in damages.

Appearing before the Virginia State Corporation Commission on January 3, 1977, Kyle gave testimony that showed his hand not only to Universal but to the public as well. He hinted that he would most likely be prepared to up the ante to Universal stockholders when the time was appropriate. Kyle spent almost an entire day on the witness stand, testifying that, among other things, he might be able to sweeten the deal because he had been able to increase Congoleum's financial base through the Canadian negotiations. With the extra money, the offer of $32.50 per share for any of Universal's stock could be raised to $35.

Crenshaw's report to stockholders following a January 21 special meeting was one he took great satisfaction in sending. He announced that almost 90 percent of the stockholders had been present or represented and that 96.5 percent had voted to amend company articles to require 80 percent of the shareholders to approve certain mergers, consolidations, and other business transactions. The remainder of the statement expressed thanks for the stockholders' support. The company had won a significant legal and psychological battle.

On January 25, Universal was once again back in court, this time at its own instigation. During a twelve-hour hearing in Richmond's district court, it formally asked the judge for a preliminary injunction to derail Congoleum's takeover bid.

Even before all the arguments were heard in the district court, Universal filed another motion with the State Corporation Commission requesting that the six-bank consortium that agreed to finance the takeover be required to submit information statements. The banks, the motion argued, would be the prime beneficiaries of a successful takeover because they were charging Congoleum a high interest rate and stood to obtain some of Universal's banking business as well.

On February 8, the Richmond district court ruled against Universal, but the company again took the offensive when it appealed the decision to the Fourth Circuit Court of Appeals. The company had a taste of the victory that was to come when, on May 19, that court ordered the district court judge to reconsider his denial of the preliminary injunction. The appeals court directed him specifically to proceed with the assumption that, unless restrained, Congoleum "will make a tender offer which probably will result in its acquisition or control of Universal." Included in the opinion was an order to seek an interpretive ruling from the Federal Reserve Board as to whether a credit agreement between Congoleum and the banks was in compliance with federal regulations. Clearly, more litigation was yet to follow.

During the litigation, Congoleum had learned a great deal about the tobacco business, but the knowledge had come too late to be of use. Universal had warned the company that if the takeover were successful, Universal's top officers would walk out and take the business with them. They had even made an offer to put Congoleum people in contact with major Universal customers abroad. When Congoleum finally took the advice, the company's agents returned from Europe with confirmation of what Universal officers had predicted: foreign customers would withdraw their business from Universal if it became part of a nontobacco conglomerate.

Universal finally had its day when officers were summoned to a hastily called meeting with key Congoleum people. The meeting was scheduled to take place in New York City and involve the two opposing attorneys; however, representatives of both litigating parties were asked to be on hand. Although no settlement was reached, Universal's people judged that they held the winning hand. The sweetness of victory was near, except for the bitter pill Universal had to swallow in the form of paying some of Congoleum's legal expenses.

On June 9, Crenshaw sent stockholders a letter that began with a victorious statement, but the concluding paragraph brought the sting. In it Crenshaw said the company was covering Congoleum's legal expenses to the tune of $1.2 million. "In retrospect, it was a bargain," Crenshaw recalled, but years after the settlement many at Universal harbored feelings of anger for having to give money away to the would-be raider. In Universal's offices and halls the feeling at the time was one of righteous indignation, tempered, however, by a sense of relief.

Ironically, the takeover bid had one positive side effect. Company stock was selling for less than $25 a share before Congoleum announced that it was prepared to up the ante to $32.50. When news of the offer was made public and it seemed that Congoleum had the wherewithal to achieve victory, the price immediately jumped to the point that the company's shares actually began trading above what Congoleum proposed in its offer.

That Universal was able to defeat the Congoleum takeover was attributable primarily to the fact that it set up roadblocks that for more than eight months frustrated Congoleum's efforts to make a public tender offer. Chandler expressed it succinctly when he said, "We fought like cats and dogs."

The frustrating ordeal had both its positive and negative effects on the company. There are, for example, those at Universal who contend that the crisis brought not only the entire staff, but particularly top management, closer together. The observation has been made that an already close team closed ranks even further because they realized that to win they had to be of like mind. Such closeness, though, had its negative side; some perceived that, for whatever reason, management had become less approachable than in pre-Congoleum days. On the positive side, several middle-level managers suddenly found themselves exercising greater authority within the company, simply because those at the top did not have, at least temporarily, sufficient time for the business of tobacco.

The overall effect of the Congoleum matter, trying though it was, was basically good for the company. The loss of the $1.2 million aside, the lesson learned was that the business climate of the 1970s was radically different from that of previous eras.

Finally, one additional point. Both government and public sentiment regarding tobacco have changed markedly in the recent years. Companies that for decades could count on tobacco as their sole asset no longer enjoy that luxury. Diversification is now seen as the most practical and pragmatic way to continue business, and, had Universal's top people known or recognized this at the time, the Congoleum crisis may not have arisen. One of the things that made Universal look so attractive as a takeover target in the 1970s was that it had an abundance of surplus cash on hand. Congoleum reasoned correctly that, if it were both careful and methodical, it would be able to use Universal's own nest egg to complete a transaction that it could not complete on its own. After the end of the Congoleum affair, Universal actively used its money to diversify, as discussed earlier in this chapter. Congoleum doubtless taught Universal about changes that were taking place in the corporate world, so that when the company began its own forays into other, and disparate, kinds of ventures it could rely on a backlog of bitterly won experience. Universal was no longer, as Chandler once described it, "another good old Virginia gentleman company." The takeover attempt took it outside the world of tobacco and into a business climate it had not formerly known. In this new climate deals were done confrontationally rather than with a handshake.

Epilogue

The most recent major change to take place at Universal centers on the appointment of Henry H. Harrell as the company's president in 1987. A native Richmonder, Harrell graduated from the city's St. Christopher's school and later from Washington and Lee University, where he was a Phi Beta Kappa English major. He joined Universal in 1966 and, as all newcomers, was sent off to the factories. His introduction to the company was through a lifelong friendship with Jan Laverge, who at first had serious reservations about the young man's ability to fit into the tobacco world.

When Harrell was job hunting following his discharge from service as a U.S. naval officer, he had several offers, all of which were more immediately lucrative than the one extended by Laverge. He settled, however, on Universal. When Laverge questioned him regarding his decision, Harrell said, "Mr. Laverge, if I didn't think I could be president of this company within fifteen years, I wouldn't think of taking the job."

Five years after his appointment he was already in sales and operating on the international level. He became an assistant vice president in 1972, vice president in 1974, senior vice president in 1980, and president in 1987. Following Crenshaw's retirement in October 1988, Harrell became chief executive officer. Like Crenshaw before him, Harrell is a consensus manager, but he has pushed Universal Corporation ahead on several fronts, as his closest colleague Allen King noted. His tenure thus far has been "primarily a continuation," King observed. "But we have expanded the tobacco business considerably through acquisitions, and we have reviewed our diversification strategy, one important result being the spin-off of our title insurance company." Introspective and unassuming, Harrell is an avid golfer, flower gardener, wine collector, and fisherman.

Henry Harrell's chief strength before assuming the company's top post lay in his abilities with foreign operations. While in the Navy he had served in the Mediterranean and prior to that had been a student of Victorian literature and culture at the University of London, and had thus had a good look at life outside the United States. When he entered sales, he at first worked with the Japanese account, but soon was responsible for coordinating all aspects of Universal's foreign interests, a job at which he was most successful. Like so many others in the company, his primary concern is with tobacco, but in his position as head man, he also is of necessity centrally involved with non-tobacco interests as well.

Another significant event in recent Universal history occurred at the October 1987 annual stockholders' meeting, at which time company officers asked formal approval of the creation of a holding company that would bear the name Universal Corporation, thus moving the name Universal Leaf Tobacco Company, which had defined the business since its inception, into a lesser position. Management and the board believed that it was in the company's interest to create a corporate structure that would result in a clearer delineation, separation, and understanding of the different businesses in which it was involved. Over the years it had diversified through acquisition and expansion both geographically and by product line. Despite the company's new name, tobacco remains the primary concern. Harrell has made a concerted and successful effort to increase its sales worldwide. In addition to its tobacco interests, the company trades in products such as rubber, coffee, tea, and sunflower seeds from the countries of origin to various customers in the consuming industries throughout the world. It also is involved in lumber distribution in Holland, Belgium, and Germany. Diversification has come in response to a changing world and changing attitudes, particularly in the United States, toward the one product on which Universal has from its inception depended.

Opposition to the use of tobacco has never been so strong worldwide, particularly in the developed countries, as it has since the epoch-making surgeon general's report of 1964 followed by a more recent surgeon general's highly publicized effort to make American society smoke-free by the year 2000. Despite increased taxation and mounting health concerns, however, the demand for tobacco is still strong. Far from leveling off, it rises annually on a worldwide basis. As late as the summer of 1990, for example, with public use of tobacco being banned in locale after locale, even reaching into the tobacco capitals of Virginia and North Carolina, Universal had more orders than ever. Before the harvest began, company officials had worried that supply might fall below demand. And this in a season when the crop looked exceptionally good.

The increasing importance of American blend cigarettes in world markets and the major manufacturers' commitment to leaf from the United States has led to this demand and to obviously larger domestic crops as the decade of the 1990s begins. Export sales of cigarettes from American manufacturers, for example, rose an astonishing 64 percent from 1987 to 1990, while marketing of flue-cured tobacco was up to almost 800 million pounds, an increase of more than 16 percent over the volume sold in 1987. At the same time, burley tobacco was up almost 9 percent over the 1987 crop.

Net income for the last year of Crenshaw's leadership was almost $61 million, up $5 million from the previous year. The company also saw a 9 percent increase in earnings on a per share basis, and gross revenues of nearly $2,500,000,000. When Crenshaw assumed the top post in 1966, gross revenues were $329,952,000.

Nor were there signs of anything other than continued growth, as the first annual report issued by Harrell the following year indicated. With worldwide tobacco consumption on the rise, particularly in the form of cigarettes for developing countries, many manufacturers were turning more and more to independent leaf dealers such as Universal to fill their needs. Thus the company showed a 30 percent increase in processing volume between 1988 and 1989.

The company's international operations also handled an increased volume of tobacco, and Universal entered into partnership with a Turkish company for the purpose of exporting Turkish Oriental tobaccos. A modern processing plant constructed in Turkey is now in operation. Other vital interests continue to grow in Africa, Asia, South America, Europe, and the Far East; the company's involvement in tobacco worldwide is still growing.

Alone in its decline in the Universal family was Lawyers Title Insurance, whose fifteen nationwide offices reported a sharp decline in the late 1980s, primarily because of a softening in the national real estate market and an increase in claims. Universal has spun off Lawyers Title into an independent company, giving Universal shareholders one share in Lawyers Title for each four owned in the parent company.

One of the major goals of the emerging Harrell years has been to make Universal a smoothly running international organization. In the summer of 1991 a territorial management system was implemented. For example, in the Far East one man was formerly in charge of the Philippines, another in charge of Thailand, and a third in charge of

Korea, while a London office was looking after India and still another office overseeing China. That system was recently replaced; now one man is responsible for each region, and each man reports to Allen King.

Perhaps indicative of things to come at Universal, King is the first person to reach the top ranks of the company without first having served an apprenticeship on the auction floors and in the factories. He started in the accounting department in 1969 and worked his way through the business end of the company until in the mid-1970s. Crenshaw made him an offer that led to his entering line management. King was educated at Richmond's Thomas Jefferson High School and the city's Virginia Commonwealth University. He and Harrell work as the company's top team.

The African operation is a good example of the way the international part of the company does business. In the past the company had separate organizations in Zimbabwe and Malawi, while Tanzania was run from a distant United Kingdom office. One man, who lives in Malawi, now coordinates them all. Similarly, France, Spain, Italy, Greece, and Turkey are headed by one person. South America has also been reorganized along similar lines. As Harrell expressed it, "We now have a series of head men rather than offices. It's all based on the individual." Each of these individuals functions as a member of a board that advises King and Harrell.

Other current concerns at the company center on tobacco expansion as well as diversification. During Harrell's brief tenure, Universal has acquired Thorpe-Greenville, a leaf dealer based in Rocky Mount, North Carolina, the German-based trading company Gebrueder Kulenkampff, and a major competitor, Casalee, with extensive worldwide activities. A significant acquisition took place in the late summer of 1993 when Universal acquired controlling stock in Nyidofer Tobacco Processing Company. Hungary's leading processor, Nyidofer has some four hundred employees and contracts with approximately ten thousand Hungarian producers. It is Harrell's conviction that growth in tobacco plus prudent and manageable diversification is the way of the future for Universal Corporation.

For western tobacco interests, probably one of the most significant recent worldwide events has been the collapse of communism and the opening of former Iron Curtain countries to western tobacco business. Although the figures are not yet available, Universal is selling significant amounts of tobacco in Central European countries, while at the same time its customers are sending vast quantities of cigarettes in. An idea of the market's magnitude can be judged by the fact that the Soviet Union recently extended to the tobacco world a 50 billion cigarette contract.

For Universal, an important alliance took place in the fall of 1993 when Philip Morris announced an agreement with the government of Kazakhstan, a republic of the former Soviet Union, to acquire 49 percent of the state cigarette company. Universal is scheduled to work with Philip Morris in the venture; its specific task will be to develop and implement a comprehensive agronomy and leaf-processing program.

Looking to the future, Harrell hopes to articulate clearer goals for the company as it prepares to enter the twenty-first century. In ten years, he hopes the company will see significant product diversification, although he admits it is far from realizing a definite goal.

On the brink of the twenty-first century, Universal, the small business that began life some seventy-five years ago as a fledgling American leaf tobacco dealer, is now a worldwide company, with tobacco leaf still dominating its center. Of necessity, one begs the question in order to ask, "How did Universal do it? How has this business, founded in the shadow of the American Civil War and in the blighted and beaten American South, managed to be the leader among the world's independent leaf tobacco dealers?" The definitive answer is uncertain, but several observations, taken together, may offer at least a partial explanation.

First and foremost, leaders at Universal have from the beginning kept in mind the ambitious name of their company and have made efforts to move into new foreign markets. Universal was the first leaf tobacco dealer to attempt organization on a global level, an initial advantage that paid well as success bred success. In addition, Universal's foresight led it to be a pioneer in the use of science, technology, and engineering in the processing of tobacco. Its laboratory, efforts at quality control, and constant monitoring and updating of mechanical facilities (such as the super plants) have all helped give the company a competitive edge. Universal was also a pioneer among tobacco companies in the area of diversification, although not always successful.

Moreover, all activities of the company have been presided over by men whose vision reached much farther than tobacco. A strong liberal arts undertone permeates the company's highest ranks (Henry Harrell's studies in Victorian literature before he joined the company; Thomas Towers's lifelong hobby of military history; and Jan Laverge's avocation of collecting seventeenth-century Dutch art, to mention only three). Universal's leaders, well and broadly educated, are concerned with far more than tobacco; most enjoy a knowledge of what is going on in their communities and in the world at large, as well as in the worlds of books and the arts. Company personnel at various levels have served and continue to serve on countless local and statewide philanthropic committees and institutional governing boards that have no relation whatever to tobacco. Such activities have given Universal people an overview that might otherwise be absent.

In its business dealings, Universal, despite its conservative stance, has always taken risks in cultivating customers with long-range potential. Numerous tobacco manufacturers around the world owe their success at least in part to the company's willingness to finance them when they were starting, and such risks have usually paid well. One prime example is that of Dr. Anton Rupert. Arriving unknown and unannounced at the end of a work week, he received aid that put him on the road to worldwide prominence. Along the way he became, and remains, one of the company's most highly valued customers. In like manner, Philip Morris, once a small company, has remained a Universal customer during its climb to international status. That relationship is based on Universal's willingness to be there when needed years ago.

Probably the two most central words in defining Universal, however, are "trust" and "continuity." In the panoply of American businesses tobacco dealers occupy a unique spot in that absolute trust is imperative. Within Universal an atmosphere of trust comes from each individual's knowledge that he or she alone is in charge of a particular job and the better it is done the more everyone will prosper. There is little competition within the company; rather people of like minds and like cultural backgrounds work together to deliver to customers the best product they can.

Almost all the people who run Universal are recruited locally and therefore have shared philosophical outlooks. Although diversity of temperaments exists, seldom is found the worker who has a personal agenda to implement. Similarly, in the foreign satellites, the company places indigenous people in charge and allows them to operate on their own with as little control as possible from the Richmond office. In short, the sprawling worldwide company works as a team with maximum freedom and support and minimum interference given each key player. At Universal there is surprisingly little bureaucracy, especially given the international scope of the business. Junior employees know that senior executives' doors are open and they may enter without formal appointments whenever the need arises. In an atmosphere such as this, impromptu meetings, sometimes on matters of considerable significance, can be hastily called. Also, because key officers are often key account executives, they have an overview that serves them efficiently when dealing with large sums of company money.

Moreover, with one exception, nowhere within the executive ranks at Universal is there a person who did not start out sweeping floors, sharing modest meals with hourly workers, or working round-the-clock shifts in 100-degree-plus heat in tobacco factories or on tobacco auction floors. When company executives periodically visit the factories, they still are ribbed in a spirit of camaraderie by former bosses for the ways they performed years ago when they were starting out. The company leaders served apprenticeships as difficult as in any American business in the twentieth century. They did so, however, with full knowledge of the rewards that waited at the top as they worked their way, in a classical example of American capitalism, step-by-step up the company ladder.

Trust is also the operative word in customer relations. Loans to customers are approved quickly following authorization, sometimes by only one company executive. Orders are taken and filled by verbal agreement, often based on a telephone conversation between the various world offices and an executive in a country thousands of miles away. Bonds based on business over time blend into bonds of friendship as customers become first business associates, then friends, then the families become lifelong friends. Examples are Pierre Warwick's friendship with Portugal's Mello family; one of Jim Abernathy's Mideast customers insisting that Mrs. Abernathy stay with his family when Abernathy was hospitalized; and Will Tuggle's discovery and admission of a major financial error he made in billing Philip Morris. The Philip Morris contact person simply said to make a counter-mistake for the same amount in order to solve the problem.

Universal's methods of operating are also based on continuity. The company almost always promotes from within rather than recruiting from outside. Therefore employees—Henry Harrell, for example—can set their goals high and know that if they are good enough they can expect to achieve them. No one will be hired from the outside and placed in a position someone within the company had an eye on. In corporate America of the twentieth century the rule is most often to canvass the country to find nationally the best-qualified candidates to fill high-level positions. Universal's theory is exactly the opposite: it assumes that the best candidate is already in the company's ranks and that it is only a matter of identifying him or her. Such an attitude leads to productivity, institutional loyalty, informed leadership at the top, and aspiring young people in the lower ranks. It also means that Universal executives are personally known by employees at all levels of the company.

Continuity offers another reward, especially as it pertains to top officers. Long tenures by the leaders, each of whom contributed something unique to Universal, has tended to give the company a personality, even a heritage, that permeates its day-to-day life. In a very real sense, Fred Harrison set the moral tone of the company in the 1930s and 1940s, while Herbert Jackson pointed it on its conservative, and highly successful, business path in the years following World War II. Recently Gordon Crenshaw modernized the company and thrust it into a worldwide arena.

Continuity and commitment have over time given a style to Universal. Bucking the national trend, the company has fewer than five attorneys, keeps as low a profile as possible, does not advertise, and is rarely the subject of newspaper and magazine articles. Office doors are always open, even when business is being discussed, and people work without suit coats, an obligatory item of dress in many businesses. When one telephones an executive at Universal one's call is routed directly to that executive's office instead of to an intermediate secretary. Most executives answer their own phones; Universal's theory is that when people are accessible, business is conducted with fewer delays. When the daily lunch hour arrives at 1 P.M., the whole executive branch departs in groups, some together, some to lunch with other company employees. Finally, anyone walking the halls at Universal is likely to see behind some of the desks people who have long since retired but who still come to the office for at least a few hours or days each week just to keep a hand in.

APPENDIX 1:
A Short History of Tobacco Consumption

Although the exact date is lost, we know that tobacco was first cultivated by the Mayans of southeastern Mexico and Central America in the centuries before Columbus made his 1492 voyage to the Caribbean. At that time, tobacco was being used not only in the immediate Caribbean area but also by other native North Americans who were soon to feel the full force of European colonization.

Two of Columbus's men were the first Europeans to see tobacco being smoked. While on an inland scouting mission, Louis de Torres, Columbus's official interpreter, and Rodrigo de Jerez, able seaman, saw natives inhaling the burning plant and reported their discovery to the admiral.

Within fifty years of this late fifteenth-century discovery, the Spanish had begun to produce tobacco on their own in the West Indies. Soon the plant was known in Spain, particularly around the seaport towns, and in Portugal, where in 1560 the French Ambassador Jean Nicot sent some seeds to Catherine de Medici, who at the time was visiting France. She began using the leaf as snuff, thus putting royal approval on tobacco. She also called tobacco *nicotaine*, thus forever after associating Jean Nicot's name with the product.

During the next twenty-five years the English discovered tobacco, and by 1585 it was soon enjoying great favor among the colonists in Sir Walter Raleigh's ill-fated settlement in what is now North Carolina. Raleigh introduced tobacco to the English court, further popularizing its use both there and elsewhere in Europe.

One of the earliest significant advancements in the growing of tobacco occurred in 1612 when Virginia colonist John Rolfe, remembered also as the husband of Pocahontas, defied Spanish restrictions by smuggling tobacco seeds from Caracas and Trinidad. After risking his life in this venture, Rolfe accidentally hit upon the combination of soil and seed to produce the best tasting tobacco of the time. Indeed, it was tobacco that saved the Jamestown colony and ensured the permanent English presence in the New World. Soon there was such a demand for Virginia tobacco that the colonists were growing it for export in the main street of the tiny Jamestown community.

Physicians and other learned men of the time soon began to study, debate, and write about tobacco. England's King James I vehemently denounced it, arguing that smoking produced "a perpetual stinking torment," but others were not so harsh. The medical world of the day thought that tobacco use was good for the lungs and the brain, that it cured coughs and evaporated phlegm. It was often used as a medicine, particularly during London's Great Plague of the 1660s. Soon English school children were required to bring pipes and tobacco to school so they could be taught to smoke properly. By the time of Queen Elizabeth I's death in 1603 all classes of English society accepted smoking.

Portugal was the next country to play a major role in the spread of tobacco use. Portuguese sailors, along with those from other countries, carried tobacco across the world by way of the major sea routes of the day. The leaf was soon being used in Holland, India, Japan, Turkey, and South Africa. Russia was also introduced to tobacco, and the Thirty Years War (1618-48) spread it to all countries involved in that conflict. By the late eighteenth century, the Siberian Eskimos had become acquainted with tobacco, and the commodity soon made its way to Australia and New Zealand with the British colonists. As a matter of fact, tobacco caught on so firmly around the world that during the American colonial era as many as two hundred ships laden with tobacco would annually leave the Chesapeake Bay in convoy, sailing together to thwart hostile navies and avaricious pirates. Soon ships' captains, plantation owners, and English merchants were becoming wealthy by dealing in the plant. Throughout the colonies tobacco was legal tender.

At the time of Columbus's arrival, Native Americans chewed and smoked tobacco and also dipped snuff. They daily paid homage to their gods by spreading tobacco on the waters of local rivers, carried it with them to assuage hunger on long hunting trips, and smoked it ceremoniously in pipes.

Apart from the religious rites, early Europeans followed the same customs, but soon fashion intruded and made tobacco the object of numerous fads. By the end of the eighteenth century smoking was going out of style and snuff dipping, with the tobacco carried in all sorts of elaborate, often bejeweled boxes, was all the rage. In the nineteenth century, clay and metal pipes gave way to briar, which burned cooler, and cigars increased in popularity.

The Crimean War (1853-56) saw the rise of the cigarette throughout Europe and soon in North America as well. By 1885 the Prince of Wales was serving them at formal lunches, and Frances Folsom Cleveland, the U.S. president's wife, followed suit in the White House just four years later. Tobacco was firmly entrenched in all walks of life—from the day-laborer who took solace in his inexpensive pleasure to the visitor to the chief executive's mansion; but tobacco has always had detractors.

Tobacco has sparked controversy since its introduction into European society in the sixteenth century. From the early days to roughly the mid–twentieth century few scientific studies of its possible adverse health effects were conducted, and even today the Tobacco Institute continues to question the results of numerous investigations centering on tobacco. Although they are the most far-reaching ever conducted, modern studies have their precursors in centuries-old aversion to tobacco.

As early as 1603 King James I mounted a campaign against the leaf; "Counterblast to Tobacco" was one of the first published attacks against its use. In 1612 tobacco was banned in both China and Japan, and in 1617 a Mogul emperor placed the death penalty on both smoking and snuff dipping.

Tobacco fared badly in many other places throughout the world in former times. In Persia, hot lead was poured down the throats of tobacco merchants, and in 1634 the Czar of Russia had snuffers' noses amputated, while a host of other national figures with the power to do so banned tobacco and persecuted users in numbers of ways. For example, in the mid–eighteenth century, the Empress of Russia ordered all snuff boxes brought to church to be confiscated, and the Duke of Wellington forbade junior officers to smoke by a 1845 directive. Clearly, tobacco has been at the center of a storm almost constantly since the Europeans discovered and started using it.

The bombshell dropped, however, in 1964 when the surgeon general of the United States released a report to a nation of smokers informing them of research that directly linked smoking to cancer and heart disease. This was no Carry Nation, who was jailed in 1907 while lecturing against tobacco, nor was it a Billy Sunday, the fiery professional baseball player turned evangelist who mounted a 1916 campaign against tobacco. Indeed, this was the full force of the United States government issuing a stern warning to its citizens.

The surgeon general's 1964 report actually had its origin in government actions that began almost a decade earlier. As early as 1955, the Federal Trade Commission ordered the cigarette industry to make no health claims in its advertising, a practice that had formerly been standard procedure. Two years later the surgeon general made public a statement based on statistical findings that cigarette smoking was a causative factor in lung cancer. In 1964, however, tobacco was characterized as "a health hazard of sufficient importance . . . to warrant remedial action." Four years later the FCC proposed a ban on broadcast cigarette advertising, and such advertising has been prohibited since January 1971. By that date, cigarette packages were required to carry the statement: "The Surgeon General Has Determined That Cigarette Smoking is Dangerous to Your Health."

Following a spate of regulations and warnings, the government once again put its weight behind its antitobacco stance during the Carter administration, when the secretary of Health, Education, and Welfare announced in May 1976 that one of the administration's top priorities would be to decrease the number of smokers in the U.S. The following month, he announced plans to put his department behind a vigorous antismoking campaign. By the fall, the plans were beginning to be implemented. They recommended a yearly "no-smoking" day, an end to federal tobacco programs, social welfare programs to ease losses of small tobacco farmers, additional taxes on cigarettes, and similar measures.

Two years later, on the fourteenth anniversary of the surgeon general's report, the secretary went even further; he initiated a mail campaign to the nation's top five hundred corporate executives asking them to impose smoking restrictions in their buildings. Over the ensuing months, tobacco came under closer and closer government scrutiny until, in 1979, the surgeon general issued a report on smoking and health at the expense of a quarter of a million dollars.

Although much of the information in the twelve-hundred-page report reiterated previous government caveats, the intent was both obvious and revolutionary: the government had as its ultimate goal the halting of tobacco use by the American public. In 1983, the tax on a package of cigarettes doubled from eight to sixteen cents; another four-cent increase was added in 1991. By that date Congress had also voted to bar smoking on all domestic airline flights of six hours or less, which meant all those within the continental United States.

Where future legislation will leave the American tobacco industry is by no means clear. Although the government is centrally involved in its campaign to make America "smoke free" in the foreseeable future, and although American tobacco companies are diversifying in order to meet the financial challenge, major countries are still consuming large quantities of tobacco. Moreover, new political alliances following the end of the Cold War will doubtless affect the tobacco business in unforseen ways.

APPENDIX 2
Universal Corporation
Annual Earnings

Universal Corporation Historical Data on Annual Earnings (in thousands)

Year	Net Income	Revenues	Assets	Equity
1918	1,291		13,848	7,044
*1920	@3,769		28,244	19,832
1921	270		31,593	20,103
1922	438		29,419	20,647
1923	1,450	14,200	28,369	20,632
1924	179	18,924	20,019	16,365
1925	1,018	13,312	19,128	16,146
1926	1,221	18,344	19,897	16,493
1927	1,169	17,620	13,083	11,903
1928	1,284	17,900	14,149	12,244
1929	1,312	21,254	13,912	12,612
1930	964	14,466	14,414	11,929
1931	1,228	14,182	15,139	11,973
1932	861	12,310	14,686	11,303
1933	1,242	17,362	13,184	12,147
1934	1,503	13,983	12,944	11,827
1935	1,589	18,012	13,765	12,416
1936	1,631	20,973	14,927	12,966
1937	1,636	27,361	14,193	13,116
1938	1,538	24,917	14,397	13,282
1939	1,529	21,676	16,550	13,490
1940	1,520	33,908	16,719	13,697
1941	1,445	22,710	16,022	13,914
1942	1,379	33,688	16,150	14,004
1943	1,408	55,854	16,641	14,375
1944	1,475	57,528	17,152	14,784
1945	1,421	82,139	22,108	15,282
1946	1,492	76,992	32,673	16,025
1947	1,501	73,596	26,373	16,181
1948	2,010	58,184	21,831	17,145

Historical Data, continued

Year	Net Income	Revenues	Assets	Equity
1949	1,897	79,558	24,827	17,603
1950	2,003	75,335	26,110	18,503
1951	2,202	108,910	28,368	19,209
1952	1,917	78,014	36,525	19,539
1953	2,244	96,035	33,467	22,014
1954	2,746	100,729	27,427	23,064
1955	2,480	93,134	35,657	23,898
1956	2,677	119,386	43,173	25,040
1957	2,752	111,540	40,404	25,962
1958	2,593	118,413	43,511	26,623
1959	3,018	143,676	36,525	27,826
*1960	3,462	131,120	57,740	29,323
*1961	4,565	214,984	98,222	45,498
1962	6,156	251,085	126,507	48,453
1963	5,363	233,508	121,432	50,985
1964	6,362	265,603	110,925	54,770
1965	7,163	309,925	119,322	60,242
1966	7,266	348,351	121,834	60,887
1967	7,568	367,729	139,151	64,410
*1968	@7,755	#396,244	~127,637	+74,861
1969	7,827	397,281	143,070	73,415
*1970	7,513	#410,354	143,469	+75,381
1971	8,273	463,349	144,814	79,855
*1972	@8,672	#499,545	~140,508	+83,188
*1973	9,988	*545,406	186,629	88,046
1974	11,398	626,231	212,855	94,812
1975	13,992	760,649	237,198	103,414
*1976	17,989	#700,813	172,995	115,804
1977	19,581	737,586	182,103	127,731
1978	21,294	839,465	208,796	136,618
1979	25,491	978,458	215,337	147,893
1980	28,368	992,887	402,062	160,575
1981	31,272	1,041,835	405,779	178,868
*1982	34,271	#934,306	~356,264	197,236
*1983	36,641	#1,046,221	~417,242	215,430
*1984	38,282	#891,790	~454,397	233,263
*1985	46,386	#1,088,833	389,013	261,017
*1986	47,106	#1,047,123	~737,523	293,774
1987	55,973	1,700,900	819,021	325,745
1988	60,719	1,996,673	870,461	356,874

Historical Data, continued

Year	Net Income	Revenues	Assets	Equity
1989	54,035	2,462,608	900,288	386,438
1990	45,105	2,389,346	1,011,012	397,059
1991	20,224	2,896,464	1,275,621	389,829
1992	70,721	2,989,018	1,261,449	301,696
1993	80,242	3,047,213	1,561,995	417,913

Explanations:

*1920: No Income Statement available. Used Surplus as Net Income
    @: Includes difference in Surplus 1918 and 1920

*1960: Includes Universal Leaf Tobacco Co. and Wholly Owned Subsidiaries

*1961: Includes Universal Leaf Tobacco Co. and Consol. Cos.

*1968: Used revised amounts from 1969 statement:
    @, #, ~, +: Reflects restatement for pooling of interest

*1970: Used revised amounts from 1971 statement:
    #: Includes dividends
    +: Reflects change in Income reserved for business use

*1972: Used revised amounts from 1973 statement:
    @, #: Reflects change in dividends received and equity in net income in
        unconsolidated companies
    ~: Reflects change in stocks of affiliated companies
    +:Reflects change in earnings retained for business use

*1973: Used revised amounts from 1974 statement:
    #: does not include equity in net income of unconsolidated companies

*1976: Used revised amounts from 1977 statement
    #: Reflects change in sales and other operating income

*1982: Used revised amounts from 1987 statement
    #: Reflects change in sales and other operating income
    ~: Reflects an overall change in all asset balances

*1983: Used revised amounts from 1987 statement
    #: Reflects change in sales and other operating income
    ~: Reflects an overall change in all asset balances

*1984:Used revised amounts from 1987 statement
    #: Reflects change in sales and other operating income
    ~: Reflects an overall change in all asset balances

*1985: Used revised amounts in 1987 statement
    #: Reflects change in sales and other operating income

*1986: Used revised amounts in 1987 statement
    #: Reflects change in sales and other operating income
    ~: Reflects an overall change in all asset balances

1985-1991 Revenues and Assets restated to equity basis for Lawyers Title

APPENDIX 3
Tobacco Grades

Following is a government-originated calendar of the various grades of tobacco commonly found on the U.S. tobacco markets. Tobacconists at all levels of the business must be intimately familiar with these categories in order to make sound judgments regarding the leaf. *This explanation refers only to flue-cured.*

I. CLASS

Based on characteristics connected with varieties, soils, climatic conditions, or method of cultivation, harvesting, or curing. The primary criterion for class distinction is based on how long the tobacco leaves were ripened while still in the field. Leaves are "pulled" from the stalk at different intervals to create different classes.

II. TYPE

A. Grade

A subdivision of type, based on a combination of group, quality, and color.

1. **Group.** The first and basic factor of a grade, based on certain characteristics related to stalk position, body, or the general quality of the tobacco. Groups in flue-cured tobacco are

   a. **Wrapper (Grademark A).** Leaves from either leaf or cutters, mature to ripe, elastic, with small and blending fibers and a low percentage of injury.

   b. **Leaf (Grademark B).** Usually found at or above the midportion of the stalk, leaves have a pointed tip, tend to fold, are usually heavier in body than other groups, and show little or no ground injury.

   c. **Smoking Leaf (Grademark H).** Usually found at or above the midpoint of the stalk, leaves show a high degree of maturity, more open leaf structure than those in B group, and a material amount of injury characteristic of very ripe leaf tobacco.

   d. **Cutters (Grademark C).** The leaves of this group are usually grown at or just below the midportion of the stalk; they have a tendency to roll, thus concealing the stem, and usually have a rounded tip, are thin to medium in body, and show some ground injury.

e. **Lugs (X).** Usually grown near the bottom of the stalk, most leaves have a blunt tip and open face and show some ground injury characteristic of the group.

f. **Primings (P).** Round-tipped leaves from the lowest portion of the stalk; such leaves ripen prematurely as a result of starvation and show a material amount of injury characteristic of leaves grown close to the ground.

g. **Nondescript (N).** Common tobacco that does not meet the minimum specifications or that exceeds the tolerance of the lowest grade of any other group except scrap.

h. **Scrap (S).** A by-product of stemmed and unstemmed tobacco accumulated from handling of the plant in farm buildings, warehouses, packing and conditioning plants, and stemmeries.

2. **Quality.** The second factor of a grade, based on the relative degree of one or more elements of quality. Quality takes into account such factors as the tobacco's ripeness, accuracy of grading, cleanliness, and whether or not it has been burned by the sun or damaged by the weather.

   a. **Choice (1)**
   b. **Fine (2)**
   c. **Good (3)**
   d. **Fair (4)**
   e. **Low (5)**
   f. **Poor (6)**

3. **Color.** The third factor of a grade, based on the relative hues, saturations of chromas, and color values common to the type.

   a. **Lemon (L)**
   b. **Orange (F)**
   c. **Orange Red (FR)**
   d. **Red (R)**
   e. **Variegated (K)**
   f. **Walnut (D)**
   g. **Green (G)**
   h. **Lemon Greenish (LV)**
   i. **Green Lemon (GL)**
   j. **Green Orange (GF)**
   k. **Green Red (GR)**
   l. **Green Variegated (GK)**
   m. **Gray Green (GG)**

    n. Variegated Lemon (KL)
    o. Variegated Orange (KF)
    p. Variegated Greenish (KV)
    q. Variegated Mixed (KM).
    r. Lemon Slick (LS)*
    s. Orange Slick (FS)*
    t. Rank Red (RR)*
    u. Rank Green (RG)*
    v. Lug Side (XL)*

*Combination symbols

Key to Standard Grademarks

For example, cutters (C) of good quality (3) in orange color (F) would be written C3F. Each symbol used in a federal grade for tobacco has therefore a definite and known meaning.

Group	Quality	Color	Color
A Wrappers	1 Choice	L Lemon	GG Gray Green
B Leaf	2 Fine	F Orange	KL Variegated Lemon
H Smoking Leaf	3 Good	FR Orange Red	KF Variegated Orange
C Cutters	4 Fair	R Red	KV Variegated Greenish
X Lugs	5 Low	K Variegated	FV Orange Greenish
P Primings	6 Poor	D Walnut	KM Variegated Mixed
N Nondescript		G Green	LS Lemon Stick*
S Scrap		LV Lemon Greenish	FS Orange Stick*
		GL Green Orange	RR Rank Red*
		GF Green Orange	RG Rank Green*
		GR Green Red	XL Lug Side
		GK Green Variegated	

APPENDIX 4
Company Officers and Directors

Abernathy, James H., Jr.: assistant vice president, 1954; vice president, 1966; senior vice president, 1974; retired, 1983.

Aliberti, Giovanni: assistant vice president, 1984; resigned, 1986.

Andrews, Robert M.: assistant treasurer, 1922; assistant secretary, 1923; resigned, 1924.

Baldwin, Sterling T.: assistant vice president, 1982; vice president of Universal Leaf Tobacco Co., 1984.

Beale, Cyrus W.: vice president and director, 1918; resigned, 1918.

Bell, Donald F.: senior vice president, 1983; died in office, 1987.

Benson, Edward H.: director, 1968; died in office, 1980.

Berry, William H.: director, 1968.

Blanchard, Lawrence E., Jr.: director, 1975; retired, 1991.

Campbell, F. Scott, III: assistant vice president, 1978; vice president of Universal Leaf Tobacco Co., 1982.

Cary, Lucius F., III: assistant vice president, 1970; vice president, 1974; executive vice president, 1982; died in office, 1983.

Carr, Charles S., Jr.: assistant vice president, 1957; vice president, 1958; director, 1962; retired, 1975.

Carrier, Ronald E.: director, 1979.

Carter, Charles H., Jr.: assistant treasurer, 1970; vice president of Universal Leaf Tobacco Co., 1985.

Chandler, Wallace L.: assistant secretary, 1953; secretary, 1963; general counsel and secretary, 1966; director, 1966; vice president and secretary, 1969; senior vice president, 1974; executive vice president 1982; vice chairman, 1986; vice chairman of new holding company, Universal Corporation, 1987; retired, 1989.

Christian, Stuart G., Jr.: vice president, 1969; senior vice president, 1974; retired, 1986.

Clark, Robert E.: assistant vice president, 1944; vice president, 1946; director, 1950; retired as vice president, 1960; retired, 1963.

Cobb, John B.: director, 1918; resigned 1919.

Cone, Howard B.: vice president, 1967; senior vice president, 1974; retired, 1984.

Connell, Cleveland E.: assistant vice president of Universal Leaf Tobacco Co., 1982.

Coronado, William J.: controller, 1990.

Covington, James E.: director, 1933; vice president, 1941; executive vice president, 1955; retired as executive president, 1956; retired and elected director emeritus, 1969.

Covington, Robert L.: vice president, 1983; senior vice president and processing director of Universal Leaf Tobacco Co, 1987.

Crenshaw, Gordon L.: assistant vice president, 1954; vice president, 1958; director, 1962; president, 1965; chief executive officer and president, 1975; chairman and chief executive officer, 1982; chairman and chief executive officer of new holding company, Universal Corporation, 1987; retiredas chairman, 1991; retired as director, 1992.

Cullman, Joseph F., Jr.: director, 1918; resigned, 1918.

Cullman, Joseph F. Sr.: director, 1918; resigned, 1924.

Davis, Edward G.: assistant treasurer, 1946; resigned, 1951.

Dawson, Robert C.: director, 1985; vice president of new holding company, Universal Corporation, 1987; retired, 1989.

Devries, Willem L.J.: assistant vice president, 1982; vice president of Universal Leaf Tobacco Co., 1983.

Dozier, Curtis M.: assistant treasurer and assistant secretary, 1920; secretary, 1922; secretary and assistant treasurer, 1923; director, 1924; retired as secretary, 1951; retired, 1962.

Dozier, Curtis M., Jr.: assistant secretary, 1948; secretary, 1951; retired, 1963.

Dozier, O. Kemp: treasurer, 1975; vice president and treasurer, 1986; treasurer of new holding company, Universal Corporation, 1987; vice president and treasurer, 1989.

Eagelburger, Lawrence S.: elected director, 1993.

Edwards, K.R.: director, 1922; vice president, 1924; resigned, 1938; reelected director, 1946; retired, 1966.

Foster, Charles H., Jr.: director and vice president, 1989; resigned, 1991..

Funkhouser, A. Paul: director, 1976.

Garrett, R.M.: director, 1939; died in office, 1955.

Gay, Peter M.: vice president, 1971; resigned, 1983.

Gaylord, Richard W.: assistant vice president, 1969; vice president, 1970; resigned, 1983.

Godthep, Jaap: elected director, 1991.

Goodson, William A.: director, 1955; retired, 1960.

Gordon, R.L.: director, 1920; treasurer, 1920; resigned, 1922.

Gorman, Patrick H.: director, 1918; vice president, 1918; resigned, 1929.

Gray, Elmon T.: director, 1977.

Gregory, John M.M.: assistant vice president, 1977; vice president, 1982; senior vice president of Universal Leaf Tobacco Co., 1987.

Gregory, Oscar C.: director, 1918; vice president, 1923; died in office, 1930.

Grubbs, Wirt L., Jr.: director of human resources, 1982; retired, 1989.

Hamlett, H.W., Jr.: director of internal audit, 1977; corporate director of internal audit for new holding company, Universal Corporation, 1987.

Harrell, Henry H.: assistant vice president, 1972; vice president, 1974; senior vice president, 1981; executive vice president, 1982; director, 1984; president, 1986; president of new holding company, Universal Corporation, 1987; president and chief executive officer, 1988; chairman and chief executive officer, 1991.

Harrison, Frederick N.: director, 1919; vice president, 1923; president, 1924; resigned as president and elected chairman of the board, 1946; resigned and elected director emeritus, 1968.

Harrison, James P.: director, 1922; assistant secretary, 1923; vice president, 1924; on military leave, 1942; vice chairman, 1947; chairman of the board, 1950; retired, as chairman of the board, 1965; acting chairman of the board, 1966; reelected chairman of the board, 1967; died in office, 1968.

Hatcher, Vance R.: assistant vice president, 1944; vice president, 1946; director, 1950; resigned, 1956.

Hatcher, Wirt H., Jr.: assistant vice president, 1965; vice president, 1969; retired, 1986.

Henderson, Joe F.: assistant treasurer, 1923; treasurer, 1923; director, 1924; vice president and treasurer, 1946; vice president, 1955; retired as vice president, 1956; retired, 1963.

Hessels, Jan-Michael: director, 1987; resigned, 1989.

Hildt, Thomas: director, 1920; resigned, 1923.

Hitchcock, Harry: director, 1960; retired, 1966.

Hobgood, Alfred L., Jr.: director, 1966; retired, 1987.

Holder, Richard G.: elected director, 1922.

Holt, Bernard S., Jr.: assistant vice president, 1970; corporate director, Information Services, 1987; vice president of Universal Leaf Tobacco Co., 1990.

Howe, M. Norton, Jr.: assistant vice president, 1970; vice president, 1974; senior vice president, 1981; senior vice president of Universal Leaf Tobacco Co, 1987; resigned, 1989.

Humphreys, Edwin W.: vice president, 1957; director, 1958; senior vice president, 1966; retired as senior vice president, 1974; retired, 1977.

Jackson, Herbert W., Jr.: director, 1933; vice president, 1933; president, 1946; chairman of the board and chief executive officer, 1965; died in office, 1966.

Jennings, Joseph A.: director, 1973; retired, 1990.

Johnston, J.E.: assistant secretary, 1920; resigned, 1923.

Johnston, P.H.: director, 1919; resigned, 1924.

King, Allen B.: assistant treasurer, 1977; assistant vice president, 1978; vice president, 1981; senior vice president, 1985; vice president of new holding company, Universal Corporation, 1987; director, 1989; executive vice president, 1989; president and chief executive officer, 1991.

Lacy, William C.: vice president, 1976; senior vice president of Universal Leaf Tobacco Co, 1982.

Laverge, Jan: assistant vice president, 1946; vice president, 1951; director, 1953; senior vice president, 1966; retired, 1978.

Leavell, John N.: assistant vice president, 1957; vice president, 1970; retired, 1976.

Lelong, Chaffraix A., Jr.: assistant vice president, 1983; vice president of Universal Leaf Tobacco Co., 1988.

Lewis, James E.: assistant vice president, 1977; vice president, 1982.

Lowden, Francis V., III: assistant general counsel, 1977; assistantsecretary, 1989; secretary and associate general counsel, 1987; assistant secretary, 1991.

Luckett, William S.: director, 1918; vice president, 1918; resigned, 1922; re-elected director, 1923; resigned, 1924.

McAdams, Thomas B.: director, 1925; resigned, 1926.

Meredith, John F.: assistant vice president, 1977; retired, 1980.

Miller, James I.: director, 1918; vice president and treasurer, 1918; resigned as treasurer, 1919; resigned, 1924.

Moore, David C.: assistant vice president, 1986; vice president of Universal Leaf Tobacco Co., 1990.

Moore, T. Justin, Jr.: director, 1969; resigned, 1973.

Morris, Joseph B.: assistant treasurer, 1922; resigned, 1923.

Mullen, James: president, 1918; director, 1918; resigned as president, 1918; retired, 1963.

Munford, John D.: director, 1988.

Owen, Leroy D.: assistant secretary, 1964; retired 1985.

Parnell, John Q., Jr.: director, 1980; retired, 1982.

Parrish, Hamilton P.: vice president, 1978; died in office, 1981.

Pettus, Hunter R.: director, 1930; vice president, 1933; resigned, 1946.

Phillips, D.C.: treasurer, 1919; resigned as treasurer, 1920; secretary/assistant treasurer, 1920; resigned, 1922.

Pollard, Fred G.: director, 1976; retired, 1988.

Poulson, James H.: director of management information services, Universal Leaf Tobacco Co., 1985.

Powell, W.R.: director, 1982; resigned, 1984.

Ratcliffe, Clyde H., III: assistant vice president, 1976; director corporate development, 1990.

Roark, Elijah B., Jr.: controller, 1973; retired, 1986.

Robertson, Walter S., Jr.: assistant vice president, 1961; vice president, 1964; senior vice president, 1986; retired, 1987.

Robins, Charles R., III: assistant vice president, 1986; vice president of Universal Leaf Tobacco Co., 1988.

Robins, W. Randolph: assistant vice president, 1981; vice president, 1983; senior vice president of Universal Leaf Tobacco Co., 1990.

Robinson, William L.: director, 1939; vice president, 1939; resigned, 1941.

Roper, Hartwell H.: assistant controller, 1977; assistant vice president, 1981;

vice president, 1983; vice president and controller, 1985; controller of new holding company, Universal Corporation, 1987; vice president and controller, 1989; vice president, 1990.

Rose, John D., Jr.: vice president, 1970; director, 1973; senior vice president, 1974; died in office, 1978.

Ruffin, Roulhac: assistant vice president, 1964; retired, 1966.

Schaaf, Edward M., III: assistant vice president, 1981; vice president, 1983; senior vice president of Universal Leaf Tobacco Co., 1990.

Shivers, S.J.: assistant secretary and assistant treasurer, 1918; resigned, 1921.

Stallard, Hubert R.: elected director, 1991.

Starkey, James H., III: vice president, 1983; senior vice president of Universal Leaf Tobacco Co., 1987.

Stone, L.K.: assistant secretary, 1920; resigned, 1922.

Sutton, F.T., IV: assistant vice president, 1983; vice president of Universal Leaf Tobacco Co., 1985.

Taylor, Herbert D.: assistant treasurer, 1949; died in office, 1953.

Taylor, Jaquelin E.: director, 1944; retired, 1974.

Taylor, Jaquelin P.: director, 1918; chairman of the board, 1918; resigned, 1922.

Taylor, Ronald J.: assistant controller, 1985; assistant vice president, 1988; corporate director, 1990. (Remains corporate director, administrative liaison of Universal Leaf Tobacco Co.)

Taylor, William L.: vice president, 1990.

Tompkins, Seldon T.: assistant vice president, 1977; vice president of Universal Leaf Tobacco Co., 1982.

Towers, Thomas R.: assistant vice president, 1961; vice president, 1964; director, 1966; executive vice president, 1969; president, 1982; vice chairman, 1986; retired as vice chairman, 1987.

Tucker, Edwin W.: assistant vice president, 1946; resigned, 1949.

Tuggle, Aubrey, G.: assistant vice president, 1969; vice president, 1974; died in office, 1978.

Tuggle, Richard W.: assistant treasurer, 1953; assistant vice president, 1959; vice president, 1967; senior vice president, 1981; retired, 1982.

Veinouis, A.J.: assistant secretary, 1925; resigned, 1933.

Walker, Walter M., Jr.: director of transportation, Universal Leaf Tobacco Co., 1985.

Warwick, Pierre C.: vice president, 1946; director, 1950; senior vice president, 1966; retired as senior vice president, 1971; retired and elected director emeritus, 1975.

Watson, R.P.: director, 1921; died in office, 1932.

West, Hugh P.: assistant vice president, 1954; resigned, 1961.

West, James W., Jr.: assistant treasurer, 1957; retired, 1973.

White, James M., III: assistant secretary, 1970; secretary, 1973; secretary and general counsel, 1982; secretary and general counsel of new holding company, Universal Corporation, 1987.

Williams, Fielding L.: director, 1963; retired, 1975.

Williams, Lewis C.: secretary and treasurer, 1918; director, 1918; resigned, 1918.

Willingham, E.W.: director, 1922; vice president, 1924; resigned, 1932.

Willingham, William A.: director, 1918; vice president and secretary, 1918; president, 1923; chairman of the board, 1924; died in office, 1945.

Wilson, George P.: assistant vice president, 1924; died in office, 1962.

Winfree, William A., Jr.: assistant treasurer, 1953; treasurer, 1955; director, 1963; director of corporate relations, 1975; retired as director of corporate relations, 1977; retired, 1983.

Winstead, William A., Jr.: director, 1918; died in office, 1962.

Winston, Henry S., III: assistant vice president, 1985; vice president of Universal Leaf Tobacco Co., 1988.

Wood, Mildred J.: assistant treasurer of Universal Leaf Tobacco Co., 1983.

Yarbrough, Fred W.: assistant treasurer, 1970; corporate director of administrative services, 1987; retired, 1989.

Yuille, Thomas B.: director, 1918; president, 1918; resigned as president, 1923; resigned as director, 1923; reelected director, 1929; resigned, 1933.

Bibliographical Note

Unpublished Sources

The story of Universal Leaf Tobacco Company as told in this book is based, above all else, on some two hundred interviews conducted with company officers, employees, and former employees between 1982 and 1992. There are no archives containing individuals' or company correspondence; such materials are discarded periodically. Chief among the interviews was the information collected from Jan Laverge, who joined Universal in 1934 and who, in the early 1990s, was still coming to the office almost daily. His interview, taped over a period of several years, runs well over five hundred pages and contains an array of information that could, in itself, be the subject of a separate volume. John N. Leavell, A.I. McOwan, E.D. Allen, and R.W. Tuggle provided particularly valuable and lengthy oral commentaries as well.

Other major interviews—with senior officials, factory workers, customers, competitors, market buyers, and supervisors from throughout the United States and beyond—were granted by James H. Abernathy, Jr., E.D. Allen, Wayne Baggett, W.S. Bost Sr., James T. Botkin, C. Stuart Carr Jr., Garland Carter, Wallace L. Chandler, M. Deane Cheatham Jr., Stuart G. Christian Jr., L. Carl Cline, Harry Collie, Howard B. Cone, James E. Covington Jr., Gordon L. Crenshaw, Hugh Cullman, Joseph F. Cullman III, Robert E. de Bruyn, Glenda Davis, Mr. and Mrs. E.A. Dinnsen Sr., Sam H. Donnell, Murray E. Dunlop, James B. Eggleston, E. Agnew Galloway, Esther L. Garrett, William A. Goodson Jr., Wirt L. Grubbs Jr., Enoch Haley, Mrs. Grace J. Hall, Louise T. Hankins, Fred N. Harrison Jr., Mrs. Fred N. Harrison Sr., Mrs. J. Pinckney Harrison, Wirt H. Hatcher Jr., C.H. Hinnant Jr., Harry E. Hichcock, A.L. Hobgood Jr., Bernard S. Holt Jr., Robert B. Horine, H. Neal Howard Jr., M. Norton Howe Jr., Mrs. Edwin W. Humphreys, William Thomas Hunt, E. Hilda Johnson, W.L. Jordan, Bruce E. Koonce, Gabriel J. Kremer, William C. Lacy, A.T. Laverge, M.L. Dawson Jr., Henry H. Harrell, Joseph J. Lepine, Howard Todd Livesay, Alma Lucas, George W. Macon Jr., John E. Markle, Mr. and Mrs. A.I. McOwan, John F. Meredith, Marcella W. Minshew, Ann Morton, M.R. Nelson, Guy Norton, W.E. Parham, Kenneth Pittman, W. W. Pritchard, Jr., Walter Raiford, Elijah B. Roarke Jr., Mrs. Walter S. Robertson Sr., Walter S. Robertson Jr., A.C. Robinson, J. Lee Rogers, Paul G. Roland, Gerhard W. Schoenbach, Benjamin E. Schramme Jr., Leo T. Stephenson, Jaquelin E. Taylor, C.W. Thomas III, Mrs. Ralph Thompson, Thomas R. Towers, Henry K. Towler, J.C.

Waddell, A.W. Walker, Mrs. Pierre C. Warwick, Hugh P. West, J.J. White, William A. Winfree Jr., and James B. Winstead. These interviews, all now transcribed, constitute perhaps the most comprehensive oral history yet attempted of a major segment of the tobacco business.

Following is a list of other sources we found useful:

Books

Anon. *"Sold American!" The First Fifty Years, 1904-1954.* New York: American Tobacco, 1954.

Axton, William F. *Tobacco and Kentucky.* Lexington: Univ. Press of Kentucky, 1975.

Badger, Anthony J. *Prosperity Road: The New Deal, Tobacco, and North Carolina.* Chapel Hill: Univ. of North Carolina Press, 1980.

Brooks, Jerome E. *The Mighty Leaf: Tobacco through the Centuries.* Boston: Little, Brown, 1952.

Chesson, Michael B. *Richmond after the War, 1865-1890.* Richmond: Virginia State Library, 1981.

Count Corti. *A History of Smoking.* Trans. Paul England. London: Harrap, 1931.

Dabney, Virginius. *Richmond: The Story of a City.* Garden City: Doubleday, 1976.

_____. *Virginia: The New Dominion.* Garden City: Doubleday, 1971.

Daniel, Pete. *Breaking the Land: The Transformation of Cotton, Tobacco, Rice Cultures since 1880.* Urbana: Univ. of Illinois Press, 1985.

DeBardelben, Marian Zalis, comp. and ed. *Dictionary of Tobacco Terminology.* New York: Philip Morris, 1980.

Finger, William R., ed. *The Tobacco Industry in Transition: Policies for the 1980s.* Lexington, Mass.: North Carolina Center for Public Policy Research, 1981.

Fite, Gilbert C. *Cotton Fields No More: Southern Agriculture, 1865-1980.* Lexington: Univ. Press of Kentucky, 1984.

Fisher, Robert Lewis. *The Odyssey of Tobacco.* Lichfield, Conn.: Prospect, 1939.

Hagan, Jane Gray. *The Story of Danville.* New York: Stratford House, 1950.

Hamilton, A. E. *This Smoking World.* New York: Century, 1927.

Howe, Harold R. *Tobacco Under the AAA.* Washington, D.C.: Brookings Institute, 1935.

James I, King of England. *A Counterblast to Tobacco.* Newcastle Upon Tyne: Pattison and Ross, 1843.

Lefler, Hugh T., and Albert Ray Newsome. *North Carolina.* 3rd. ed. Chapel Hill: Univ. of North Carolina Press, 1973.

Marin, Carmen M., comp. *Tobacco Literature: A Bibliography.* Raleigh: North Carolina Agricultural Research Service, 1979.

Middleton, Arthur Pierce. *Tobacco Coast.* Baltimore: Johns Hopkins Press, 1953.

Mordecai, Samuel. *Virginia, Especially Richmond, in By-Gone Days.* Rev. ed. Richmond: West and Johnson, 1860.

Pollock, Edward. *Illustrated Sketch Book of Danville, Virginia; Its Manufacturers and Commerce.* Danville: Waddill, 1885.

Robert, Joseph C. *The Story of Tobacco in America.* Chapel Hill: Univ. of North Carolina Press, 1949.
Shideler, James H. *Farm Crisis.* Berkeley: Univ. of California Press, 1957.
Tait, Lyal. *Tobacco in Canada.* Canada: T. H. Best Printing, n.d.
Tennant, Richard B. *The American Cigarette Industry.* New York: Archon, 1971.
Tillie, Nannie May. *The Bright-Tobacco Industry, 1860-1929.* Chapel Hill: Univ. of North Carolina Press, 1948.
_____. *The R.J. Reynolds Tobacco Company.* Chapel Hill: Univ. of North Carolina Press, 1985.
Tindall, George B. *The Emergence of the New South, 1913-1945.* Baton Rouge: Louisiana State Univ. Press, 1967.
The Tobacco Industry. New York: Barney, [n.d.].
Virginia and Tobacco. Washington, D.C.: Tobacco Institute, 1960.

Newspapers and Periodicals

Business Week
Durham (North Carolina) *Morning Herald*
Richmond (Virginia) *News Leader*
Raleigh (North Carolina) *News and Observer*
New York Times
Richmond Times-Dispatch
Tobacco International
Tobacco Reporter
Tobacco Weekly
U.S. Tobacco Journal
Universal Leaf Tobacco Co. Universal News
Wall Street Journal

Dissertations

Cox, Reavis. "Competition in the American Tobacco Industry." Ph.D. diss., Columbia University, 1932.
Schlotterbeck, John T. "Plantation and Farm: Social and Economic Changes in Orange and Greene Counties, Virginia, 1716-1860." Ph.D. diss., Johns Hopkins University, 1980.
Sigel, Frederick F. "A New South in the Old: Sotweed and Soil in the Development of Danville, Virginia." Ph.D. diss., University of Pittsburgh, 1978.

Miscellaneous

Universal Leaf Tobacco Co. annual reports, corporate records, minute books, and press releases, 1918-93.

Index